Augustine's Theology of Angels

References to the good angels in the works of Augustine are legion, and angels also play a central role in some of his major works, such as *City of God* and the opening of *On the Trinity*. Despite Augustine's interest in angels, however, little scholarly work has appeared on the topic. In this book, Elizabeth Klein gives the first comprehensive account of Augustine's theology of the angels and its importance for his thought more generally. Offering a close textual analysis of the reference to angels in Augustine's corpus, the volume explores Augustine's angelology in relationship with his understanding of creation, of community, of salvation history and of spiritual warfare. By examining Augustine's angelology, we glimpse his understanding of time and eternity, as well as the meaning and perfection of created life. Klein's book is foundational for a proper understanding of Augustine's angelology and has far-reaching implications not only for Augustinian studies, but also the broader history of Christian angelology.

Elizabeth Klein is an assistant professor of theology at the Augustine Institute in Denver, Colorado.

Augustine's Theology of Angels

ELIZABETH KLEIN

Augustine Institute, Denver, Colorado

CAMBRIDGE
UNIVERSITY PRESS

University Printing House, Cambridge CB2 8BS, United Kingdom

One Liberty Plaza, 20th Floor, New York, NY 10006, USA

477 Williamstown Road, Port Melbourne, VIC 3207, Australia

314–321, 3rd Floor, Plot 3, Splendor Forum, Jasola District Centre, New Delhi – 110025, India

79 Anson Road, #06-04/06, Singapore 079906

Cambridge University Press is part of the University of Cambridge.

It furthers the University's mission by disseminating knowledge in the pursuit of education, learning and research at the highest international levels of excellence.

www.cambridge.org
Information on this title: www.cambridge.org/9781108424455
DOI: 10.1017/9781108335652

First published 2018

Printed in the United States of America by Sheridan Books, Inc.

English translations of many of Augustine's works are used with the permission of the Augustinian Heritage Institute.

A catalogue record for this publication is available from the British Library.

ISBN 978-1-108-42445-5 Hardback

Contents

Acknowledgments

First and foremost, I am grateful to my husband without whom my pursuance of an academic career would not have been possible.

I would also like to thank my doctoral advisor, John Cavadini, whose enthusiasm for my project made the burden of writing light, and who always provided insightful comments and steadfast encouragement. My other committee members – Ann Astell, Lawrence Cunningham and Brian Daley – were likewise a wonderful support and each offered an invaluable perspective on my work.

I extend a special thank you to Daryn Henry, who made detailed comments on the manuscript on short notice, and also to Peter Widdicombe, who not only read the manuscript, but has offered me unfailing help in all of my academic endeavors.

The Social Sciences and Humanities Research Council of Canada and the University of Notre Dame graciously provided the financial support needed for me to complete the dissertation on which this book is based. The Augustine Institute and its faculty have also been incredibly supportive as I completed the manuscript, especially John Sehorn, whose library has been at my disposal.

There are many others in the Notre Dame community who deserve my thanks for patiently listening throughout the writing process and offering their friendship and support, including Michael and Anna Petrin, Kate Mahon and Kristen Drahos.

October 2, 2017 (Feast of the Guardian Angels)

Abbreviations of Augustine's Works

adn. Job	Comments on Job
b. vita	On the Happy Life
c. Adim.	Against Adimantus
c. adv. leg.	Against Adversaries of the Law and the Prophets
c. ep. Parm.	Against the Letter of Parmenian
c. Faust.	Against Faustus, a Manichee
c. Iul.	Against Julian
c. Iul. imp.	Against Julian, an Unfinished Book
c. litt. Pet.	Against the Letters of Petilianus
c. Max.	Against Maximinus, an Arian
c. mend.	Against Lying
c. Sec.	Against Secundinus, a Manichee
civ. Dei	The City of God
conf.	The Confessions
cons. eu.	On Agreement among the Evangelists
cresc.	To Cresconius, a Donatist Grammarian
cura mort.	On the Care of the Dead
doc. Chr.	On Christian Teaching
divin. daem.	On the Divination of Demons
div. qu.	On Eighty-Three Varied Questions
Dulc. qu.	On Eight Questions, from Dulcitius
en. Ps.	Expositions of the Psalms
ench.	A Handbook on Faith, Hope and Love
ep. Jo.	Homilies on the First Epistle of John
ep.	Letters
exp. Gal.	Commentary on the Letter to the Galatians
Gn. adv. Man.	Genesis Commentary Against the Manichees
Gn. litt. imp.	Unfinished Literal Commentary on Genesis

Gn. litt.	*Literal Meaning of Genesis*
gr. et pecc. or.	*On the Grace of Christ and Original Sin*
haer.	*On Heresies*
Jo. ev. tr.	*Homilies on the Gospel of John*
lib. arb.	*On Free Will*
loc. in Hept.	*Sayings in the Heptateuch*
pecc. mer.	*On the Merits and Forgiveness of Sins and on Infant Baptism*
qu.	*Questions on the Heptateuch*
retr.	*Reconsiderations*
s.	*Sermons*
s. Casin.	*Sermones in bibliotheca Casinensi editi*
s. Denis	*Sermones*, ed. Michel Denis
s. Dolbeau	*Sermones*, ed. François Dolbeau
s. Dom. mon.	*On the Lord's Sermon on the Mount*
s. Erfurt	*Sermones Erfordienses Bibliothecae Amplonianae*, ed. Isabella Schiller, Dorothea Weber and Clemens Weidman
s. Guelf.	*Sermones ex collectione Guelferbytana*, ed. Germain Morin
s. Morin	*Sermones*, ed. Germain Morin
spir. et litt.	*On the Spirit and the Letter*
symb. cat.	*On the Creed, to Catechumens*
trin.	*On the Trinity*
util. cred.	*On the Usefulness of Belief*
vera rel.	*On True Religion*

Introduction

We do not see the angels as present; this is something hidden from our eyes, something that belongs to the mighty commonwealth of God, our supreme ruler. But we know from our faith that angels exist, and we read of their having appeared to many people. We hold this firmly, and it would be wrong for us to doubt it.[1]

Augustine here expresses a simple fact of ancient Christian faith: that angels, invisible rational creatures, exist. The ubiquity of angels in the biblical text could hardly go unnoticed by such a great and prolific exegete, and indeed the angels feature in all of Augustine's major theological works and in his homilies. The angels are prominent in his discussion of the text of Genesis and are important for his doctrine of creation. The angels are the founders of the city of God and so of creaturely communion as Augustine understands it. The angels also play a pivotal role in salvation history, as well as in the story of each individual Christian's struggle against temptation.

Despite the attention that Augustine gives to the angels, there has been little scholarly interest in the place of the angels in his writings and in patristic angelology broadly speaking. The only modern monographs which substantially treat the early Christian understanding of angels are Jean Daniélou's *Angels and their Mission According to the Fathers of the Church* (1953) and Ellen Muehlberger's *Angels in Late Ancient Christianity* (2013).[2] Both Daniélou and Muehlberger begin their books

---

[1] *en. Ps.* 103.1.15.
[2] Jean Daniélou, *The Angels and Their Mission According to the Fathers of the Church* (New York: Newman Press, 1957), and Ellen Muehlberger, *Angels in Late Ancient Christianity* (Oxford: Oxford University Press, 2013). Neither of these texts focus on

by offering something of an apology for their chosen subject; the study of angels, it seems, necessitates a justification for the modern reader. Perhaps an interest in the angels could be seen as an indulgence in idle speculation. After all, the charge brought against the scholastics – who are said to have wondered how many angels could dance on the head of a pin – was that of utter irrelevance. Or, perhaps we are leery of a curiosity about angels which corresponds to an overactive imagination about the spiritual world, something which is not highly regarded in contemporary academic discourse. On the surface, it would seem that for us moderns the angels have little use, are of little interest and a study of them has no serious intellectual merit.

Although the mediation of angels seems to have little hold on the imagination of modern scholars, this was not the case for an ancient religious adherent. The *daimones* of Homer and Hesiod are inherited by Socrates, and in turn by the Platonists and the Neo-Platonists.[3] Celestial beings and divine mediators play a central role in Roman religious practice as well as in various forms of Gnosticism (including Manicheanism). In Augustine's time, the world is understood to be populated by spirits whose role in religious life is as important as it is contested. In a word, the existence of spirits such as angels and demons is assumed in antiquity. How they are understood to participate in religious worship and indeed everyday life is not consistent across time and place, but the interaction of human beings with celestial spirits of various kinds is a basic element

---

Augustine. The recent dissertation by Gregory Wiebe on Augustine's demonology, however, does have a significant treatment of the good angels in the first part of the text. See Gregory Wiebe, "Demons in the Theology of Augustine" (Ph.D. Diss., McMaster University, 2015). The only other substantial scholarly discussions on the topic of Augustine's angelology come from Augustinian encyclopedias – in English, Frederick Van Fleteren, "Angels" in *Augustine through the Ages* (Grand Rapids: Eerdmans, 2009 [1999]), ed. Allan Fitzgerald et al., 20–22; and in French, Goulven Madec, "Angelus" in *Augustinus Lexicon*, vol. 1 (Basel: Shwabe & Co., 1986), ed. Cornelius Mayer, 304–315 – in addition to one article in Italian by Manlio Simonetti. See Simonetti, "Gli angeli e Origene nel *De civitate Dei*" in *Il De Civitate Dei* (Rome: Herder, 1996), ed. Elena Cavacanti, 167–178. Other short discussions of Augustine's angelology occasionally appear in works concerned with medieval angelology, such as Steven Chase, *Angelic Spirituality: Medieval Perspectives* (Mahwah: Paulist Press, 2002), David Keck, *Angels and Angelology in the Middle Ages* (Oxford: Oxford University Press, 1998) and *A Companion to Angels in Medieval Philosophy* edited by Tobias Hoffman (Leiden: Brill, 2012). We may note this lack of scholarly material does not seem to correspond to a widespread lack of interest, as popular and spiritual titles on the topic of angels steadily appear.

3 For a study of the *daimon* in Plato's thought and its reception through to the Neo-Platonists, see Andrei Timotin. *La démonologie platonicienne. Histoire de la notion de Daimon de Platon aux derniers néoplatoniciens* (Leiden: Brill, 2012).

of ancient Greco-Roman religion. The nature of the angels and their relationships with human beings was of significant pastoral import for Augustine, and our lack of interest in the matter does not correspond well with the reality of ancient religion.

It is not surprising, therefore, that the existence of angels has far-reaching theological implications for patristic authors generally and for Augustine in particular. The presence of angels at many pivotal moments in the biblical narrative demands some account of them, and the question of the angels' role in Christian worship is still an open one in the fourth century. Although Augustine has no single work that treats the angels as a separate subject, he develops a surprisingly consistent way of speaking about them and of understanding them. He expends significant energy doing so, and the angels are integrated into fundamental aspects of his theology. It is not an overstatement to say that there are many ways in which we cannot fully understand his theology (and his world) without them.

To get a sense of the patristic orientation toward angelology, Daniélou describes the two theological extremes of angelology as he sees it: of mythology on the one hand, and of abstraction on the other, and it is helpful to imagine that Augustine (like other writers of ancient Christianity, according to Daniélou) navigates these two extremes.[4] On the one hand, given Augustine's Manichean background, it is crucial for him to develop a proper understanding of angels in order to defend the goodness of creation and to reject a dualistic worldview. It is imperative for Augustine that the angels were created good, with good intent, and that many persisted in that good. This very concern is one of the reasons why Augustine takes such keen interest in the book of Genesis and the angels' role in creation. The angels are not mythological beings, with their own narrative apart from that of scripture. On the other hand, as an exegete Augustine must interpret the numerous references to angels in the biblical text, particularly their interactions with God's people in the Old Testament. As Augustine notices, the angels in the Bible have a personal quality and are creatures in their own right.

For Augustine, then, the Christian angels are not the demons of mythology, but are personal, created spirits. A consideration of the angels is related to a number of theological questions, yet angels remain actual

---

[4] Daniélou, *Angels and their Mission*, vii. He speaks of these extremes as the unhealthy interest of spiritism or theosophy on the one hand (what I call mythology), and our tendency to think of angels and demons as merely the personifications of psychological realities on the other (what I call abstraction).

creatures and do not merely stand in for a theological concept. Put otherwise, Augustine seeks to understand the proper relationship of the angels
with the rest of creation in a way that maintains the personal quality of
their being. Augustine deals with this issue perhaps most significantly in
City of God where he imagines the angels not only as a part of this great
city, but as its primordial members. But in other texts, Augustine also
speaks of the angels as our "neighbours,"[5] as our "friends,"[6] as "fellow
citizens"[7] and reminds us that although God uses angels to communicate
with human beings, he does not thereby always "trumpet out from heaven
through an angel"[8] in some kind of imperious fashion. God allows both
angels and human beings to participate in the economy of salvation, each
according to ability and station.[9]

By avoiding both mythology and abstraction, then, Augustine shows
that he understands the angels *as* created. On the one hand, they are
good, they are made spiritual, and the good angels persist in perfection,
but on the other hand, they are not so unlike us. Since they are created,
they serve God and worship him, they seek God as their end, and they
are our neighbors and fellow-citizens in the city of God. But since they
are perfected, the angels also serve as a kind of litmus test in Augustine's
theological thinking. If the good angels embody the blessed state for
which the elect are also destined, by looking at them we might see what
constitutes perfection for Augustine, and what theological categories
he uses even when speaking about the blessed life of heaven. Against
the angels, we can measure the relative importance of many theological
themes in Augustine's writing; we can ask whether or not a certain way
of speaking about God, about the body or about worship persists in the
angelic life or not. The good angels help to show us the meaning and perfection of created life.

The Organization of This Work

In this book, then, we will see what Augustine says about angels and
where in his corpus he is most interested to say it. This book is primarily

[5] *doc. Chr.* 1.31.
[6] *adn. Job* 20.
[7] See *en. Ps.* 90.2.1 and 136.1, for example.
[8] *doc. Chr.* preface 6–7.
[9] For example, Augustine interprets the ascension as the angels carrying Christ up toward
heaven as an act of worship (or service) done by the angels, that is, Christ allows the
angels to worship him but does not have any need to be carried. See *en. Ps.* 90.2.8.

concerned with the good angels (although the demons necessarily make an appearance) and with the question of how these good angels function theologically for Augustine, including the angels' role in his pastoral theology. The material on angels is somewhat disparate, and so dividing it up thematically, as I do in this work, runs the risk of atomizing Augustine's reflections on the angels and interpreting them apart from their original context. Each chapter, therefore, is centered on a specific text or group of texts, as well as a specific theme, and each chapter concludes with a suggestion about how Augustine's conception of angels is related to larger questions in Augustinian studies.

In chapter 1, Augustine's treatment of the creation of the angels as well as the role of the angels in creation is discussed. Augustine's Genesis commentaries are considered in chronological order, namely, *On Genesis: A Refutation of the Manichees, The Unfinished Literal Commentary on Genesis, The Literal Meaning of Genesis,* the final books of *The Confessions* and book XI of *City of God.* We will see how Augustine fits the angels into the creation story, and that his persistent efforts to do so are founded on his desire to combat a mythological understanding of spiritual creatures. For example, Augustine argues, both in *Literal Meaning of Genesis* and *City of God* that the creation of everything (including angels) is described by the Genesis narrative. He says that he is unable to believe that the angels are not included in the biblical text, however obscurely, because in Genesis it is written that God created *in the beginning*, implying nothing happened beforehand, and that on the seventh day God rested from all his works, implying nothing could have been created afterwards.[10] The angels do not have an extra-biblical narrative of their own. Moreover, Augustine insists that his interpretation of *let there be light* as the creation of the angels is literal and not metaphorical; the creation of the angels and their subsequent activity (the night/day cycle) is truly signified by these biblical words.[11] Augustine thereby seeks to emphasize that the angels are part of the created order. He is insistent, both in the Genesis commentaries and elsewhere, that the angels do not create, but that this activity belongs to God alone.[12]

---

[10] See *civ. Dei* XI.6, XI.9 and *Gn. litt.* V.5.
[11] *Gn. litt.* IV.45.
[12] This is noted by Goulven Madec in his encyclopedia entry on angels. See Madec, "Angelus," 304–315. Madec also draws from an earlier article by Aimé Solignac; see Solignac, "Exégèse et Métaphysique, Genèse 1,1-3 chez saint Augustin" in *In Principio: Interpretations des premiers versets de la Genèse* (Paris: Études augustiniennes, 1973), 154–171.

The way in which the angels interact with creation, moreover, has implications for the goodness of creation and the goodness of the economy of salvation. Some scholars have argued that the sacraments are merely external signs for Augustine, with no lasting meaning or ultimate effectiveness.[13] The image of the angelic life in the Genesis commentaries challenges this notion. Augustine persists in using the language of signification and receptivity in the life of heaven which parallels our liturgical life here (such as the image of angelic reading). Signs and sacraments are ultimately taken up into Augustine's vision of the angelic life rather than simply surpassed in order for us to obtain something even better. For the angels, the contemplation of what God has created redounds to God's glory eternally, not just for a time until the external can be completely discarded in favor of the internal or spiritual.

City of God books IX–XII are the focal point of chapter 2. In these books, we find Augustine's vision of the angelic community, its sacramental life, and our interaction with and imitation of that life. Muehlberger's claim, that the angels are "divine drones" with no will of their own, and whose primary function is to serve as a heavenly placeholder or guarantor of a blessed afterlife, is contested.[14] The angels are not automatons, as Muehlberger suggests, but are icons of worship, since they both embody perfect worship of God and also mediate it. They are not un-free in being aligned with the will of God, but absolutely free in loving, willing and clinging to God. They are, in a way, guarantors of the blessed life to come, but they are also aids and exemplars to the church sojourning below.

Not only is the chapter on angelic worship the hinge chapter of the *City of God* (book X) but the understanding of proper worship is critical to the work as a whole. The *City of God* as a project, after all, attempts to envision two communities, the heavenly and the earthly, and these two cities are defined by the order of their desire, "the one enjoying God, the

---

[13] Phillip Cary is perhaps the most vigorous proponent of this view, writing (for example) that "in Augustine's Platonism words and sacraments have their significance and their use, but they cannot give us the inner good they signify. So it is not by turning to them that we find the knowledge of God but by turning inward, looking in a different dimension from all bodily things." See Phillip Cary, *Outward Signs: The Powerlessness of External Things in Augustine's Thought* (Oxford: Oxford University Press, 2008), 4.

[14] See, for example, Muehlberger, *Angels in Late Ancient Christianity*, 5. She argues that Augustine's use of angels in *City of God* is primarily polemical. In short, Augustine pictures the angels as stable and blessed in order to demonstrate the superiority of the Christian God and the Christian heaven to the gods and afterlife of Roman religion. In this regard, Muehlberger follows the general argument of Simonetti.

other swelling with pride."[15] Angels have a more significant role to play in Augustine's understanding of that city than might be first apparent. The angels are already citizens of that city and represent our end. And so, as the first members of the city of God, angels are critical for Augustine's conception of the beginning, course and end of the city. They are an essential part of its composition. How, therefore, are we to understand the bodies of angels, and our future bodies in relation to them? If the angels present a perfect image of worship, how does our worship here on earth (particularly the *sacramenta*) correspond with heavenly worship? We again find significant evidence that Augustine has a "sacramental" understanding of the angelic life, as he uses the imagery of eating as well as the language of sacrifice to describe the angel's heavenly activity.

In short, *City of God* is about two communities, and both of them have their beginning among the angels. As John Rist writes, "it is human society as a whole, with its divine and diabolical associates, which is the subject matter of *City of God*."[16] But perhaps one of the most striking things about Augustine's work is that this statement can, and perhaps ought to be, reversed: it is angelic society, with its human associates, which is the subject matter of *City of God*. The city of God is not anthropocentric, and this entails that Augustine work, at times, on a completely different register.

It becomes clear, in the course of chapter 2, that since angels have a role to play in embodying perfect worship, they are exemplars for the church. In chapter 3, however, the human side of the question comes to the fore; how do angels interact with the human race throughout history in order to aid in its salvation? The main text for consideration is *On the Trinity*, in which Augustine asserts that all Old Testament theophanies are appearances of angels. In this respect, he departs from earlier traditions which regard these theophanies as appearances of Christ. In rejecting this position, he is able to solve the problem of confusing singular and plural references in some of these theophany texts, as well as to maintain what he sees as the uniqueness of the event of the incarnation. But he also thereby gives to the angels a privileged place in salvation history, and the implications are many. Again, Augustine works to affirm that the angels are created and so their role in the economy is one arranged by

---

[15] *civ. Dei* XI.33.
[16] John Rist, "On the Nature and Worth of Christian Philosophy: Evidence from *City of God*" in *Augustine's City of God: A Critical Guide*, ed. James Wetzel (Cambridge: Cambridge University Press, 2012), 214.

providence for their benefit and ours, but there is no room for an alternative myth in which angels work apart from God, nor does God have any inherent need for the angels to exact his will. Augustine solidifies this vision of angelic mediation by frequently pairing the work of angels with the work of prophets. By bringing angels down to the level of human mediators, so to speak, he also creates a unified vision of how creatures in general – angelic or otherwise – participate in the economy of salvation.

In chapter 4, the challenge that spiritual warfare does not feature prominently in Augustine's theology is addressed.[17] The primary texts considered in this chapter are Augustine's *Expositions of the Psalms*. In these sermons, Augustine does make frequent reference to demonic interference in the everyday life of the Christian, as well as in the scriptural narrative. He often interprets the Psalms as pertaining to spiritual warfare, and he sees the temptation of the devil and his angels as commonplace in Christian experience. Reading his *Expositions of the Psalms* in this light, a basic account of his teaching on spiritual warfare is given. He considers the devil's attacks to be real and dangerous, but recommends reliance on God as the foremost defense against them. He advises that we cultivate this dependence on God through the liturgy and prayer, as well as by following the example of holy men and women. The martyrs sometimes serve as this example, but Augustine prefers the biblical figure of Job as a model of a successful spiritual combatant.

In this chapter, we come to see that Augustine's teaching on spiritual warfare in his sermons is consistent with his angelology articulated elsewhere, that is, Augustine affirms angels are created beings involved in the economy of salvation, but not in the arcane cosmic struggles of myth. Thus he does not imagine spiritual warfare to be angels fighting demons over the control of souls, and rarely speaks about demons tormenting individuals or angels defending them. He insists that any power which the devil has is power permitted him by God, and that the devil's mastery

---

[17] Muehlberger distinguishes between genres of literature in which the angels appear. She designates the writings of Evagrius as "cultivation" literature, concerned with spiritual development, ascetic practice, etc., whereas Augustine's *City of God* is deemed "contestation" literature, concerned with political and theological argumentation. This distinction leads her to emphasize the polemical nature of Augustine's angelology. Spiritual warfare and cultivation are not part of Augustine's main concern, according to Muehlberger, but rather in aiming to give "an authoritative account of the world and of world history" Augustine "imagined angels to be eternally secure, in the happy circumstance of being assured of their stability with God. As Christians would be in the future ... already aligned with the will of God and working according to that will" (*Angels in Late Ancient Christianity*, 57).

of any human being involves the acquiescence of that person to the power of the devil. This understanding of spiritual warfare is consonant with Augustine's view of how the angels and demons form a community with us in *City of God*.

In pursuing these four main topics of discussion, we see that Augustine does not treat the angels as an abstract idea, but as creatures of God, whose existence has wide-ranging theological and pastoral implications about the body, about the sacraments, about salvation history and about everyday spiritual life. Augustine's angelology helps us to see his vision of the beatific community, and that understanding perfect communion is central to understanding the logic of (and perfection of) creation.

I

Angels and Creation

To discuss creation first is fitting not only because we will thereby begin *in the beginning*, but also because Augustine's understanding of Genesis is without doubt central to his understanding of angels. Augustine's keen interest in the text of Genesis is due in part to his own intellectual and spiritual journey, as we read in *Confessions*,[1] and defending this text against the dualism of the Manicheans seems to have been an imperative task for him after his conversion.[2] The Manicheans' claim that Genesis does not make any sense in the bare letter of the text and their rejection of allegorical readings as a viable alternative,[3] along with Augustine's own profound interest in the creation story, leads him to comment repeatedly on the book of Genesis. He persists until he is finally able to give, as he sees it, a literal account of the Genesis narrative.

In his Genesis commentaries, Augustine develops a set of concerns and a way of reading Genesis which ultimately necessitates that he

---

[1] See, for example, *conf.* III.5.9.

[2] Augustine considered *On Genesis: A Refutation of the Manichees* (one of his earliest works) to be a continuation of an earlier (more erudite, and less accessible) refutation of the Manicheans (as he mentions in *Gn. adv. Man.* 1.1). Augustine saw the task of commenting on Genesis as one of his first and most important tasks as a new catholic, particularly for guarding the uneducated against the Manichean heresy. In his *Reconsiderations*, Augustine also indicates that he wanted to set right whatever wrongheaded interpretations he may have espoused as a Manichean (*retr.* 1.10). Michael Fiedrowicz suggests that part of this concern may have come from the role the exposition of Genesis played in Christian catechesis. See the introduction to Augustine, *On Genesis*, trans. Edmund Hill (New York: New City Press, 2002), 28.

[3] See Fiedrowicz, Introduction to "Unfinished Literal Commentary on Genesis," in Augustine, *On Genesis*, 107.

deal extensively with angelic creation. He seeks to take on the Genesis narrative whole, against the Manicheans who dissect its parts and point out obvious inconsistencies in order to advance their own cosmogony as a counternarrative. In *Literal Meaning of Genesis*, it becomes apparent that in order to argue that Genesis is one cohesive unit, and so finally to defeat the mythological claims of the Manicheans, Augustine must account for the creation of angels and for the seeming double creation of light (on days one and four). His primary concern, therefore, as will emerge in this discussion, is to depict the angels precisely as created. Angels do not have a separate story apart from that of creation; they do not have a different set of rules or a different blessedness, or even, ultimately, a different kind of sin than that of human beings.[4] Angels are not powers coeternal with God, but have their origin and end in God. There must be no gap in the Genesis narrative where myth or an alternative cosmogony can take hold, and in some ways, the most critical territory for the proponents of myth is this celestial territory, the territory of light and darkness, of angels and demons. In addition to affirming that the angels are created *ex nihilo*, Augustine must also develop and defend a doctrine of the angels in which they are created good.[5] There can be no stable principle which opposes God, uncreated or otherwise, and both Satan and his fallen angels must become evil from their own will, not from some defect or maliciousness in the creator. Augustine therefore develops a view of the angels which is fundamentally anti-Manichean (to be specific) but anti-mythological (to speak more broadly); above all, he is concerned to show that the status of an angel is unequivocally that of a creature, created good just like everything else in those seven days. Constructively, therefore, we can see that Augustine's view of the angels helps us to understand his doctrine of creation. The angels, just like human beings, come into their own perfection by understanding their created status and their relationship to God, a relationship which is characterized by praise, but also imaged in sacramental language.

To see how these concerns develop in Augustine's thinking, his Genesis commentaries will be considered in turn: first, *On Genesis: A Refutation of the Manichees* (c. 388–389), followed by the *Unfinished Literal*

---

[4] On the similarities and differences between human and angelic sin, see Wiebe, "Demons in the Theology of Augustine," 93–104.
[5] Joseph Torchia points out that for Augustine, these two doctrines are inseparable. Since God is the author of all natures (creator of everything *ex nihilo*) therefore all natures are good. See N. Joseph Torchia, *Creatio ex nihilo and the Theology of Saint Augustine* (New York: Peter Lang. 1999), 147–148.

Commentary on Genesis (c. 393–394), *Confessions* books XII and XIII (c. 397), and finally, *Literal Meaning of Genesis* (c. 415) and *City of God* books XI and XII (c. 417).

On Genesis: A Refutation of the Manichees
(c. 388–389)

In this early work, Augustine does not yet deal with the matter of angels, but some of the concerns that will come to play a significant role in his angelology are nascent here. First, he develops a hermeneutic for reading Genesis, or at least one might say, he recommends an attitude for reading that will persist throughout his five commentaries. It is necessary for Augustine to articulate this proper disposition, since the Manicheans thrive on ensnaring unlearned Christians by "casting slurs on the scriptures"[6] and so causing the weak to doubt. This early commentary is written especially for the sake of less educated Christians – who could not digest Augustine's "other books"[7] – and so he explains to them, that it is of course "the easiest thing in the world"[8] to find fault with the scriptures, and to parade about its seeming errors, but that this is the practice of heretics. Augustine sets up a different spirit of reading, whereby those of "sound faith"[9] take the coherency of the scriptures as their starting-point. They ask that they may receive, they knock that the door may be opened,[10] and if the Manicheans were to adopt this position "of reverent inquiry rather than captious fault-finding,"[11] they indeed would no longer be Manicheans but catholic Christians. The Manicheans want to "find what they are seeking" behind the text, rather than seeking so that they may find.[12]

Here Augustine evokes one of his best-known principles, that of faith seeking understanding. In this case, he asks the faithful to assume the

---

[6] *Gn. adv. Man.* I.2.
[7] Hill suggests that Augustine has in mind *The Catholic Way of Life and the Manichean Way of Life*, that is, the book which Augustine lists directly before *Genesis Against the Manichees* in his *Reconsiderations*.
[8] *Gn. adv. Man.* I.2. This is how Hill renders *facile possit reprehendi*.
[9] Ibid.
[10] He cites this biblical phrase (Matt. 7:7; Luke 11:9) three times with regard to interpreting the text of Genesis, once in *Gn. adv. Man.* I.2 and twice in *Gn. adv. Man.* II.3.
[11] *Gn. adv. Man.* II.3. *si non reprehendentes et accusantes, sed quaerentes et reuerentes Manichaei mallent discutere, non essent utique Manichaei, sed daretur petentibus et quaerentes inuenirent et pulsantibus aperiretur.*
[12] Ibid.

coherence of Genesis and seek to uncover it, rather than panic in the face of seeming inconsistencies and concede to the Manicheans. His general strategy in this commentary is not to provide one definitive "literal" interpretation of a given passage (though he contends such an interpretation is both possible and laudable, if difficult to find),[13] but to consider the questions prompted by perplexing passages and to give a plethora of readings, mostly figurative. In this way, he endeavors to invite the reader to contemplate the text, and, by showing that the text can be read in *many* different ways, to deflate the Manichean criticism that there is simply *no* way to read Genesis and have it make any sense. Assuming Augustine's hermeneutical attitude, one has no need for myth to supplement Genesis, but rather only to make oneself more open to the mysteries of Genesis itself. Moreover, the Manichean idea that there are two principles of light and darkness, which are coeternal and antithetical,[14] is not consonant with the Genesis narrative, nor is it needed to explain creation as it is described by the text. Although Augustine tends toward figurative interpretation in this commentary, he is laying the groundwork for his future repeated attempts at a "literal" reading of the entire seven days as one coherent narrative.

So Augustine is already undercutting interpretations that would attempt to place certain celestial events behind or before the Genesis narrative. For example, the Manicheans wonder why it should "suddenly take God's fancy"[15] to create the heavens and the earth, and ask what God was doing before he created. Augustine responds that, by claiming God "suddenly" (*subito*) resolved to create, the Manicheans are supplying a detail that helps to levy their critique, namely, that God had spent some length of time idle, lounging around in nothingness, before he impetuously decided to create the world. But no time at all could have passed, Augustine argues, since time itself is created by God.[16] Although Augustine does not mention angels, he is already rejecting the idea that some story could occupy the time prior to Gen. 1:1, as well as insisting that everything which is not God (including time itself) must be understood as created. As for why it pleased God to create, Augustine responds, God created because it was good. Here again,

---

[13] Ibid.
[14] For a brief summary of the Manichean cosmogony, with an eye to Augustine's theological concerns, see Torchia, *Creatio ex nihilo*, 65–97. For a reflection on the Manicheanism Augustine knew and how it shaped his theological interests, see Kevin Coyle, "Saint Augustine's Manichean Legacy," *Augustinian Studies* 34 (2003): 1–22.
[15] *Gn. adv. Man.* 1.4; *quid placuit deo subito facere caelum et terram?*
[16] Ibid., 1.3–4.

he wants to cut off the possibility of some creation which is evil, or which exists apart from the single intention of God as expressed in Genesis. He correspondingly insists that the source of sin in the world can be found in the text of the fall story, and nowhere else. On the terms of Genesis, he argues, Eve's sin cannot be blamed on God, since the story tells us that God created everything good, nor can it be blamed on the creation or an act of the devil, because God created him good as well. The sin rests in Eve's consent. We ought not to blame God for allowing the devil access to Eve, but to blame Eve for giving the devil access to herself; she was made good so that "if she hadn't wanted to, she wouldn't have done so."[17] In fact, in order to be reconciled to God and to reenter the garden one must repent of the idea that evil can be blamed on some "extraneous nature"[18] and not on oneself.

In this commentary, then, Augustine lays the foundations for the rejection of an alternative creation myth, first by recommending a holistic reading of Genesis in an attitude of humility, which *de facto* eliminates the need for an alternative narrative to help explain seeming problems in the text. Second, he interprets Genesis so as to exclude potentially mythological elements, such as rejecting any time previous to the Genesis story or the existence of some external source of evil. Further groundwork is laid in this commentary which becomes critical for Augustine's angelology, particularly in how he exposits Gen. 1:1-3, since he will later understand these verses to describe the creation of the angels. For example, in support of dualism, the Manicheans note that in Genesis God is said to create out of some preexistent matter rather than *ex nihilo*. In verse 2, the earth seems already to have been created, although it is formless and shapeless, and it is from this shadowy material that God creates everything else. Augustine argues that Gen. 1:1 "God made heaven and earth" does indeed describe some initial creation of everything, but it was yet without form or shape, as explained in verse 2. He thus attempts to read the verses in context and to show that the story coheres; verse 2 simply clarifies verse 1. In the six days following the proclamation that God created heaven and earth (Gen. 1:1), then, God duly arranges everything although creation is still entirely *ex nihilo*. Moreover, the light which is made following in Gen. 1:3 does not imply, as the Manicheans think, that God was sitting around in

---

[17] Ibid., II.42.
[18] Ibid., II.41; *extraneam naturam*. Similarly, in *Confessions* Augustine recalls how Manicheanism appealed to his pride by providing him an external scapegoat for his sin (see *conf.* V.18.10).

the darkness beforehand, but rather that God enlightened creation. This light is not the kind seen "with the eyes of the flesh" (since this is made on day four).[19] Moreover, God is not said to make darkness, since darkness is only the absence of light.[20] Although some of these points of interpretation may seem quite familiar to us from Augustine's later works, here he tentatively lays down principles which will be developed to include an understanding of angelic creation and indeed angelic life: first, that somehow God created everything in Gen. 1:1 but it unfolds in seven days, second, that the light created on day one is not visible or corporeal light, and third that God did not create the darkness.

The Unfinished Literal Commentary (c. 393–394)

In the *Unfinished Literal Commentary on Genesis*, Augustine continues to develop the work he began in his first commentary, still very much in an anti-Manichean key.[21] In this work, he attempts for the first time a truly "literal" reading of Genesis, which he felt was necessary to ultimately thwart the Manicheans (even if a figurative reading is still entirely appropriate and even necessary).[22] Augustine operates with a similar hermeneutical strategy as in the first commentary, both in his approach of "faith seeking understanding" and also in his reluctance to insist on a certain interpretation, which he warns can turn out to be sacrilege, merely "the rash assertion of one's uncertain and dubious opinions."[23] In this work, he is also more explicit about the subordination of his interpretation to the rule of faith, in part, because he is newly ordained.[24] He gives a summary of the creed at the beginning of his commentary, and draws special attention to the statement that God is creator of "all things both visible and invisible." Augustine elaborates on this phrase: it means that God created everything, "whether intellectual or corporeal"[25] and that

[19] Ibid., 1.5.
[20] Ibid., 1.7.
[21] Fiedrowicz in *On Genesis*, 107. Solignac, however, argues that although the commentary has anti-Manichean concerns, Augustine's exegesis is still driven by the Genesis text itself, not by these external critiques. See Solignac, "Exégèse et Métaphysique," 158.
[22] See Fiedrowicz in *On Genesis*, 105.
[23] *Gn. litt. imp.* 1.1. In light of this, Fiedrowicz, among others, claims for Augustine "a healthy dose of skepticism." See *On Genesis*, 110. Solignac likewise notes this "caractère aporétique" of Augustine's Genesis commentaries; "Exégèse et Métaphysique," 158.
[24] Fiedrowicz, *On Genesis*, 106.
[25] In this passage, the creed, scripture and its interpretation are tightly knit. Augustine notices that the creed clarifies the phrase "creator of heaven and earth" (cf. Gen. 1:1) to

these things "are not born of God, but made by God out of nothing, and
… there is nothing among them which belong to the Trinity except what
the Trinity created."[26] It is therefore "not lawful to say or believe that
the whole creation is consubstantial or co-eternal with God."[27] In other
words, the creed clearly distinguishes between the created order and the
divine nature. To confuse them is to defy the opening statement of the
creed, and thus the basis of Christian faith. Augustine is also quick to
add that creation is "very good" and that God did not create evil itself
nor anything evil.[28] Again, in describing the appropriate approach to the
biblical text, he excludes possible mythological interpretative strategies.

   Unlike in his first commentary, Augustine speaks about the angels almost
immediately after he lays down this rule of faith. Perhaps this change is
due to the emphasis he places on the clear distinction between God and
creation, which we have just noted, that is, he must immediately consider how God created everything, "whether intellectual or corporeal."[29]
This creation includes celestial creatures, and Edmund Hill suggests that,
although Augustine is relying on Neo-Platonic vocabulary, he would have
understood the idea of "intellectual creation" or "subsistent intelligences"
to refer specifically to angels.[30] The question of the creation of the angels
emerges from Augustine's consideration of the first phrase of Genesis *in
the beginning*. Augustine posits that *in the beginning* can mean in Christ,
who is the "very Wisdom of God,"[31] and the beginning of all things. Or, *in
the beginning* could refer to the first thing made, that is, heaven and earth.
But, he asks, could heaven and earth have been the first thing made "if
angels and all the intellectual powers were made first, because we have to

---

mean creator of "all things visible and invisible" (cf. Col. 1:16). Augustine himself then
further clarifies that "all things visible and invisible" means *everything* "whether intellectual or corporeal," but notes that the creed expresses this same idea in a biblical
idiom. So, although Augustine interprets Genesis in light of the rule of faith, he also
demonstrates that the creed is already interpreting scripture. The back and forth between
the creed and the Genesis text is happening at every turn; next he affirms the goodness
of creation, not, of course because it is next in the creed, but because it is next in the text
of Genesis and is a crucial qualifier of the phrase "creator of heaven and earth."

[26] *Gn. litt. imp.* I.2.
[27] Ibid.
[28] Ibid., I.3.
[29] Ibid., I.2.
[30] See Hill's footnote to *Gn. litt. imp.* I.2.
[31] *Gn. litt. imp.* I.6, referring to 1 Cor. 1:24. Augustine is fond of this interpretation and
repeats it many times; see *Gn. adv. Man.* I.3, *conf.* XIII.5.6, *Gn. litt.* I.2, *Gn. litt.* I.9 and
civ. Dei XI.32. It is an interpretation also employed by Origen and Ambrose; see Solignac,
"Exégèse and Métaphysique," 155.

believe that the angels too are God's creation and were made by him?"[32] As in his earlier commentary, Augustine is attentive to the problem of the integrity of the Genesis narrative, and now he expands this concern to include the precise timing of the creation of angels. He wonders if the angels were created first, then what of time? Were the angels created before time, in time or simultaneously with time?[33] Augustine had already made clear in his first commentary that time was created, and here he reiterates that point.[34] The angels are dealt with similarly, and the problem of the creation of angels, although as obscure as that of time, is merely a matter to be considered, not a reason to abandon Genesis or deem it deficient. As is his custom in these commentaries, he goes on to provide many plausible answers to these questions, again laboring to defang the Manichean claim that the narrative is sheer nonsense, and so completely uninterpretable. It is possible, Augustine contends, that the angels were created before time and then time was made on day four, along with the lights in heaven. Or, it is possible that the days of creation signify something entirely unrelated to time as we know it, but the narrative is arranged into days "in this order to help human frailty."[35] In that case, the timing of angels' creation is somewhat a moot question. Another possibility is that time was created on day one, but not time yet demarcated by days and years, rather some celestial time in which the angels can move.[36]

Augustine shortly returns to the question of the angels, in his discussion of verse 3, the creation of light. He must interpret the light of the first day already looking forward to day four, the creation of "the lamps in the sky, which are set out after this light here."[37] Knowing that the light of day four must somehow represent corporeal light or time as we know it now, Augustine considers it quite plausible to understand the first light of day one as "an incorporeal light, if we say that in this book it is not only the visible creation but the entire creation that is being set before us."[38] Whatever this first light is, he insists, "we are still, surely, obliged to take it as something made and created," since God makes it in the same way he makes everything else.[39] Given, then, that the first light is both

---

[32] *Gn. litt. imp.* 1.7.
[33] Ibid.
[34] See *Gn. adv. Man.* 1.3.
[35] *Gn. litt. imp.* 1.9. See also *Gn. litt. imp.* 1.28.
[36] *Gn. litt. imp.* 1.8.
[37] Ibid., 1.20.
[38] Ibid., 1.21.
[39] Ibid., 1.20.

invisible and definitely created, and, moreover, that people wonder when
it was that the angels were created, Augustine suggests that it is in verse 3
(the *fiat lux*) that angelic creation comes into being.[40] He is tentative and
concedes that this reference to angelic creation would be brief indeed,
but that these words would still "most aptly and suitably" refer to that
creation.[41]

As Augustine himself laments, this matter of angels is "most abstruse,
quite impenetrable to human guesswork."[42] So why should this discussion hold his attention here? He speaks about angels at some length,
both when he comments on *in the beginning* and in his discussion of day
one, as we have just seen.[43] Augustine has already told us: it is because
"the angels too are God's creation and were made by him,"[44] and because
it "is not only the visible creation but the entire creation that is being set
before us."[45] To contemplate the origin of angels, then, is properly done
alongside a contemplation of the rest of the created order, in the context
of reading Genesis. Genesis has the whole story, so to speak, and it is thus
primarily in this text where we should seek to find out about the angels
and their origin. Augustine concludes his discussion of *in the beginning*
by harkening back to his citation of the creed, saying that regardless of
our exact opinions about the angels, it "assuredly has to be accepted in
faith, even if it exceeds our habits of thought, that everything created has
a beginning and that time itself is something created, and this itself also
has a beginning and is not co-eternal with the creator."[46] Whatever one
might think about angels, Genesis makes clear that they have a beginning, a shared beginning with the rest of creation, and that in Genesis one
may contemplate their creaturely status like that of any other creature.

The Confessions (c. 397)

In books XII and XIII of *The Confessions*, Augustine interprets Genesis once
again, although the character of this work is quite different from that of
his earlier commentaries. His concerns with the Genesis text are always
shaped to some extent by his encounter with Manicheanism, although in

---

[40] Ibid., 1.21.
[41] Ibid.
[42] Ibid., 1.7.
[43] Ibid., 1.7–8; 21–28.
[44] Ibid., 1.7.
[45] Ibid., 1.21.
[46] Ibid., 1.8.

The Confessions he is not so overtly polemical. The final books of *The Confessions*, moreover, are not a line-by-line exposition of the text of Genesis, but rather a rumination on its significance. Augustine ends his search to find his "rest in God"[47] with a consideration of Genesis and its promised rest of the seventh day. As he began with his own childhood, so he ends with the creation of the world, as if his life echoes all the way back and all the way forward. In short, this commentary on Genesis is not an attempt at a "literal" reading, but Augustine is led on through the creation story by a contemplation of its images.

In book XII of *The Confessions*, Augustine considers the first two verses of Genesis, when God creates the heavens and the earth and the darkness is over the waters. Augustine's primary interest is to consider what is meant by the initial reference to the creation of the heavens and the earth (in verse 1), and to establish the origin of the formless matter from which creation is subsequently brought forth. His interpretation is that "heaven" indicates intellectual creation, and "earth" indicates the unformed substrate that is to become both the world and heavenly bodies, i.e. the substrate of all corporeal creation. Augustine never uses the word *angelus* in book XII, but, in the course of attempting to explain the meaning of God's initial creation of an unformed heaven and earth, he argues for the creation of a spiritual creature, immune to time, which he calls the "heaven of heaven" (cf. Ps. 113:16). His use of the phrase "heaven of heaven" (*caelum caeli*) for intellectual creation has attracted much scholarly attention, and many have sought to establish what Augustine thinks about form and matter and to what extent his interpretation in book XII is influenced by Greek philosophical ideas.[48] As opposed to the way in which he imagines angels, however, Augustine tends to think of the heaven of heaven primarily as a place, which he calls, for example the "house" of God.[49] The angels, it seems, inhabit (or perhaps, constitute) this place,

I do not find anything which I may more fittingly judge should be called "the heaven of heaven, which is the Lord's" (cf. Ps. 113:16) than your own house, which contemplates your delight without any fault of going to another, a pure

---

[47] *conf.* I.I.I.
[48] See, for example, Gerd Van Riel, "Augustine's Exegesis of 'Heaven and Earth' in Conf. XII," *Quaestio: Annuario di storia della metafisica* 7 (2007): 191–228. Van Riel engages with the history of the debate over the phrase, including the seminal work by Jean Pépin.
[49] For example, in *conf.* XII.15.19–22.

mind, most harmoniously one by the established peace of holy spirits, citizens of your city in heavenly places above these present heavens.[50]

The passing reference to the angels suggests that Augustine does consider the heaven of heaven and other spiritual creatures to be related and perhaps co-dependent, but he does not refer to the angels' relationship to the heaven of heaven in any other place.[51] In *City of God*, for example, he does not designate the city founded by the angels as the heaven of heaven. Nevertheless, this "house" of God is described in terms which he commonly uses for angels, as we will see; it is a stable spiritual creation which cannot fall and it clings to God through contemplation.[52] Augustine also contends that the biblical text should include an account of the creation of the heaven of heaven, just as it must account for the angels, however obscurely.[53] While he clearly understands the heaven of heaven to be outside of time in this exegesis, he will later understand the angels to be within some order of time.[54] Since the relationship between angels and this living house of God is unclear, perhaps he does not intend the angels to be included in the timelessness of the heaven of heaven.

When Augustine comes to consider Gen. 1:3 in book XIII (the creation of light), he discusses the angels more directly. At the beginning of this book, he emphasizes the dependence of all creation on God. Still contemplating the significance of the first two verses of Genesis, he meditates on creation *ex nihilo*, asking "what claim did corporeal matter have upon you, merely to be invisible and without form, since it would not even be except you made it? Hence since it did not exist, it had no claim on you to exist."[55] Even if God had created out of some primordial matter, which was without

---

[50] Ibid., XII.11.13.
[51] Wiebe seems more confident about equating the heaven of heaven with the angels; see "Demons in the theology of Augustine," 44.
[52] Augustine speaks of the heaven of heaven as adhering (*cohaerendo*) to God in contemplation of the Word (*conf.* XII.11.13). That angels "cling" or "adhere" to God is Augustine's principle way of describing the angelic life and activity, as discussed below.
[53] Against those who would say that he is over-reading the Genesis text by introducing this idea of the heaven of heaven, Augustine mentions that seraphim and cherubim are nowhere explicitly mentioned in Genesis, but they must have been created (*conf.* XII.22.31). As he develops a more "literal" understanding of Genesis, he insists that the creation of angels must be accounted for by the Genesis text, but he tends toward this interpretation even in his earlier commentaries (as noted above).
[54] Time, after all, seems to have been made on day four, as noted in the earlier commentaries. It is hard to say what might cause Augustine to later reject that angels are outside of time, other than a more sustained interest in the created status of angels and how they interact with time.
[55] *conf.* XIII.2.3.

form and shape, such matter would still have been created by God and be dependent on God. Moreover, even after God brought this matter into existence, he would not have been obliged to shape it. Augustine continues with *fiat lux* (verse 3). This verse, he suggests, seems to apply

to spiritual creation, since there was already some sort of life you might illuminate. But just as it had no claim on you to be such a life as could be illuminated, so also, now that it existed, it had no claim on you to be given light. Nor would its formlessness be pleasing to you unless it were made light, not by merely existing but by beholding the light-giving light and adhering (*cohaerendo*) to it. Hence the fact that it lives in some way, and that it lives happily, it owes entirely to your grace.[56]

What we have noted in previous commentaries is now on full display: the angels are created *ex nihilo* and spiritual creation is entirely gratuitous, just like the shapeless matter. Genesis proclaims a series of completely free acts done by God out of his goodness, and nothing he creates binds him to act in one way or another. Illuminating creation is not incumbent upon God, and yet he would not have done otherwise because of his goodness.

Note that, for Augustine, the origin of spiritual creation and the intention in which it was made already entails its end. The shapeless matter needed to be formed such that it could receive God's illumination and behold it, but also so that it could adhere to the light (*cohaerendo*). Augustine often speaks of angelic beings adhering to God, using verbs such as *adhaerere*, *cohaerere* and *inhaerere*.[57] All of spiritual creation was made to behold the light and to be held by the light in perpetuity. After announcing the nature of this light, in fact, Augustine moves into a contemplation of the light itself (i.e. the Trinity) in reference to Gen. 1:1b, the Spirit of God sweeping over the waters. Seamlessly, Augustine moves on to the division of the light from the darkness, when day and night are named. He will later explicitly take this division to be the moment of the angelic fall, and here he also seems to be contemplating that event. He writes:

The angel fell away; man's soul fell away. They pointed out the abyss of all spiritual creation and its darksome depths, unless you had said from the beginning "let light be made," and light was made, and every obedient intelligence in your

---

[56] Ibid., XIII.2.4.
[57] Augustine's use of these verbs with respect to the angelic life is ubiquitous from early (e.g. *lib. arb.* III.34) to late (e.g. *Gn. litt.* IV.49), but is especially prominent in *City of God* (see, for example, *civ. Dei* XI.29, XII.1, XII.5 and XII.9).

heavenly city had cleaved to you (*inhaereret tibi*) and found rest in your Spirit ... otherwise even the heaven of heaven would be a darksome deep within itself, but now it is light in the Lord.[58]

The entire celestial drama plays out in an instant, and the parallel of the human and the angelic falls is striking, because Augustine, of course, is not commenting on the story of Adam and Eve. But the fall of the angels is parallel to the fall of human beings; both are an (inexplicable) failure to cling to God. Any creation that does not adhere to God reverts into the darkness from which it sprang, that is, into non-being.[59] Augustine's emphasis remains on the utter sufficiency of God and the utter insufficiency of creation to exist apart from God. The angels, as human beings, are nothing without God and their fall into darkness points this out with great clarity. Augustine has obviated any notion that the creation of the angels or the condition of their fall has any essential difference from that of human beings, and in this, his anti-Manichean aims once again come into view. The fall of the angels does not imply a God who must struggle against some coeternal darkness, nor an evil creation, but quite the opposite:

The very restless misery of spirits flowing away and displaying their own darkness, when stripped of the garments of your light, you sufficiently reveal how great you made the rational creature. For in no way is any being less than you sufficient to give it rest and happiness, and for this it is not sufficient to itself.[60]

The evil angels who have fallen now wander restlessly, and prove that God has made all creation only for himself, and this is the highest honor. There is no other origin or end for the created order, but all is in darkness which does not cling to the light. All of these images, of course, remind us of Augustine's

---

[58] *conf.* XIII.8.9.
[59] James Wetzel suggests that Adam undergoes an "angelization" in Augustine's imagination when he is attempting to explain Adam's fall. It is certainly true that the problems of Adam's fall and of the angels' fall end up being exactly parallel for Augustine; how could a creature, created good, with every advantage possibly choose its own destruction? But it seems as if it might be better to speak of angels undergoing an Adam-ization. Augustine must think about the angelic fall in light of his rigorous theological reflections on the human fall, and not vice versa, since the biblical information regarding the angelic fall is so slim. In any case, the problem is how to extricate God completely from the creation of evil while retaining that God created everything (human being or angel) to be very good. See Wetzel, "Augustine on the Origin of Evil: Myth and Metaphysics" in *Augustine's City of God: A Critical Guide*, ed. James Wetzel(Cambridge: Cambridge University Press, 2012), 167–186. The problem is discussed more in depth in *Literal Meaning of Genesis*.
[60] *conf.* XIII.8.9.

own restless heart which for so long sought for happiness in things external. In the good angels, Augustine sees the image of rest completed and turns from this discussion to cry out,

Give me yourself, O my God! Restore yourself to me! Behold, I love you, and if it be too little, let me love you more strongly ... this alone I know, that apart from you it is evil with me not only outside myself, but also in myself, and that for me all abundance that is not my God is but want.[61]

Augustine comes to see that his own end is already proclaimed on day one of creation, when God creates the light. Apart from God, nothing – neither angels nor Augustine – can find rest, but only an unstable listlessness, deficiency, want and ultimately non-existence.

The honor, however, which is peculiar to the good angels is that they receive full enlightenment along with their creation, since they are both created and illuminated in the *fiat lux*.[62] The good angels know no other existence. In human beings, however, there is a distinction in time between when we are made and when we are enlightened, and in our present state we are ever "being converted to that unfailing light."[63] Human beings must look upon the firmament above (which Augustine takes to be an image of scripture, unfurled like the scroll of heaven), whereas the angels read the book of Christ (i.e. the Word).[64] In light of this angelic blessedness, Augustine writes,

let the supercelestial peoples, who are your angels praise you, they who have no need to look up at this firmament or by reading to know your Word. They always behold your face, and without any syllables of time, they read upon it what your eternal will decrees. They read your will, they choose it, and they love it. They read forever and what they read never passes away.[65]

---

[61] Ibid.
[62] Ibid., XIII.10.11.
[63] Ibid.
[64] Ibid., XIII.15.18.
[65] Ibid. *laudent te supercaelestes populi angelorum tuorum, qui non opus habent suspicere firmamentum hoc et legendo cognoscere uerbum tuum. Uident enim faciem tuam semper [Matt. 18.10] et ibi legunt sine syllabis temporum, quid uelit aeterna uoluntas tua. legunt, eligunt et diligunt; semper legunt et numquam praeterit quod legunt.* The image of eternal reading appears also in *s.* 57.7: "We shall [in heaven] be seeing the Word itself, listening to the Word itself, eating it, drinking it, as the angels do now. Do angels need books, or lectures, or readers? Of course not. They read by seeing, since they see Truth itself *(uidendo legunt: uident enim ipsam ueritatem)*." In *en. Ps.* 119 we find a similar discussion. The angels, Augustine says, enjoy God's Word in the heavenly city "without reading, without letters, for what is written on the page for us they behold in the face of God" *(ibi omnes iusti et sancti, qui fruuntur uerbo dei sine lectione, sine litteris; quod enim nobis per paginas scriptum est, per faciem dei illi cernunt; en. Ps.* 119.6). In these two passages, as in *conf.*, Augustine rejects that the angels read in a physical sense

In this arresting image of eternal reading, Augustine attempts to represent how angels always have their face turned toward God and love him. He is also beginning to use Genesis as source material for understanding the life of the angels, particularly to develop an understanding of angelic knowledge. I will return to the idea of angelic knowledge and to eternal reading, as it takes the fore in *The Literal Meaning of Genesis*.

There is one last reference to angels in book XIII which warrants our attention. It comes at the very end of *Confessions*, when Augustine at last asks how we are to understand God, and fittingly, how we are to find our rest in him on the seventh day. He asks, "what man will give it to a man to understand this? What angel will give it to an angel? What angel to man? From you let it be asked. In you let it be sought."[66] Just as he began his reflection on Genesis with the emphatic proclamation that angels come from God and find their rest in him, so he ends on the same note. A human being cannot give rest to another any more than an angel could give it to another angel. Angels, in the order of creation, seek their happiness in God, as should human beings. Finally, not even an angel can give rest to a human being, one last reminder that myth does not promise the omnipotent God as its end, but only some shoddy replacement which must, according to Augustine, itself be a creature. Genesis, on the other hand, demands that both angels and human beings knock and seek God himself; "thus, thus is it received, thus is it found, thus is it opened to us."[67]

What we have noted in Augustine's earlier commentaries remains true in *The Confessions*. Augustine understands the angels in terms of their creaturely status, and emphasizes the total sufficiency of God. In so doing he reduces the status (or, we might say, the allure) of the angel of myth, the archon, who is formidable enough to oppose God, or to have some origin outside of God.[68] Those angels of myth are actors in their own celestial

---

(they do not read the syllables of the scriptures), but rather they read the Word forever. Angels do read in heaven, but they do not have books (*codices*), readers (*lectores*), pages (*paginae*) or readings (*lectio*). Likewise in *s. Dolbeau* 3.12, Augustine tells us that in the angelic life there is no preaching (*evangelizare*); the angels need the Word (*uerbum*) but not voices (*uoces*), which are time-bound and fleshly. On the whole, in these homiletic contexts, Augustine seems to be thinking of certain aspects of the liturgy (the turning of pages, readings, preaching) being surpassed or transformed in the angelic life, since all explanatory and exegetical practices cease. Reading, nevertheless, reaches its perfection in heaven where the angels read the Word always without any passing of time.

[66] *conf.* XIII.37.52.

[67] Ibid.

[68] This is not a claim about a particular moment in the Manichean myth, but only of the abilities of archons in general in various gnostic systems, although the powers of darkness clearly pose a threat to the realm of light in the Manichean myth.

drama into which humankind can be drawn, but Augustine's angels do not enjoy this kind of autonomous power. From Augustine's perspective, however, he has raised the status of angels to the highest it could possibly be, because God made angels from his own free will and for himself, just as he made human beings. The good angels even have a special blessedness to be envied, because they "knew no other state"[69] than to abide in God's rest. By looking at them, we have an image of the life to come, for which Augustine expressly longs and which he articulates in the image of eternal reading. He has thus also gone farther in *The Confessions* than in his previous commentaries in contemplating the nature of the angelic life, and what it means for the promised end of human life.

City of God and Literal Meaning of Genesis
(c. 415; 417)

Both *City of God* and *Literal Meaning of Genesis* represent Augustine's mature attempts at interpreting Genesis. It is here where he gives, at last, a complete "literal" interpretation of the creation story, and where he deals with the question of the angels most extensively. As in his earlier commentaries, in *The Literal Meaning of Genesis* Augustine interprets the text verse by verse, and operates under the same hermeneutic of faith seeking understanding. He reaffirms that although allegory is a perfectly suitable and edifying way of reading the text, it is his goal and intention to give an interpretation of Genesis in its primary sense.[70] He also maintains a certain reticence to give final approbation to a particular reading, always leaving open the possibility that someone else may be able to give a better interpretation.[71] And yet, in *Literal Meaning of Genesis* he does offer more concrete conclusions than we have seen in any of his other commentaries. He is thorough – perhaps, for the modern reader, too thorough – in thinking through each alternative interpretation and its every implication, in order to exclude those that cannot possibly fit the text. As a result, he often does arrive at some sense of the proper meaning, even if he allows latitude within his final determination. Books XI and XII of *The City of God*, on the other hand, are not strictly a commentary on Genesis, but part of an exposition of the whole of scripture which is intended to show "the origin, and progress, and destinies of the two cities

---

[69] *conf.* XIII.10.11.
[70] *Gn. litt.* I.2.
[71] For example, see *Gn. litt.* IV.45.

(the earthly and the heavenly)."[72] In these two books, Augustine discusses the foundation of the two cities which "were originally laid in the difference that arose among the angels."[73]

Although these two texts have different aims and organization, they will be treated together, as they are written around the same time and in them Augustine expresses many similar ideas with respect to angels.[74] First Augustine's interpretation of the first and the fourth days of creation will be discussed. Unsurprisingly, he pays significant attention to the creation of light(s) on these two days, where considerable material on angels is to be found. His vision of angelic knowledge, which arises from his discussion of the meaning of the days of creation, will be of special interest. This idea was alluded to briefly in *The Confessions*, but in these texts becomes a topic of sustained meditation. Then, Augustine's understanding of the angels' role in the act of creation will be explored. He repeatedly affirms that the angels are creatures and not creators, even if they help God in some way, and he favors agricultural imagery to describe the work of the angels. Augustine is careful to avoid any suggestion that the angels created some part of the world on their own, which resonates with his earlier anti-mythological concerns. Lastly, the fall of the angels will be considered. This topic is of particular interest in *City of God*. Just as Augustine insists that the creation of the angels is described in Genesis, however briefly, so also he prefers an interpretation of the angelic fall which is contained within the text. The devil has no time or narrative space whatsoever apart from the Genesis story.

The Creation of Light and Angelic Knowledge

Augustine spends almost the entirety of book I of *The Literal Meaning of Genesis* inquiring whether or not the light created on day one is corporeal. He has pursued the answer to this question before, but here the discussion is much expanded as he considers every conceivable way in which the light of day one could have been bodily. Having ruled out all the possibilities, he concludes that the first light created is not corporeal but rather spiritual, and seems to be related to enlightenment.

---

[72] *civ. Dei* XI.I.
[73] Ibid.
[74] Admittedly, in *City of God* Augustine's comments are much briefer, and so I use *Literal Meaning of Genesis* as my main source. For an overview of what he discusses vis-à-vis Gen. 1:1–3 in *City of God* in comparison to *Literal Meaning of Genesis*, see Solignac, "Exégèse et Métaphysique," 170–171.

The light, moreover, must be understood as created and does not refer to the Word or to some other light within the divine nature.[75] He has tread this ground before, but in the course of his more rigorous investigation another problem comes to his attention. Even if the creation of the first light is properly understood as spiritual, why does Genesis use the language of "morning and evening" prior to day four when the sun (and thus time as we know it) would seem to have been created? Although he has suggested in previous commentaries that the use of the word "day" may be an accommodation for human weakness, here the question becomes pressing, since he will not allow himself recourse to allegory.[76] Even if Genesis uses the words evening and morning as adaptations to the human mind, they must signify something literal about creation. Augustine leaves off the first book with this question, then: if we say the *fiat lux* is a literal creation of spiritual light, in what way could it possibly take place on or in a literal day?

Although Augustine seems to leave the question behind and move on to the creation of the firmament, in book II he quickly returns to the troubling matter of the signification of the morning–evening cycle. To the former problem is added a new textual detail: day one, the creation of light, is the only day which does not feature repetition. So God says "let there be light," but the text does not follow and say "thus light was made." Such repetition does occur on each of the other days of creation.[77] In book IV, when he discusses the seventh day and in what way God can be said to rest on a day, these problems inevitably resurface: "once again, therefore, we find ourselves slipping back into the same problem from which we seemed to have extricated ourselves," namely, "how light could circulate to produce the alternations of day and night, not only before the lamps of heaven, but even before heaven itself."[78] It is here finally, after he has discussed the rest of the seventh day, where a solution is reached. All of the elements which he has been juggling – that the light of day one must be both created and spiritual, that the morning–evening cycle must refer to something which "actually happened"[79] and that day one seems

---

[75] *Gn. litt.* I.3.
[76] Augustine starts to make some suggestions about the night/day cycle pertaining to the fall and redemption, but quickly ends this line of discussion since "we undertook ... to talk here about the scriptures according to their proper meaning of what actually happened, not according to their riddling, enigmatic reference to future events" (ibid., I.33).
[77] Ibid., II.16.
[78] Ibid., IV.38.
[79] Ibid., I.33.

peculiar in its lack of repetition – lead him to propose that the references to morning and evening in the entire Genesis narrative (both prior to and after day four) refer to the movements of angelic knowledge.

Thus, on day one the angels are created. They are spiritual creatures whose beginning is fittingly described in the words *fiat lux* since they receive enlightenment along with their being.[80] The following cycle of evening eclipsed by morning and overtaken by evening does not signify any amount of time as we know it, but rather indicates the angels beholding all things as they already exist in the mind of God (day) and then looking at creation, and knowing the created order as it is in itself (evening). When the angels then refer the good of the created order back again to the praise and glory of God "it is as if morning has dawned in the minds of those who contemplate them."[81] Therefore,

> the evening of the first day is also its [the spiritual creation's] self-knowledge that it is not what God is, while the morning after that evening, which marks the conclusion of the one day and the beginning of the second, means its turning to refer what it was created as to the praise of the creator, and to receive from the Word of God knowledge of the creation which is made after itself.[82]

On day one the angels receive knowledge of God first, then of themselves in the evening. The next morning, they return to the Word aglow with praise for their own creation and glimpse again what will be created on day two, the firmament. They then "look back, over their shoulder, as it were"[83] to see what has been created during the evening, which they again refer to the praise of God and so on for six days. Aimé Solignac fittingly describes these noetic movements as three "conversions:" the "conversion transcendante et formatrice" (day), the "conversion immanente et conscientielle (ou descendante et contemplatrice)" because the angels look at creatures below (evening) and the "conversion ascendante et laudatrice" (morning).[84] Solignac's threefold distinction and his use of

---

[80] Ibid., II.17.
[81] *civ. Dei* XI. 29.
[82] *Gn. litt.* IV.39
[83] Ibid., II.17. The Latin has only *respicientes*, but I have indulged and cited Hill's translation, which expands the text to "make the image more vivid," as he says.
[84] Solignac, "Exégèse et Métaphysique," 164. He also raises the question of Plotinian influence. He suggests these movements of angelic knowledge could be considered an "application" of three phases of the constitution of the *nous* in the fifth *Ennead* (specifically, V.1.6 and V.2.1), but it is difficult to parse how this application might function, even if we allow that the influence may not be direct. The angels are not really analogous to the *nous*, but rather Augustine insists precisely that the *fiat lux* describes a created *other* and not the Word (with which the *nous* is normally associated). Although the return to

the concept of conversion captures the Augustinian text well. Augustine is speaking both of internal turning, a continual conversion of the angelic mind, but he also evokes motion: transcending, descending and ascending, to borrow Solignac's paradigm. The so-called downwards turn (to look at creation) is also an immanence, as the angels become self-aware. The repetition which Augustine had noted earlier – "and thus it was made" – indicates this same activity of the angels. When God speaks in order to make something, Augustine explains, this signifies the angels seeing by God's Word what is about to be made in the way in which it already exists in the mind of God. The repetition represents the thing actually coming into being. The repetition does not occur on day one, since there are no angels to witness the thing as it exists in the mind of God, and since the angels are made and enlightened all in one word.[85]

This interpretation of Augustine is novel, and Goulven Madec, following the suggestion of Solignac, claims that Augustine's incorporation of the angels into the creation story is his greatest achievement in angelology.[86] Neither Madec nor Solignac, however, says exactly why this should be so, beyond the sheer innovation of it. It is true that Augustine's attentiveness to the nuances of the text is remarkable, and that the interpretation which arises is as surprising as it is profound. The interpretation, however, also has considerable implications for Augustine's thought more broadly speaking. Although we could draw much from the wealth of this exposition, I will here suggest three ways in which we might consider the wider import of his interpretation. First, it implies creation itself is pedagogical and spectacular from the beginning. Second, it gives us some insight into Augustine's understanding of the creaturely status of angels and so the status of creation itself. Third, it suggests that (human) time has a sacramental quality.

As we have noted, Augustine from his earliest commentaries suggests that the days of creation are so named as an accommodation for human

the begetter (*enn.* v.1.6) is described by Plotinus as love, it occurs by sheer necessity and could not be understood as anything like praise (which is Augustine's primary way of referring to the angels' matinal motion). It is certainly true that the Neo-Platonic notion of the movement of the mind and of its return to God shapes Augustine's imagination, but the idea has been so changed by the biblical context and Augustine's other theological interests that it does not much illuminate the present discussion.

[85] *Gn. litt.* II.16.
[86] Goulven Madec, "Angelus," 315. The passage to which Madec refers is Solignac, "Exégèse et Métaphysique," 161; "l'intrègre de façon cohérente le monde des anges à l'ensemble de la creation," Solignac remarks, is "l'apport le plus remarkables d'Augustin dans la tradition des commentaires de Genèse 1,1-3."

understanding.[87] But, since these days in their literal and proper sense indicate the movement of angelic knowledge from God to creature, and then back to God again, it would seem that these days are pedagogical. They are the literal referent to angelic education. The repetition of God speaking the Word of creation and then the making of that creation is in some way done for the sake of the angels, so that they may see creation unfold as a spectacle. Although it may not be proper to speak of the angels learning something through this process, as they are enlightened immediately and possess the fullness of knowledge, still it seems that through the morning and evening cycle the angels are shown something. Although the angels already have knowledge of creation in the morning it "is again known in its specific kind by that light, which had already known in the Word of God that it was to be made."[88] The angels are also described as *seeing*, "glancing down below"[89] and then *referring* what they see back to God.[90] In other words, the angels seem to experience something new in the actual unfolding of creation, even though they can behold the blueprint for the whole created order from the first moment of their existence. They respond to this experience by praising God. The idea that the days are pedagogical, even for the angels, is further implied by Augustine's suggestion that morning and evening knowledge may be contemplated simultaneously in the angelic mind. Perhaps,

> the angels of the loftiest heavens do not successively gaze, first upon the ideas of creatures which are there unchanging in the unchangeable truth of the Word of God, next upon the creature themselves, and thirdly refer their own knowledge of them to the praise of the creator, but their minds have the marvelous facility of being able to do all three things at once. All the same, they [those who may argue this point] will surely not say – or if anyone does, we should certainly not pay any attention – that those thousands of angel citizens of the heavenly city either do not contemplate the eternity of the creator or are unaware of the mutability of creatures, or are not prompted also by that lower kind of know-ledge of theirs to the praise of the creator ... they may be able to do all this simultaneously; let them do it all simultaneously. Then they can and they do; so then they simultaneously have day and evening and morning in themselves all together.[91]

---

[87] See *Gn. litt. Imp.* 1.9 and 1.28.
[88] *Gn. litt.* IV.39.
[89] Ibid., IV.41. The passage mentions seeing as well as referring: *infra despicientes eamque referentes ad illius laudem.*
[90] See, for example, *Gn. litt.* IV.41 (cited above), but Augustine employs *refero* throughout his discussion of the cycle of angelic knowledge.
[91] Ibid., IV.46.

In this passage, Augustine suggests what the angels could gain in the cyclical revelation of morning succeeded by evening, even though they already know the Word before they know themselves. He calls the angelic knowledge of creatures, the evening knowledge, "their own knowledge" (*in se ipsis cognitionem*), meaning that although the angels had full knowledge of the Word first in the day, they somehow come to make that knowledge their own in the evening, that is, they come to possess it fully as creatures.[92] Moreover, the idea that angelic knowledge may behold all these things in an instant (which implies creation itself was also simultaneous)[93] does not at all diminish the importance of the concept of unfolding or of the language of days. In fact, Augustine insists that no one would be so foolish as to deny that the angels have knowledge of God and of the creature and that they praise God for it. That is, no one would deny the logical movement of the angelic mind, from God to creature and back to God, in a morning–evening motion. Even if creation is simultaneous, it is still ordered with proper "measure and number and weight."[94] If angels do see creation unfold in an instant, moreover, the suggestion that they learn something through creation would be more plausible, since all of creation would be included in the simultaneous and full enlightenment of the angels, rather than happening in some subsequent time.

Whether the angels contemplate everything simultaneously or in stages, Augustine's insistence that the morning–evening cycle applies literally to the movements of the angelic mind portrays the act of creation as performative and informative from the beginning. Genesis is not

---

[92] See also *civ. Dei* XI.29.
[93] If the angels know both the form and particularity of creation all in one instant, this implies that all of creation also came into being in one instant, since the angels could not possess the full knowledge of the created order in itself until its actual creation. See Augustine's discussion *Gn. litt.* IV.51–53.
[94] Wis. 11:20. Augustine is extremely fond of using this verse to describe the orderliness of God's creation and it is cited in the context of the proper ordering of angelic knowledge (see *Gn. litt.* IV.7–12, but also *Gn. litt.* III.25, IV.52 and VI.27). Solignac suggests that the three movements of angelic knowledge correspond to this threefold metaphysical structure – measure, number, weight – as well as to the triad of *modus, species* and *ordo*. To draw the parallels out: number/modus is day, measure/species is evening and weight/ordo is morning. The triadic scheme of angelic knowledge should also then be seen then as the archetype of the triad *mens, notitia* and *amor* (Solignac, "Exégèse et Métaphysique," 164–165). Certainly, these triads suggest a Trinitarian dimension, but it is difficult to press these comparisons too far. Augustine never links the threefold movement of angelic knowledge with the Trinity nor does he speak of it in an explicitly Trinitarian way. Wiebe, however, is more confident in the Trinitarian implications, see "Demons in the Theology of Augustine," 36.

merely a literary husk which seeks to contain an unfathomable mystery, although it is that, but in the very literary form a quality of creation is preserved.[95] The word "day" is an accommodation to human language, but the idea of order, unfolding, of going and coming, of seeing and loving, of setting and dawning points to the reality of the act of creation and indeed created life, even if we cannot fully grasp what this looks like in its perfection (i.e. the angelic life). Genesis as a didactic text about creation actually matches with the event itself; Genesis is a mode of instruction that imitates in form the original mode of angelic instruction, that is, creation itself.

In light of this view, we must imagine that, for Augustine, Genesis is the record of a witness, and so its genre might be understood more like that of the Gospels rather than as some rote dictation given to Moses. Augustine even suggests that this angelic witness is a traditional source of the Genesis text as we know it. Scripture testifies about the nature of the creation of the world, but

was the prophet present when God made the heavens and the earth? No; but the wisdom of God, by whom all things were made, was there, and the wisdom insinuates itself into holy souls and makes them friends of God and his prophets, and noiselessly informs them of his works. They were also taught by the angels of God, who always behold the face of the Father, and announced his will to whom it befits. Of these prophets was he who said and wrote "in the beginning..."[96]

Moses could not have seen the events of Genesis, but he was inspired by God's Word who was present, or by the angels who were present and who always see God's face. Likewise, of Eve's creation, Augustine comments that although God did not need to make Eve in the way in which he did, he fashioned her thus in order "to signify something ... foretelling in his actual works the fruit to be derived in the age to come from the very origins of the human race."[97] The creation of Eve and its full meaning would then "in due course ... be revealed to his servants, whether by tradition through successive generations or by his Spirit or by the ministry of angels, and then written down to provide evidence

---

[95] In his *Unfinished Literal Commentary* Augustine speaks of the days of creation as an accommodation for our intellect, but an accommodation that presents, as Hill translates, "a spectacle for our very eyes to gaze on" (*Gn. litt. imp.* 1.28). Although the concept of a spectacle is not quite present in Latin, there is the suggestion that the text of Genesis, arranged in days, allows us to perceive creation as with our eyes: *per huius modi ordinem sermonis exposita quasi istis oculis cerneretur.*

[96] *civ. Dei* XI.4.

[97] *Gn. litt.* IX.23.

both of promises for the future being made and their fulfillment being acknowledged."[98] Augustine recognizes that the author of Genesis and subsequent human beings, even human beings who lived prior to the writing of Genesis, could not have witnessed the creation of the human race and therefore might be unaware when its prophetic vision came to fruition. Therefore, whether through human beings, the Holy Spirit or the angels who were present, the events were handed down from generation to generation and, of course, eventually written.

The second theological implication of Augustine's discussion of angelic knowledge, the question of creaturely status, follows naturally from our initial observations. Although he calls the evening knowledge a "lesser degree of knowledge,"[99] it would seem that this lesser knowledge is still a vital part of the angelic education, as shown above. The angels must know both God and then themselves as creatures, and they know these things by looking at creatures *in themselves* and not just as they exist in the eternal Word. This knowledge has its own character, "there is, of course, a very great difference between knowledge of a thing, whatever it may be, in the Word of God and knowledge of it in its own specific nature."[100] It seems obvious to Augustine that the good angels, enlightened first by the Word, would go on to contemplate creation in itself as well. But one might well ask, if the angels have the fullness of knowledge in the day, which by all accounts is a superior form of knowledge, why look down at creation at all? An answer has already begun to suggest itself. It is both fitting and good, according to the creaturely status of angels, to come to possess this knowledge fully as their own. The knowledge which the angels receive in the evening is knowledge about creation in itself, but this is also relational knowledge, i.e., knowledge about how creation is

---

[98] Ibid.
[99] Ibid., IV.39.
[100] Ibid., IV.40. An almost identical sentence (and accompanying discussion) appears in *civ. Dei* XI. 29. In Dods' translation, however, at one point Augustine seems to imply that the angels know creation in the Word only and not in itself, having rendered *quam in ea ipsa sciunt* in the passage as contrasting rather than comparing. Babcock, however, translates correctly "they [the angels] also know every creature better there (*quam in ea sciunt*) – that is, in God's wisdom, as in the very design by which it was made – than they know it in itself, and so they know even themselves better there than they do in themselves, although of course, they also know themselves in themselves. For they were made, and they are other than the one who made. In him, therefore, they have a kind of daylight knowledge, while in themselves they have a kind of twilight knowledge as I said previously. For there is a great difference between knowing something in the exemplar according to which it was made and knowing it in itself."

related to God.[101] The angels' lesson on the first evening is that they are not "what God is,"[102] and that "they were created and are different from their creator."[103] The good angels come to know themselves as creatures, and it is this very thing which prompts them to turn and praise God for the first time. As James Wetzel puts it, "they are exquisitely attuned in their angelic nature to the logic of creation."[104]

In short, the movement of angelic knowledge proves the goodness of creation. Looking down at what is created is good, because creation is good and thus the goodness of beholding creation does not disappear even in angelic perfection. Contemplating God and contemplating creation need not be in competition, but it would seem both the goodness of God and the creature are amplified by mutual appreciation. Creation redounds to God's glory, which adds nothing to God but only to the creature who praises God. Recall the passage from *The Confessions* pertaining to eternal reading, which images this paradox. The angels have no need to read, yet "they read your will, they choose it, and they love it (*legunt eligunt et diligent*). They read forever and what they read never passes away."[105] The image of reading deftly captures both angelic receptivity and activity. On the one hand, the angels are given the full knowledge of the Word already written before all ages, but, on the other, the angels themselves read the word forever with their own voice.[106] They read the

---

[101] I.e., by knowing what is and is not God. In *civ. Dei* XI.29 Augustine notes that the angels have perfect knowledge because of their presence to the Word and their comprehension of the proper relations within the Trinity. Then, in the proper knowledge of the three-in-one, they know all other things. We could perhaps further reflect on this concept (of angelic knowledge defined by relations) by exploring the relationship between Augustine's epistemology and the great chain of being. For some thoughts on this matter, see Paul Kuntz "From Angel to the Worm: Augustine's Hierarchical Vision" in *Jacob's Ladder and the Tree of Life* (New York: Peter Lang, 1987), 41–55. Kuntz argues that Augustine's exploration into the concept of the chain of being is peculiarly relational, that is, Augustine does not ask only where a subject *is* in the hierarchy, but where it is with respect to other beings and where it is going.

[102] *Gn. litt.* IV.39.

[103] *civ. Dei* XI.29.

[104] Wetzel, "Augustine on the Origin of Evil," 177.

[105] *conf.* XIII.15.18.

[106] The angels read "with their own voice," so to speak, because for Augustine an image of reading would be an image of speaking as well. Augustine considered silent reading to be highly unusual, as famously demonstrated in *conf.* VI.3.3, when he is impressed to find Ambrose reading silently to himself. Although it has long been accepted that ancients almost exclusively read aloud (whether due to preference or ability), this is perhaps less normative than Augustine's experience would imply (see, for example, A. K. Gavrilov, "Techniques of Reading in Classical Antiquity" *The Classical Quarterly* 47.1 (1997): 56–73). Even if silent reading was more popular than Augustine seems to think,

Word which they are choosing and loving. Rowan Williams writes that, for Augustine, in order for us to image God we must be "at home with our created selves (our selves as produced, derived),"[107] but I can think of no more fitting way to describe the perfection which the good angels have achieved. Augustine's angelology, then, reflects a deep commitment to the idea of a created good. That which is not God, the angels, are created to be something other than God, and to know that they are not God but also to know themselves in themselves. And yet this self-knowledge truly is good because it has its origin and end in God, and in the morning it is referred back to God. So the good angels are stable and always at rest, and yet somehow always receiving themselves back again.

Augustine's conception of the created good, along with his understanding of the perfection of angels, allows him to defend the doctrine of creation in book XI of *Literal Meaning of Genesis*. He explains that in light of the unhappy outcome of Gen. 3, some think it would have been better for God to have made Adam and Eve unable to sin.[108] Augustine responds that while being securely without sin is surely a superior nature, God has already created this good in the holy angels.[109] These angels are made to "find absolutely no joy in anything unlawful" but human beings are made with the ability "to check unlawful enjoyment."[110] Although the angelic nature is "the better one,"[111] human nature is also good and it adds the joy of restraining evil to the joy of always choosing the good. Perhaps one can accept that human beings have their goodness, even if they sometimes put it to bad use, but what of the devil? God's magnanimity applies to him as well, because "while God knew he [the devil] was going to turn out bad of his own free will and so do much harm to the good, he still created him"[112] and even brought good from him. The fact that angels exist in one state and human beings in another is not proof of God's deficiency or favoritism, but proof of his abundance, that is, proof of God's intention to create various kinds of good, both the kind

---

it remains that Augustine (at least) would have imagined reading to also entail speaking. He does not think the angels make an audible noise, of course, but I use this phrase to evoke angelic activity or responsiveness.

[107] Rowan Williams, "*Sapientia* and the Trinity: Reflections on the *De Trinitate*" in *Collectanea Augustiniana: Mélanges T. J. van Bavel*, ed. B. Bruning, M. Lamberigts and J. van Houten, Leuven: Peeters, 1990, 321.

[108] *Gn. litt.* XI.8–9.

[109] Ibid. XI.9.

[110] Ibid.

[111] Ibid.

[112] Ibid., XI.29.

that is issued perfect, and the kind that judges between perfect and imperfect.[113] So with the devil. We must accept that the creation of the devil
does not indicate any failure on God's part, but rather God's ultimate triumph, because no evil use of creation could make creation evil, nor could
it cause God to withhold his goodness from any part of his creation.
Creation is not homogeneous; therefore, it remains differentiated, but all
of creation is made good, and not even the devil's plans could prevent this
goodness from being bestowed upon him.

That Augustine unambiguously affirms the goodness of creaturely
status should come as no surprise, given his concerns in the earlier
Genesis commentaries. As repeatedly noted above, he emphasizes
that the angels are created, and he insists on fitting the whole angelic
narrative into that of Genesis.[114] But this affirmation of the goodness
of creation has further implications beyond simply reiterating, against
various opponents,[115] that God created the whole world good, just as
he created the angels. First, it suggests he has high regard for the angelic
will. Ellen Muehlberger, writing about the difference between Eastern
and Western ideas about angels, notes that Augustine's angels are stable.
She argues that Augustine's angels, due to their unwavering allegiance
to God, serve a political and rhetorical purpose in *City of God*, because

---

[113] In *lib. arb.* III.xi.32, Augustine makes the case even more strongly. Here, he says that
creation would have been deficient without angels and human beings, i.e. every kind of
rational good: "If there were no souls occupying the highest rank in the universe, such
as would have power to shake and weaken the universe if they should choose to fall
into sin, that would be a great defect in creation. That would be lacking which secures
the stability and unity of the universe. Such are the good and holy and sublime souls of
the powers celestial and super-celestial, over whom God alone rules, and to whom the
whole world is subject. Without their just and perfect offices there can be no universe.
Again if there were no souls who, whether by sinning or not sinning, make no difference
to the order of the universe, again there would be a grave defect." Presumably the late
Augustine muted this point, since it could seem to imply God was required to make
angels. Nevertheless, he still sees a fittingness in God's thorough creation of goods.

[114] He perhaps says this most clearly in *civ. Dei* XI.9: "But that they [the angels] were
wholly omitted, I am unable to believe, because it is written that God on the seventh
day rested from all his works which he made; and this very book itself begins 'in the
beginning...' since, therefore, he began with the heavens and the earth – and the earth
itself ... and then all the things which are recorded to have been completed in six days
were created and arranged, how should the angels be omitted, as if they were not among
the works of God, from which on the seventh day he rested?"

[115] The Manicheans, but also the Platonists and Origen, whom Augustine mentions by
name in *civ. Dei* XI.21–23. Moreover, Augustine in *de haeresibus* mentions six groups
who, he claims, believe that angels created the world, or who worship angels (see *haer.*
2, 3, 8, 38–39, 59 and 70.2).

they are Augustine's assured guarantee of the heavenly city of which he speaks, in contrast to the uncertain promises of Roman religion.[116] Angels have no will of their own, she claims, but simply stand in for God by serving as his mouthpiece, and she describes them as "divine drones."[117] In chapter 3, we will discuss how the angels serve as God's messengers, and in what way they can be said to intercede for human beings, but even here Muehlberger's assertion can be challenged. The angels are clearly described with both imagery (such as reading) and verbs (such as seeing and referring) which demonstrate that they actively participate in the divine life and that they experience and respond to God's love. The holy angels "by a free and love-inspired choice (*electione ac dilectione*) refer the knowledge of creation back to God."[118] It is in loving God that angels become fully aware of themselves and their own created status as good, and it is in God's will that they can freely will. The holy angels

gaze so raptly upon that unchangeable substance of the creator, that they not only put the sight and love of it before everything else, but also make judgments about everything in accordance with it, and align themselves on it in order to make themselves useful and from it draw the lines on which to make use of other things.[119]

Angels do not gaze upon God in such a way as to be trapped by God, rather, by looking at God continually, they are thereby able to see everything else with perfect clarity, to judge and to act.

For Augustine, being perfectly conformed to the will of God does not mean a loss of freedom, but rather the attainment of absolute freedom. It is only in this alignment that the creature truly comes into its own, for then it knows itself. The question of free will is of course a topic of intense discussion in Augustine's anti-Pelagian writings, which, like *City of God* and *Literal Meaning of Genesis*, are written near the end of his life. Augustine's understanding of free will in these works, however, is not defined as the ability to choose between good and evil in a neutral fashion at any given time, but rather as being freed fully to love God. The choice between good and evil is only a middle level of freedom, true freedom chooses God's will.[120] This true freedom comes from God, but it is not

---

[116] Muehlberger, *Angels in Late Ancient Christianity*, 43–57.
[117] Ibid., 5. Likewise, she suggests they have no "mechanism of intention," 55.
[118] *Gn. litt.* IV.42.
[119] Ibid. X.69.
[120] Patout Burns (among others) has suggested that Adam and Eve have this middle freedom, the freedom to choose between good and evil. See Patout Burns, *The Development of*

coercive, nor is it somehow alien, imputed or forced, but it is irresistible. As Patout Burns puts it, for Augustine freedom is "an uncoerced adherence to the good."[121] By God's grace we not only "discover what ought to be done, but also that we do what we have discovered, – not only that we believe what ought to be loved, but also that we love what we have believed."[122] In other words, we do come truly to do what is good and to love it, but we only come into this freedom by the action of God. Even if the angels do not have original sin, which is a central issue of the Pelagian controversy, they are not exempt from the need for God to conform their will to the divine one. If angels did not need God's help to choose the good, Augustine explains, then they would somehow make themselves better than God created them.[123] To explain why some angels fell and others did not, he has recourse to the same answer he gives with regard to why some human beings are elect and others are not: angels who fall are not given as much divine assistance,

And thus we are driven to believe that holy angels never existed without a good will or the love of God. But the angels who, though created good, are yet evil now, became so by their own will. And this will was not made evil by their good natures, unless by its voluntary defection from the good ... these angels, therefore, either receive less of grace of the divine love than those who persevered in the same; or if both were created equally good, then, while the one fell by their evil will the others were more abundantly assisted and attained to that pitch of blessedness at which they became certain they should never fall from it.[124]

So although it may seem that since the angels are securely aligned with God's will they would have no will of their own, and are somehow entirely

---

Augustine's Doctrine of Operative Grace (Paris: Études Augustiniennes, 1980), 117–119. Jesse Couenhoven, however, argues that although early on Augustine held that Adam and Eve had this middle freedom, later Augustine understood even the primordial human freedom to be "not a power for opposites, but a power for consenting to the good in which God created human beings to delight," that is, precisely the type of freedom angels perfectly possess. See Couenhoven, "Augustine's Rejection of the Free-Will Defense: An Overview of the Late Augustine's Theodicy," *Religious Studies* 43.3 (2007): 285.

[121] Burns, *Operative Grace*, 109. Augustine's views on free will change over time, but the idea that grace is not coercive remains a constant, even if Augustine struggles to define exactly in what way the human will cooperates with divine grace. For example, in *On the Happy Life*, one of Augustine's earliest works, freedom is already defined as ease of willing, and misery as willing something which you cannot yourself effect (*beata v.* 2.11 and 4.25).

[122] *gr. et pecc. or.* 13.

[123] *civ. Dei* XII.9.

[124] Ibid.

and ecstatically seized by God at all times, their state is in fact analogous to that of human beings. It is precisely because the angelic will is perfected that good angels have the most freedom possible, that is, they are free to love God by the grace of God, not free to choose one thing over another.[125] As early as *On True Religion* Augustine describes the angels as loving God *libentissime subditi*, that is, loving him by most willing submission, but *libentissime* also means most joyful.[126] Angels have perfected the freedom which Augustine imagines for the future human will, that is, the freedom to possess God's gift fully as their own and experience it as such (not as coerced), since "Augustine's notion of freedom derives from the experience of willingness rather than from that of choice."[127] It is beyond our scope here to adjudicate whether or not Augustine's understanding of free will suffices to excuse God of any responsibility for evil (angelic or otherwise) or if it corresponds to what we might define as the freedom of the will. Perhaps it suffices to say that, for Augustine, angels are as free as the saints (i.e. beatified human beings) and certainly more free than human beings under the bondage of sin. More to Muehlberger's point, angelic freedom does not diminish personal character, so that angels are somehow more drone-like than the saints in heaven.[128] Augustine often pairs saints with holy angels, considering them to have equal blessedness, and both await us at the end of our pilgrimage.[129] So the good angels

---

[125] Burns also points out that this freedom in Augustine's thought is linked to the great chain of being. Since angels are absolutely free, they also possess the most existence, whereas the un-free demons tend toward nothingness; see *Operative Grace*, 109.

[126] *vera rel.* 26; "By willing to love God rather than themselves, angels abide firm and stable in him and enjoy his majesty, being gladly subject (*libentissime subditi*) to him alone." See also his inversion of slavery imagery in *trin.* VIII.12; angels are servants (*servos*) of love (*dilectio*) bound by the chains of holiness (*consciat vinculo sanctitatis*).

[127] Burns, *Operative Grace*, 109. Although it might seem that such a view would develop in Augustine's later works (as a way to maintain free will in the face of his doctrine of operative grace), the idea that the freedom of the will is located in our experience is present in Augustine's much earlier works; "there is nothing I feel more certainly and more personally than that I have a will, and that it moves me to enjoy this or that" (*lib. arb.* III.3). We are free because we experience freedom, or, put otherwise, because we truly come to possess this freedom as our own, even if it is entirely a gift.

[128] I seek only to use this as an analogy to show that we ought not to imagine the angels as somehow less personal and more like heavenly automatons than the saints. To discuss Augustine's understanding of the intercession of the saints would take us too far afield, but Augustine thinks of the saints in a "personal" way; we can ask for their intercession and imitate their particular Christian virtue (see, for example, *s.* 325.1). But he also affirms that the saints are assured of their salvation and aligned with the will of God, just like the angels.

[129] Some examples of the pairing of saints and angels: Job's cry "have mercy on my friends" is directed to both saints and angels (*adn. Job* 19). Saints will gain angelic abilities such

remain themselves, knowing themselves as a creature better because of their perfected will, not becoming somehow less individuated.

Augustine's high regard for the creaturely status of angels is correspondent to a high regard for their free will, even if his understanding of free will is peculiar to him. It also suggests caution in dismissing Augustine's regard for signs and sacraments. In his book *Outward Signs: The Powerlessness of External Things in Augustine's Thought*, Phillip Cary argues that for Augustine, signs are ultimately without purchase, and are surpassed and discarded in the beatific life. When human beings have ascended in Platonic fashion to behold the form of a thing, the particularity of that thing no longer has lasting meaning; for Augustine,

> freedom from the necessity of external signs such as words is thus a characteristic of the truly happy life, when we can see quite clearly the love that binds souls in one. A transparent unity of love belongs to the ultimate blessedness of souls in the city of God.[130]

According to Cary, Augustine views the sacraments like a door. They mark a threshold which we enter through to behold God's mystery, but the door has no meaning and we do not look back upon the door once we have passed through it.[131] The question of how Augustine views the sacraments in general, and the Eucharist in particular, is a thorny issue in scholarship and complicated by the later standards of transubstantiation as the hallmark of orthodoxy.[132] The life of the good angels, however, provides an excellent vantage point from which to view this problem and critique Cary's position. If it is the case that, for Augustine, all signs only lead us inward and upward, and that we ultimately discard all that is external and particular, why should the angels look at themselves and then down at creation, *after* already having seen the Word and having experienced the "transparent unity of love," which Cary describes? The angels start from a different position than human beings, they have no need to progress like us and they receive perfect enlightenment with their being. Despite this, Augustine does not abandon the language of signs

---

as moving physical objects, the ability to appear in visions and so on (*civ. Dei* XIII.18–22). The angels and saints watch us as we struggle in the contest of this life (*civ. Dei* XIV.9). God uses the spirits of martyrs like he does the angels, or angels act on their prayers (*civ. Dei* XXII.9). In short, the angels and saints together constitute the *societas* that is the city of God (see *civ. Dei* XIV.28).

130 Cary, *Outward Signs*, 83.
131 Ibid., 170.
132 For a good summary of the contentious issues surrounding Augustine's view of the Eucharist, see Pamela Jackson, "Eucharist," *Augustine through the Ages*, 330–334.

(such as reading) in the life of the good angels, and he insists the angels understand things in their particularity as well as in their form, and that the second kind of knowledge, if lesser, is still essential. The repeated use of the verb *refero* in Augustine's vision of the angelic life is also evocative of the concept of signification; signs are used precisely for the purpose of referring. The angels, simply put, look at creation even though it would seem that they have nothing left to gain from it. The angels are not using creation as a sign from which to gain some data about the signified which they will later discard. Augustine is fond of applying both 1 Cor. 13:12 and Matt. 18:10 to the angels – the angels see God face to face and always behold the face of the Father in heaven – in other words, the good angels have reached that state of transparency which Cary argues will be the termination of all forms of signification in Augustinian thought. And yet it is in a reflection on the beatific vision that Augustine's image of eternal reading appears, that is, his image of an eternal sign.

How can we understand this angelic economy of signs, if it can be so called? John Rist provides us with some direction. Although Rist agrees with Cary that, for Augustine, it would seem signs and sacraments are unnecessary in heaven (although possible), he is more skeptical about the direct and pervasive impact of Platonism on Augustine's theory of signs.[133] Augustine draws from many ancient ideas and schools of thought on the matter, Rist argues, and the Epicurean position is in fact the closest to Augustine's, although Augustine had no direct Epicurean influences.[134] To nuance our understanding of Augustinian signs, Rist speaks of Augustine's views on education more broadly. For Augustine, Rist demonstrates, experience is fundamental to education, and to learn is indeed "to make information one's own."[135] This Augustinian perspective on education corresponds well to our observations about the angelic life. In the evening, the angels do not need to gain information about creation, so to speak, but they must come to know creation as it is, and as it is related to God. They do this through their own experience of looking and then praising. Rist also alludes to a much larger problem in the study of Augustine's sacramental theology, namely, that some commentators assume that the theory of signs outlined in *On Christian Teaching* (*doc. Chr.*) can be directly applied to the sacraments without qualification. But

---

[133] John M. Rist. *Augustine: Ancient Thought Baptized* (Cambridge: Cambridge University Press, 1994), 38.
[134] Ibid., 23–29.
[135] Ibid., 33

On Christian Teaching is in essence concerned with words, the type of sign used primarily to convey information. Furthermore, words are in a sense failed signs, as Rist points out, since they do not reach the level of transparent communication about which Cary spoke. We must opine, with Rist, that if Augustine had instead attended to the meaning of performative words such as those in the baptismal formula or eucharistic prayers, whose signification is also bound up with liturgical action,[136] he may have developed his ideas quite differently.[137] In the next chapter, we will consider more fully whether the angels can be said to have a sacramental life, but here it suffices to say that the good angels, who are certainly beatified, still seem to look at external things (against Cary) and that they seem to learn in the same way as we do, by firsthand experience (with Rist). This angelic learning, moreover, is still spoken of using the vocabulary of signs and signification, even if such an economy of signs would be quite beyond our imagining.

The third implication of Augustine's exposition of the morning–evening cycle in Genesis pertains to the quality of time itself. In *Literal Meaning of Genesis*, after Augustine has finished expounding the meaning of the days of Genesis and how the details of the text sketch the contours of the angelic life, he reminds us that his interpretation is to be taken literally and not metaphorically:

And please let nobody assume that what I have said about spiritual light and about the day being constituted in the spiritual and angelic creation, and about what it contemplates in the Word of God, and about the knowledge by which the creature is known in itself and it being referred to the praise of unchangeable Truth, where first the idea was seen of the thing to be made, which once made was knowledge in itself: that none of this can be said strictly and properly, but that it all belongs to a figurative and allegorical understanding of day and evening and morning. Certainly it is different from our usual way of talking about this bodily light of every day, but that does not mean that here we have the strict and proper, there just a metaphorical use of the terms.[138]

The words "day" and "morning" and "evening" in Genesis do not refer to *our* days, but that does not mean that the text is somehow less literal. Augustine pleads with us to take him seriously when he says that he believes that these words, which to us imply ordinary time, can literally

---

[136] Augustine himself makes a distinction between regular words and words working in concert with liturgical action, for example, in *Jo. ev. tr.* 80:3 where baptism is called a "visible word."

[137] Rist, *Ancient Thought*, 39.

[138] *Gn. litt.* IV.45.

refer to angelic time, even if we cannot understand these words apart from our own ideas about bodily light. We certainly "should not rush into the assertion of any ill-considered theory" about these angelic days and must be sure they are "very, very dissimilar" to our own days.[139] And yet, Augustine is willing to posit that "these seven [our week] represent those first seven in some fashion."[140] He reminds us that although God created human time with the lamps of the sky on day four, God created the angelic day on day one, and it is this day which is repeated seven times. God does not re-create day for each occasion, but "'the day which God has made' is repeated in his works."[141] Likewise, he says, our days (which pass away) somehow still hand on the name "day" to all the days which follow them. This is in imitation of the days of creation itself, in which only one day is created but repeated six times.[142] Therefore "throughout all those days there is just one day, which is not to be understood after that manner of these days that we see measured and counted by the circuit of the sun, but in a different kind of mode," a mode which moves "not in a bodily circle motion but in spiritual knowledge, when that blessed company of angels" successively gazes at God and creation.[143] The earth even has an analog for the simultaneous experience of evening and morning in the life of the angels, since on the earth it is always day and night somewhere simultaneously, even if not at the same time in the same country.[144] In *Gn. litt.* IV.1, Augustine also suggests that the days of creation reflect the structure of human life more generally, where the morning represents the beginning of life and evening our *terminus ad quem*.[145]

Augustine's suggestion, however tentative, that our days (and even the unfolding of our lives) are somehow analogous to angelic days makes concrete his claim that the references to morning and evening in Genesis are literal. But it also implies that human beings in the very act of passing through time somehow image or share in the angelic life. Our day-in day-out drudgery is a lived anticipation of the beatific life, as well as an echo of the act of creation. Perhaps this sheds light on why Augustine should end the story of his life in *Confessions* with the story of creation. He reminds his readers that God did not need to create the world in six

[139] Ibid., IV.44.
[140] Ibid.
[141] Ibid., IV.43, cf. Ps. 118:24.
[142] Ibid., IV.37.
[143] Ibid., IV.43.
[144] Ibid., IV.47.
[145] Ibid., IV.1.

days because he required a protracted time to work, but rather to signify perfection.[146] Likewise, the morning–evening cycle is not incidental, or without intention, but we continually live in time as it was arranged by God, and in a cycle which has eternal meaning because it was founded by God.

Augustine, therefore, hints at a "sacramental" view of time, wherein our time somehow reproduces, adumbrates or reflects the operation of the angelic mind. Perhaps, then, Augustine's view of time and angelic worship are also liturgically minded. By the fourth century, the use of Psalms 148–150 in morning prayers was widespread in the Christian world.[147] Psalms 148–150 are devoted entirely to the praise of God; they declare that the creator should be praised everywhere and by all creation. Psalm 148, in particular, urges all to praise the creator, with the heavens, the angels and the heavenly hosts listed first among those who praise God (Ps. 148:1–2). The strong theme of praise used in these morning prayers,[148] combined with the invocation of all the parts of creation in Ps. 148, parallels Augustine's image of the angels praising God in the morning for what he has made.[149] Psalm 63 was another popular morning prayer, due to its mention of seeking God early (in verse 1),[150] and likewise, Ps. 141, was a popular evening prayer because it mentions an evening sacrifice (in verse 2). Although we cannot know Augustine's exact prayer regimen, morning and evening prayer with use of canonical psalms was already well established, and was a normative practice for

---

[146] *civ. Dei* XI.30 and *Gn. litt.* IV.2–14.

[147] For a brief discussion of the history of the use of the Psalms in Christian prayer, see Paul Bradshaw, *Two Ways of Praying* (Nashville: Abingdon Press, 1995), 73–89.

[148] Rebecca Weaver divides all types of prayer in Augustine's thought into two: *laus* and *oratio*. The former happens in this life but is typical of the beatific vision, the latter happens only because of our state on earth. If the general division holds, then it serves to strengthen my observation that morning prayer is tied to the angelic life (which is defined by *laus*). See Weaver, "Prayer" in *Augustine through the Ages*, 671–674. In *en. Ps.* 78.1, which is one place where Augustine draws this distinction in prayer (*oratio* vs. *laudatio*), he explicitly associates the angelic life, and our anticipation of it, with the latter.

[149] Carol Harrison (using the opening of *The Confessions* as her example) notes that Augustine shares with other patristic authors basic elements of prayer. In prayer we express that God is creator and that we have a created relationship with God, "which is the grounds of our prayer" – see *The Art of Listening in the Early Church* (Oxford: Oxford University Press, 2013), 211. If, for Augustine, the "grounds of our prayer" is a proper understanding of our created relationship with God, the angels would be a fitting model of perfected prayer.

[150] As Bradshaw notes, this meaning is not always retained in modern translation, see *Two Ways*, 76.

both so-called "monastic" and "cathedral" communities by the fourth century.[151] Moreover, it is clear these psalms were already being chosen for
their fittingness for the time of day (morning, evening) and for an attitude
appropriate for that time (praise, acknowledgment of mortal finitude).
Praising God precisely as creator is also common in these psalms, and the
Genesis story is often invoked. The ordered passing of time, the evocation
of the darkness of creation and of finitude are also evident in Ps. 104:19–23,
another text used in the West for evening prayer:

> [19] You have made the moon to mark the seasons;
>   the sun knows its time for setting.
> [20] You make darkness, and it is night,
>   when all the animals of the forest come creeping out.
> [21] The young lions roar for their prey,
>   seeking their food from God.
> [22] When the sun rises, they withdraw
>   and lie down in their dens.
> [23] People go out to their work
>   and to their labor until the evening.[152]

The passage of time, in Augustine's understanding, is something both
peculiar to the mortal condition, but also something which happens with
proper order and measure, in imitation of the life to come. In the liturgy,
these very ideas are enacted. The worshiper always turns back to praise
God in the morning, reflects on his or her own mortality in the evening,
while keeping God the creator ever before his or her eyes. These liturgical
features have powerful resonances with Augustine's understanding of the
movements of angelic worship.

The Angelic Fall

In both *City of God* and *Literal Meaning of Genesis* Augustine takes up
the question of the devil's fall. Just as he understands the creation of the
angels to have taken place within the Genesis narrative, so also does the
fall of the devil. He is, after all, already in action by Gen. 2. In *City of
God* Augustine suggests that the fall of the devil and his evil angels takes
place on day two of the creation narrative:

To me it does not seem incongruous with the working of God, if we understand that
the angels were created when that first light was made, and that a separation was
made between the holy and the unclean angels, when, as it is said "God divided the

---

[151] On this distinction, see Bradshaw, *Two Ways*, 13–29.
[152] The psalm, when read in its entirety, evokes the whole creation narrative.

light from the darkness; and God called the light Day and the darkness he called Night."[153]

Augustine further argues that the division of light from darkness would fittingly describe the fall of the evil angels because this division is not said to be good. By using the concept of division, Genesis is telling us that God passed divine judgment on the fallen angels without causing their fall.[154] This interpretation also helps to solve a problem which Augustine mentions elsewhere, that is, why on day two God should name the day "Day" and the night "Night" if God does not create time as we know it until day four; the naming indicates a distinction which God is making between good and evil angels rather than the creation of corporeal time.[155] Augustine also points out that night is not mentioned in the unfolding of the six days of creation, and so the movements of angelic knowledge are suitably said to pass only from morning to evening.[156] Night then indicates the obsession of a creature with itself, because "night never falls when the creator is not forsaken through love of the creature."[157] Morning does not dawn in the mind of the devil, who in his pride refuses to refer his own being and that of creation back to God. He remains in perpetual darkness.[158]

The most pressing matter pertaining to the devil's fall in both *City of God* and *Literal Meaning of Genesis* is again the matter of time. Even if day two indicates the devil's fall, at what time did this fall take place? Did the devil fall right away, from the beginning of creation, or did some time

---

[153] *civ. Dei* XI.19.
[154] Ibid., XI.20.
[155] Ibid., XI.19–20.
[156] *Gn. litt.* IV.42 and *civ. Dei* XI.7.
[157] *civ. Dei* XI.7.
[158] The division of light and darkness is a helpful paradigm for understanding the angelic fall, Augustine says, even if that was not the original intention of the Genesis author, so long as it adheres to the rule of faith (see *civ. Dei* XI.33). Darkness is a suitable figure for the evil angels because they are "depraved" (i.e. they lack something). The imagery works well with Augustine's understanding of evil as having only a deficient cause (on the deficient cause of the angelic fall, see *civ. Dei* XII.6–7). His understanding of the angelic fall has interested scholars for precisely this reason, that is, because it sheds light on the question of the human fall and its cause (or lack of cause, as it were), and the question of free will and theodicy in general. In an attempt to draw out different theological implications of Augustine's angelology, and to consider the good angels more properly in themselves, this study does not dwell on this particular line of inquiry. For a succinct treatment of the topic of the angelic fall, its deficient cause and its relation to human freedom, see William Babcock, "The Human and the Angelic Fall: Will and Moral Agency in Augustine's City of God" in *Augustine: From Rhetor to Theologian* (Toronto: Wilfred Laurier Press, 1992), 44–47.

pass in which he lived in angelic company? Augustine oscillates between
the two positions. On the one hand, creation is good and so God cannot
have created the devil in a state of evil. God created the devil just as he
did the other angels. So it would seem that some time must have passed
before the devil fell. On the other hand, it is impossible for Augustine to
imagine a state of blessedness, either for the good angels or the soon-to-
be fallen angels, wherein one could lack the foreknowledge of assured
blessedness.[159] If the devil had had foreknowledge pertaining to his fall,
it seems inexplicable that he would still have chosen such a course, and
if he did not have such foreknowledge then he could not be said to have
been truly blessed at any time. The good angels could hardly be said to
be blessed in heaven if there was some doubt as to their remaining with
God.[160] Augustine ponders the possible solutions to his conundrum and
notes that some people suggest the devil was a lesser angel who was not
fully blessed like the higher angels.[161] He was, nevertheless, an angelic
supervisor whose subordinates fell along with him. Perhaps, as a lower
angel of some kind, Augustine posits, Satan did not have full foreknowledge of his blessedness.[162] After all, as discussed above, Augustine does
posit that the evil angels receive less divine assistance than the good, which
explains their fall.[163] The devil in this case would not be so different from
Adam who had some measure of blessedness in Eden, but not a complete
beatification.[164]

Augustine, however, does not favor this interpretation.[165] He says that
it would be nonsense to think the devil were at any time blessed if he did
not know his fate, and there is no scriptural evidence he can muster to
support such a position. Rather, John 8:44 calls the devil "a murderer
from the beginning," and Job 40:19 speaks of the devil as being sport

[159] *Gn. Litt.* XI.18.
[160] Ibid., XI.25. In *civ. Dei* XI.11 Augustine takes a slightly different tack, saying that whether or not the wicked angels foreknew their fall, they could not have been said to be blessed, since blessedness is by definition eternal. Therefore, whether due to "fear or ignorance," they cannot be said to have been blessed.
[161] Augustine's suggestion that the devil could have possibly been a lower angel stands in stark contrast with later authors who thought of Lucifer as the most glorious of the angels. This opinion is held as early as Gregory the Great (see *Moralia* 32.23) and became standard in the Middle Ages. See Jeffery Burton Russell, *Lucifer: The Devil in the Middle Ages* (Ithaca: Cornell University Press, 1984), 94.
[162] *Gn. litt.* XI.25 and XI.33.
[163] *civ. Dei* XII.9.
[164] *Gn. litt.* XI.25.
[165] Augustine does allow for this possibility, but only "if the idea can really be maintained, and it would be most surprising if it can" (*Gn. litt.* XI.33).

for the angels from the beginning of the Lord's fashioning.[166] Augustine concludes that the devil fell from the very beginning, not the beginning of time as we know it, but from the beginning of his created life.[167] This fall happened not because God created the devil with a sinful nature, but because the devil did not accept his created goodness.[168] So on the one hand, "the devil never stood in the truth, never led a blessed life with the angels, but fell from the very beginning of his creation," but this does not mean that "he was created evil by the good God, not perverted by his own free choice. Otherwise he would not be said to have fallen."[169] Augustine rejects the idea that Satan fell because he was jealous of human beings,[170] since pride must precede jealousy, and, at any rate, the devil is already fallen by the time Adam and Eve are in the garden. Rather, the devil

> never tasted the sweetness of the blessed life of the angels. It is not that on receiving it he turned up his nose at it, but that by refusing to receive it he turned his back on it and let it slip through his fingers (*quam non utique acceptam fastidiuit, sed nolendo accipere deseruit et amisit*). Accordingly he could not have had foreknowledge of his fall either, since wisdom is the fruit of piety.[171]

These two assertions may seem difficult to hold together; that the devil was created good, but somehow was never in possession of that goodness. Through Augustine's disparate comments on the matter, however, we can discern a remarkably consistent understanding of the angelic timeline. In the *fiat lux* all the angels are created, but the evil angels fall when they fail to refer the evening knowledge of themselves back again to God, that is, on the morning of day two, when Genesis also speaks of the division of the light and the darkness. Although the angels are undoubtedly created good and fully illumined in the *fiat lux*, they come to possess that knowledge as their own in the subsequent evening. This is the moment when the devil falls in pride, not because he is created lacking goodness, but because he cannot come to terms with the fact that he is a good other than what

---

[166] Ibid., XI.26–27.
[167] In other words, from his first act of created willing. For more on the timing of the devil's fall, see Wiebe, "Demons in the Theology of Augustine," 81–93.
[168] *Gn. litt.* XI.30.
[169] Ibid.
[170] Daniélou discusses the patristic tradition that the devil fell on account of his refusal to pay homage to Adam, see *Angels and their Mission*, 45–47. Daniélou explicitly mentions that Athenagoras, Irenaeus, Methodius and Gregory of Nyssa espouse this view. Since Augustine takes care to explicitly reject this hypothesis, it stands to reason he must have had an awareness of some such tradition.
[171] *Gn. litt.* XI. 30.

God is (indeed, a good less than what God is, because his goodness is a gift). His first act of will is to separate himself from God. The image Hill uses, of goodness slipping through the devil's fingers, captures the sense of loss in the word *amisit*. The devil, turning his back on the good and letting it slip through his fingers (as Hill renders it), is an inverse image of Augustine's favorite description of the good angels clinging or adhering to God.[172] All the angels are given the same thing,[173] only the devil does not hold on to it, he refuses to receive it (*nolendo accipere*). This pride of the devil does not imply God's inadequacy, but points out vividly how grievous it is to be without God.[174] In light of the manner of the angelic fall, Augustine suggests that Ps. 73:28 "it is good to draw near to God" is true "not only of men, but primarily and principally of angels."[175]

Augustine eventually gives up on a complete and thorough understanding of the devil's fall, lamenting he would need a whole separate discourse dedicated to it.[176] But his explanation in both *City of God* and *Literal Meaning of Genesis* resonates with many of the previous concerns of Augustine's angelology which we have been discussing. First, it is profoundly anti-Manichean. Augustine allows no time – even angelic time – in which the devil was doing anything in heaven, creating, helping God, being jealous of human beings or anything otherwise. He fell immediately and has no narrative space to occupy, just as the creation of the angels has no extra-biblical story associated with it. Gregory Wiebe contends that the devil's fall "has no clear temporality and thus no story, and so is not directly perceivable by us embodied creatures bound to history. But its outcome is instantaneous, unambiguous, and irrevocable."[177] Moreover, Augustine repeatedly affirms that creation,

---

[172] In *civ. Dei* Augustine speaks of the cleaving of the angels and the not-cleaving of the demons as constitutive of the two cities. A good example is found in *civ. Dei* XII.1 ("Wherefore, if when the question is asked, why are the former blessed, it is rightly answered, because they adhere to God; and when it is asked, why are the latter miserable, it is rightly answered, because they do not adhere to God"). Augustine does not use a particular antonym for *adhaero* (here, he simply says *non adhaerere*). The verb *amitto*, however, also appears twice in *civ. Dei* XII.1 to describe the action by which the evil angels become miserable – by loss of that which makes the good angels blessed. It is not off the mark at all, therefore, to see *amitto* as the opposite of *adhaero* in the context of *Gn. litt.* XI.30, and Hill is right to suggest the sense of "slipping." On slipping, see also Couenhoven, "Augustine's Rejection of the Free-Will Defense," 287.
[173] And all angels have the same nature, as he makes explicit in *civ. Dei* XII.2.
[174] *civ. Dei* XII.1. See also *conf.* XIII.8.9.
[175] *civ. Dei* XII.9.
[176] *Gn. litt.* XI.33.
[177] Wiebe, "Demons in the Theology of Augustine," 94–95.

including the devil himself, is good. He insists this is so by maintaining the balance between God's completely good creation made *ex nihilo* and creation's own possession of that goodness (although this possession would seem to require God's aid). Shortly following his discussion of the fall of the devil, Augustine mentions that it is the goodness of creation which the heretics (presumably the Manicheans) reject.[178] But he also censures the views of Origen, who threatens the idea that the created world, both visible and invisible, is wholly good.[179] In short, at every moment he remains dedicated to the notion of a created good, and the anti-Manichean polemic never fully leaves his view even at such a late stage in his career.

The Angels' Role in Creation

Just as Augustine takes care to affirm that the creation of the angels took place by the power of God alone, so also is he hesitant to define a specific role for angels in creation. Angels certainly participate in creation, but Augustine wants to make it abundantly clear that angels cannot themselves be creators. He spends a significant part of book VIII of *Literal Meaning of Genesis* discussing how God cooperates with the human and angelic will,[180] although he does not discuss the role of angels in creation specifically in this context. In book IX, however, when he is commenting on the creation of humankind, of Eve in particular, the matter suddenly comes to the fore. As he prepares to explain the formation of Eve, he emphatically states, "now angels are not able to create any natures whatsoever, the one and only creator of any nature you like, great or small, is God."[181] He does not identify any opponent who claims that Eve was created by angels, but there seems to be some doubt as to the question, or at least there is a possibility that angels were involved, since Eve is not made from the dust but from Adam. But the angels did not help even to build Eve's body, Augustine insists, God himself created both genders, just as he had created the angels.[182] Augustine does not wish by this to imply that the angels

contribute no work at all to the creation of something, but that does not make them creators, just as we do not call the farmer the creator of crops and trees

---

[178] *civ. Dei* XI.22.
[179] Ibid., XI.23.
[180] See, in particular *Gn. litt.* VIII.17–18, 21–26 and 40–48. Most of the discussions relate to both human beings and angels, but VIII.46 pertains specifically to how God aids the angelic will internally and externally.
[181] *Gn. litt.* IX.26.
[182] Ibid.

since "neither the one who plants is anything, nor the one who irrigates, but the one who gives growth" (1 Cor. 3:7).[183]

Augustine continues to give an extended agricultural metaphor, which images the cooperation of the angels with God's creating work, while resisting the idea that the angels are in any way creators. Agricultural imagery is used by Augustine to describe the work of the angels not only in the Genesis commentaries, but elsewhere in his corpus.[184] But he is reticent to give any concrete suggestion about what the angels might actually then be said to have done. Certainly they did something, he maintains, but he avoids saying precisely what. After all, we are ignorant even of how human beings cooperate with God's creation, for example, in the process of grafting one plant from another. We would certainly not say we created the second plant. So why should we be surprised "when we are ignorant of how the angels serve God in his act of creation – we who could not know about a tree being made from the shoot of a tree in the trunk of another one, if we were likewise ignorant of how farmers serve God in his act of creating these things?"[185] In other words, even our own cooperation with God's will in the reproduction – not to say creation – of plants is obscure to us, so how much more the actions of angels? In *City of God* Augustine asks to be excused from speculating on angelic activity:

Wherefore I know not what kind of aid the angels, themselves created first, afforded to the creator in making other things. I cannot ascribe to them what perhaps they cannot do, neither ought I to deny them such faculty as they have. But, by their leave, I attribute the creating and originating work which gave being to all natures to God ... we do not call gardeners the creators of their fruits.[186]

Augustine does not wish to say anything false regarding angelic faculties, and so he leaves us only with the certainty that angels do not create, but help in some way. In *Literal Meaning of Genesis*, he offers only one small suggestion, that in helping to create Eve, "the man's rib may have been served up for the creator's work by angels."[187] Although Hill imagines a splendid picture "of angels, suitably clad in aprons, with napkins over their arms, serving Adam's rib up to God on a dish for him to carve it into being Eve,"[188] Augustine's suggestion is far from concrete.

---

[183] Ibid., IX.26.
[184] For example, see *trin.* 3.13–3.14 and *pecc. mer.* 1.37.
[185] *Gn. litt.* IX.29
[186] *civ. Dei* XII.25. He also cites 1 Cor. 3:7, as he does in *Gn. Litt.* IX.26.
[187] *Gn. litt* IX.29.
[188] See Hill's footnote to *Gn. litt.* IX.29.

So Augustine claims that we cannot really know with much certainty how an angel might help God, but only that "no angel ... can create a nature any more than it can create itself."[189] In *Literal Meaning of Genesis* he is also careful to exclude any possibility that human souls are derived from angelic souls, in order to avoid the suggestion that angels are somehow our parents.[190] Given previous discussions, Augustine's insistence on the created status of angels should come as no shock, and has obvious anti-Manichean and anti-mythological aims, but he also sees the claim as peculiarly anti-Platonic in *City of God*.[191] The Platonists wish to blame the body, or the mortal part of creation, on lesser gods who were fashioned by the demiurge. These Platonists, says Augustine, thereby fall into the dual error of thinking bodies are "the punishment of our souls" and that we ought to worship the creators of those bodies as gods.[192] These gods, who Augustine explains are actually good angels, do not create but "so far as they are permitted and commissioned, aid in the production of the things around us, yet not on that account are we to call them creators, any more than we call gardeners the creators of fruits and trees."[193] Correspondingly, angels are not to be worshiped, nor bodies disparaged. Perhaps Augustine's concern in *Literal Meaning of Genesis* to establish that Eve in particular is not created by angels is related to this anti-Platonic polemic. It was commonplace in ancient thought, of course, to associate the feminine with the lower or weaker attributes of the human mind (such as sensuality or emotion) and the male with the higher. This tendency is true also of ancient allegorical readings of Genesis, where Adam is sometimes seen as the mind and Eve as the body, or the two are seen as the higher and lower parts of the soul.[194] Perhaps, then, by insisting that Eve in particular was made by God, Augustine wants

---

[189] *Gn. litt.* IX. 27.

[190] In *Gn. litt.* VIII. 34, Augustine says *fiat lux* is not a general formula for all souls (i.e. not the creation of a proto-soul or soulish material), but that human souls are made *ex nihilo*. In *Gn. litt.* X.4, he similarly cautions against any interpretation which would make us the "daughter of angelic souls."

[191] Augustine's doctrine of *creatio ex nihilo* is, of course, anti-Platonic in other ways as well. See Torchia's comments on the philosophical background of the doctrine, *Creatio ex nihilo*, 1–65.

[192] *civ. Dei* XII.26.

[193] Ibid., XII.24.

[194] In his earliest Genesis commentary, Augustine himself interprets the Adam and Eve story in just this way. Eve represents the emotions or external senses which the devil can manipulate, Adam is the mind (*Gn. adv. Man.* 2.20–21). Even later in his life Augustine has recourse to these same basic categories; in *trin.* XII.12, for example, he interprets the woman as symbolizing the part of the soul concerned with temporal things.

to exclude any possibility that even what are called the lower parts of creation – the body, the sensual, etc. – can somehow be blamed on the angels.

Perhaps the more interesting question, however, is why Augustine insists on angelic cooperation in creation in the first place. Although this sort of mediating function for celestial spirits would have been a commonplace supposition in antiquity, he cites no biblical precedent to support this claim. Certainly, he believes that God has no need for angelic aid. Unfortunately, he does not address this question in the context of his Genesis commentaries – maybe such an angelic function is simply too self-evident for an ancient author – but he gives us a few hints. First, the strong agricultural imagery used for the work of the angels is both explicitly and implicitly linked with actual human farm work, and so conceptually with Adam's and Eve's work in the garden of Eden. Augustine questions the need for such prelapsarian work, asking: "the Lord, surely, did not want the first man to work at agriculture, did he?"[195] Such an idea seems incredible, since human beings would seem to have been condemned to labor prior to any sin. He explains the kind of work which Adam and Eve performed was for their benefit and filled them with joy, something which such work is able to do even now.[196] What God had created then "flourished in more luxuriant abundance with the help of human work." Adam and Eve are allowed to work in the garden because it is beautiful, they witness in the blooming of the garden "a wonderful spectacle."[197] Perhaps we are meant to imagine angelic work in this same way, that is, the angels would obviously be included in bringing forth creation because it is beautiful and because they would enjoy it. Such an interpretation would be fitting given our discussion above, pertaining to the movements of angelic knowledge whereby the angels become most fully themselves. Augustine hints in this direction when he explains the angelic office (that is, the office of announcing). God

certainly does not need a reporter to inform him about things lower down the scale, as if to keep him abreast of current affairs; but in that simple and wonderful way he has a steady and unchanging knowledge of all things. He does have reporters however, *both for our sake and for their own* (*propter nos et propter ipsos*), because for them to wait upon God obediently in that manner ... is good

---

[195] *Gn. litt.* VIII.15.
[196] Ibid.
[197] Ibid., VIII.16; *mirabiliusque spectaculum est.*

for them in accordance with their proper nature and mode of being (*bonum est eis in ordine propriae naturae atque substantiae*)[198]

The angels act as heralds both for our sake and their own, so that they may participate in God's economy in a way fitting for their own nature and being. It stands to reason that they help in the act of creation for the same reason, namely, for their own sake in a way proper to their nature. It would seem, then, that God makes accommodation for angelic participation and the cooperation of the angelic will in the same way he does the human, that is, he allows them to participate in his work, even if Augustine cannot fathom the many ways in which an angel might work according to God's will. Augustine, however, does not seem to question the idea that angels help in the act of creation, or offer any significant reflection on what benefit in particular this would have for angels or for God. We must postpone discussion of further implications of this question until chapter 3, in our discussion of angelic mediation.

Conclusion

In this chapter, we have discussed Augustine's Genesis commentaries and seen how his angelology develops alongside his increasing concern to exposit the text in its literal sense. In concerning himself with the double creation of light, Augustine develops an angelic narrative which is contained entirely within the seven days of creation, and which results in a picture of the angelic life which is anti-mythological and which affirms, without exception, the goodness of creation. His understanding of the cycle of morning–evening knowledge in the seven days of creation as the movements of angelic knowledge, moreover, has implications for his theology as a whole. Genesis, for him, becomes a didactic text which reports a didactic event, and his conception of angelic knowledge suggests a lasting importance of signs and sacraments. Time itself also takes on a special quality, which we may term "sacramental" or, perhaps, liturgical. In his understanding of the angelic fall, he aims to include the entire angelic narrative within Genesis, eliminating the need for Manichean mythology to explain the origins of spiritual creatures. On the whole, Augustine is concerned to demonstrate that the angels were issued good, but must always cooperate with that goodness. Like human beings, they must cling to God in charity and not fall in pride; they must accept that they are created and not creators.

[198] Ibid., v.37, emphasis added.

Augustine's interpretation of Gen. 1 as angelic witness may have further implications for his theology of inspiration. The patristic view of inspiration is deemed untenable by many modern scholars because ancient authors are thought to have a simplistic view of the process of inspiration, to de-emphasize human cooperation and to be ignorant of the human processes of editing.[199] Although Augustine's interpretation of Gen. 1 looks nothing like a modern critical historical reading, he recognizes that Moses could not have been present to record the events of Gen. 1, and he does not appeal simply to a cognitive infusion of knowledge into Moses' mind to explain its authority. Augustine suggests that the angels, the witnesses of the events of Gen. 1, may have had a part in handing it down (albeit in a human idiom). A similar suggestion is made regarding Eve's creation, and Augustine at the very least shows an awareness of human tradition. Angelic testimony is a surprising extension of the concept of tradition, but perhaps Augustine's comments can serve to further complexify our understanding of the Augustinian notion of inspiration, a task which has already been undertaken by two recent dissertations on the topic.[200]

Moreover, although angels are "eyewitnesses" only in an analogous sense, Augustine emphatically insists that they still witnessed something which *actually happened*. His appeal to angelic eyewitness, therefore, also has some potentially fruitful parallels with eyewitness research current in New Testament studies. As Richard Bauckham notes, eyewitness accounts had special authority to an antique person, not only because they communicated firsthand historical knowledge, but also because the eyewitness was in a privileged position to interpret and communicate the historical events to which they were witness.[201] Eyewitness testimony, he argues,

---

[199] See, for example Frances Young, *Exegesis and the Formation of Christian Culture* (Cambridge: Cambridge University Press, 1997), 205. Young claims that the patristic notion of inspiration was essentially that of rote dictation. Denis Farkasfalvy notes that ancient authors were ignorant of issues of oral tradition and redaction, see *Inspiration & Interpretation: A Theological Introduction to Sacred Scripture* (Washington, D.C.: The Catholic University of America Press, 2010), 58.

[200] See Christopher Evans, "Augustine's Theology of Divine Inspiration in the Production and Reading of Ecclesiastical Writings" (Ph.D. Diss., St. Louis University, 2005), and Austin Murphy, "The Bible as Inspired, Authoritative and True according to Saint Augustine," (Ph.D. Diss., University of Notre Dame, 2016). It is perhaps worth noting that, for Evans, Augustine's understanding of scriptural authority is related to its use in a liturgical context, which is an interesting observation considering the strong liturgical overtones in Augustine's description of angelic witness.

[201] For this and other reasons, Bauckham argues that the Gospel of John looks more like ancient historiography than the Synoptics. See *The Testimony of the Beloved Disciple* (Grand Rapids: Baker Academic, 2007), 93–113.

is characteristic of ancient historiography.[202] It is striking therefore to find that Augustine, in his attempt to give a fully historical and literal meaning to Genesis, appeals to the idea of angelic witness in his interpretation of the very first passage of the biblical text. As discussed further in chapter 3, moreover, Augustine believes that angels are perfect communicators and interpreters of the Word to which they are witnesses in the unfolding of creation. Augustine's view implies, therefore, that from the very first, the testimony of witness is a critical element of the biblical text. Indeed, it is not even the case that the angels just happened to be present at creation, but the structure of creation is designed *in order that* the angels might witness it. This character of revelation means that the incarnation is consistent with creation, because God seems to be in the business of acting in a way which is witness-able by created beings, but it also means that the human witness to the incarnation (the Gospels) is parallel with the angelic witness to creation (Genesis) not by happenstance but by design.

The idea that creation is witnessed by the angels is also related to Augustine's understanding of the nature of the angelic fall and the angelic vocation, and so can serve as the concluding thought to this chapter more broadly speaking. The universe is created in such a way so that the angels can witness it, but not strictly for the pleasure of the angels, or so that the angels will have private knowledge of the world which is inaccessible to human beings. The meaning of angelic witness is directly related to the meaning of angelic life, which is worship and sacrifice of praise. The angels are ultimately witnesses to God's glory, not to any scientific mechanism of creation, and the evil angels fail to be witness in that regard, whereas the good angels not only praise God but also become messengers to the human race. The good angels, in other words, are made "light" which by definition enlightens; it is the light of a will clinging to God in its own knowledge of his plan and the continual acceptance of that plan. Indeed, as we saw from *The Confessions*, all creation exists by beholding "the light-giving light and adhering to it."[203] The angels who are made light adhere to God, the light-giving light, and so they too bear light. The evil angels, by contrast, are in perpetual darkness, stripped of their "garments of light"[204] precisely because they refuse to bear witness to God's glory.

[202] Ibid., 19–20. Bauckham also makes the case in his book *Jesus and the Eyewitness* (Grand Rapids: Eerdmans, 2017).
[203] *Conf.* XIII.2.3.
[204] Ibid., XIII.8.9.

2

Angelic Community

In the course of chapter 1 we have seen some glimpses of the angelic life and noted that Augustine describes the angelic vocation as that of praising God and of clinging to God in charity. In this chapter we will continue to explore the concept of the angelic community and activity; what is the angelic life and how does it parallel or exceed human community? How do the human and angelic form one community both now and in the future? Our major text for consideration is *City of God*. It is often overlooked how much ink Augustine spills discussing celestial spirits – both angels and demons – and their respective communities, in this work. The central portion of the *City of God*, in fact, is almost entirely dedicated to a consideration of the angels, both good and evil. In the course of demonstrating that Roman imperial religion offers no benefits either in this life or the next, Augustine must dispatch the idea that the Roman gods are in any way good or that they are necessary to the religion of the one true God. In book VIII, he argues against those who deny that "the worship of the one unchangeable God is sufficient for the obtaining of the blessed life after death" and instead maintain that "in order to obtain that life, many gods, created indeed, and appointed to their several spheres by that one God are to be worshipped."[1] Augustine rejects the notion that the lesser gods, who are really demons, ought to be worshiped (an idea he attributes to the Platonists, especially Porphyry). Book IX continues in the same vein, and completes the discussion of book VIII, but here he speaks specifically of the difference among the

---

[1] *civ. Dei* VIII.1.

demons.² Augustine argues that all demons are wicked, and that God does not need mediators to prevent the defilement of the divine nature.³ He then turns in book x to the good angels and inquires whether even these creatures ought to be worshiped.⁴ Following on the heels of these three books concerning angelic worship, book xi and the beginning of book xii inaugurate the second half of *City of God*, which tells the whole of salvation history, the origin and fate of the two cities. The discussion of the origin of the two cities naturally treats the book of Genesis and the question of angels, since the two cities arose from the creation and subsequent fall of the celestial spirits, as we saw in chapter 1.

From book viii until the beginning of book xii, then, Augustine is concerned with the matter of angels and demons, how human beings ought to regard or worship them, and, finally, how their story is contiguous with the entire story of salvation. The angels therefore occupy a pivotal place in this great work, and Augustine discusses them at some length as he passes from the first part of the work (rejecting Roman imperial cult) to the second (telling the history of the two cities). There is much material which can be drawn upon from all of these books, but the focal point of our discussion will be book x, as it is in this book where Augustine deals with the good angels properly speaking. We will come to see that the good angels are in communion with God and with each other because of the proper orientation of their love, and that their life is defined by praise. This principle of their communion is also the principle which binds them to us.

To begin, the contours of what Gerard O'Daly calls Augustine's "theology of worship"⁵ must be sketched, including the place of the angels and demons in the worship of the two cities. The discussion will then turn to an examination of the implications of this theory of worship for Augustine's angelology more broadly, first by considering the resulting view of human–angelic relations in our life on earth, and then in our future life when we will be "equal to angels" (Luke 20:36). Lastly, the eucharistic imagery Augustine employs when speaking of the beatific life and its significance for understanding the human–angelic community will be explored.

---

² See ibid., IX.1–2.
³ Ibid., IX.16–17.
⁴ Ibid., X.1.
⁵ Gerard O'Daly, *Augustine's City of God: A Reader's Guide* (Oxford: Oxford University Press, 1999), 123.

Augustine's Theology of Worship

To lay a foundation for the discussion of angelic community in *City of God*, it is important to consider first Augustine's understanding of angelic worship, as this is the central issue of book x. In book x, he asks whether or not we ought to worship angels, and, having answered in the negative, he goes on to consider what constitutes properly ordered worship. He also contrasts the right worship of the city of God with the system of worship which demons create for themselves, and in which pagan religion participates. Augustine's theology of worship will here be explored by considering the object of worship in each of the two cities, the sacrifices made in each, and lastly, the disposition in which these sacrifices are made. Since the two cities are defined by their desire or love, "the one enjoying God, the other swelling with pride,"[6] they are also therefore defined precisely by whom they worship and how.

Ostensibly, in the context of *City of God*, the objects of Roman worship are the many pagan gods, whereas the inhabitants of the heavenly city pay "divine honours to the one true God, the creator of all gods," the only one to whom λατρεία (service) is truly due.[7] But this replacement of one object of worship with another is not simply an intellectual mistake, and Augustine is not merely promoting the worship of a better God about whom the Romans were hitherto ignorant. Rather, the ultimate object of worship in pagan religion is oneself, both for the demons and for those who imitate them. Augustine clearly attributes this type of self-turning behavior to demons in book x. The demons divert praise and worship to themselves for the purpose of stealing the reverence due to God, since a demon is an instrument of the devil who "longs to entangle wretched souls in the deceptive worship of many and false gods, and to turn them aside from the true worship of the true God."[8] These demons are a deceitful race, "they are filled with pride and rashness, delight in sacrificial odours, are taken with flattery."[9] For the same reason, the demons cannot be said to have any genuine concern for human affairs, but rather "have induced men to worship them only by means of miraculous works, which the heathen histories testify and by which the gods

---

[6] *civ. Dei* XI.33.

[7] Ibid., x.1. Augustine opens book x by carefully laying out different words used in the biblical context and in everyday speech to denote worship, settling on this term to describe the worship due to God alone. Dods always renders this word (λατρεία/*servitus*) as "service."

[8] Ibid., x.10.

[9] Ibid.

have made a display of *their own power* rather than having done any real service."[10] Any miraculous or powerful act performed by a demon serves only to win that demon more praise, not to provide any real aid to the human race.

Collecting honors for oneself, then, is a hallmark of demonic behavior, and it in turn is a characteristic of those who follow demons.[11] The philosophers, Augustine explains, do not reject worship of God on any sound philosophical grounds, but rather support the pagan cult as a means to gain prestige for themselves; "do you still doubt whether these [the gods] are wicked demons," Augustine asks, "or do you, perhaps, feign ignorance that you may not give offense to the theurgists who have allured you by their secret rites and have taught you, as a mighty boon, these insane and pernicious devilries?"[12] The philosophers seek honor before men, both the theurgists with whom they ingratiate themselves, and others, over whom they can lord their knowledge of occult rites. The accusation of Augustine against the philosophers goes further still. The philosophers, in directing the masses toward theurgy, not only gain benefits for themselves, but also prevent others from attaining to the higher and more prestigious intellectual life. Thus the philosophers are able to claim that intellectual achievement for their own glory as well. Although they direct the simple-minded to purification rites to receive divine revelation, Augustine charges that

you make yourself superior to these divine revelations by your intellectual life, which dispenses with these theurgic purifications as not needed by a philosopher. But, by way of rewarding your teachers, you recommend these arts to other people, who, not being philosophers, may be persuaded to use what you acknowledge to be useless to yourself, who are capable of higher things.[13]

Thus, the worship of the earthly city is a worship not of service (true λατρεία) but of prideful misdirection. The demons demand worship for themselves, and in turn the theurgists and philosophers claim the

---

[10] Ibid., x.18, emphasis mine. *Non enim se aliter colendos esse persuaserunt nisi mirabilium operum effectibus, quorum et historia gentium testis est, quarum dii se ostentare mirabiles potius quam utiles ostendere potuerunt.*

[11] Augustine expresses the same idea elsewhere quite bluntly: "I am saying that in your temples only malign spirits are worshipped. In their pride they demand sacrifices and wish to be worshipped as gods. This proves that they are malevolent and proud. Human beings who are not good behave similarly, seeking their own glory and belittling the glory of God" (*en. Ps.* 96.12).

[12] *civ. Dei* x.26.

[13] Ibid., x.27.

understanding of proper worship as a skill for themselves, as an art. They use their skill then to deceive others and turn them not even to worship of demons *per se*, but to themselves as the source of higher knowledge. The philosophers are the worst transgressors in this regard because they actually know better, but they turn people away from the highest source of knowledge in order to make themselves "superior" in their intellectual life.[14] The philosophers have preferred their "own frail and infirm human virtue"[15] to a turning in humility to Christ, and although they know that theurgy is of no use, they "recur on every opportunity to these arts for no other purpose ... than to *appear an accomplished theurgist*, and gratify those who are curious in illicit arts."[16]

The worship typical of the holy angels in the heavenly city is the antithesis of this model of pagan (that is, demonic) religion. Unlike the demons, who seek happiness by drawing praise to themselves, the good angels seek at all times to turn us to the true source of happiness, God, who has also made them happy. If the marked characteristic of the demons was their unrelenting pursuit of praise for themselves, then the life of the good angels is exactly the opposite: holy angels refuse to be worshiped themselves "for they do not wish us to worship them as our gods, but to join them in worshipping their God and ours; not to sacrifice to them, but together with them to become a sacrifice to God."[17] The good angels need and demand no worship,

for this they know is due only to the one true God, in allegiance to whom they themselves find their blessedness (*adhaerendo beati sunt*) ... such arrogance belongs to proud and wretched demons, whose disposition is diametrically opposite to the piety of those who are subject to God, and whose blessedness consists in attachment to him (*illi cohaerendo beatorum*).[18]

---

[14] See *civ. Dei* X.27. John Cavadini offers this description of Augustine's view of the philosophers, which is consonant with our discussion throughout: "Thus, Platonic spirituality, characterized by a fundamental inconsistency, boils down to the delivery of philosophy into an economy of pride, manifested in a sacramental system of deflection of sacrifice from oneself, such that one is never the sacrifice, but rather the master of the economy of sacrifice." See Cavadini, "Trinity and Apologetics in the Theology of St. Augustine," *Modern Theology* 29.1 (Jan. 2013): 61–62. See also his discussion of the Platonists' inclination to seize philosophy and knowledge of God as an accomplishment in "God's Eternal Knowledge according to Augustine" in *The Cambridge Companion to Augustine* (second edition), ed. David Meconi and Eleanore Stump (Cambridge: Cambridge University Press, 2014): 37–49.

[15] *civ. Dei* X.27.

[16] Ibid., X.28, emphasis mine; *nisi ut talium quoque rerum quasi peritus appareas et placeas inlicitarum artium curiosis.*

[17] Ibid., X.25.

[18] Ibid., X.26.

The good angels have attached themselves to God and seek to draw others into that relationship rather than to attract praise to themselves; that is the demonic impulse. The demons do not help us, for "there are no gods who care for human affairs,"[19] but the good angels offer us aid on our journey. Near the beginning of book x, Augustine sets this cosmic scene vividly. We humans are traveling here below, while the good angels above beckon us home:

> It is very right that these blessed and immortal spirits, who inhabit celestial dwellings, and rejoice in the communications of their creator's fullness, firm in his eternity, assured in his truth, holy by his grace, since they compassionately and tenderly regard us miserable mortals, and wish us to become immortal and happy, do not desire us to sacrifice to themselves, but to him whose sacrifice they know to be in common with us. For we and they together are in the city of God ... the human part sojourning here below, the angelic aiding from above.[20]

Even though we are in two different states, Augustine emphasizes our unity with the good angels, since we have a common home and a common object of worship. The good angels have true compassion, where the demons have only self-interest. Where the city of the devil is divided, with each member building up praise for himself, the city of God is united, with each building up praise for God. Augustine's image of the pilgrim church traveling to her homeland is well known, but it is easy to overlook that the good angels are often featured in these depictions (both in *City of God* and elsewhere).[21] We are headed to the heavenly Jerusalem, that "city where the angels live, the city from which we are absent like travelers abroad, groaning in our exile."[22]

As the philosophers follow after the demons in their quest for praise, so should the Christian community *in via* follow after the good angels in their effort to direct all praise to God. In this regard, Augustine holds up the example of Paul and Barnabas, who, "when they had wrought a miracle of healing in Lycaonia, were thought to be gods, and declined this honour, and announced to them the God in whom they should believe."[23]

---

[19] Ibid., x.18.
[20] Ibid., x.7.
[21] For example, see *civ. Dei* xi.33, where the demons are described as envying the angels as they gather pilgrims, and xix.23, where we are said to love the angels while on our pilgrimage. This imagery is especially prevalent in Augustine's preaching on the Psalms of Ascent, see *en. Ps.* 119.6, 121.2–3, 125.1 and 126.3. For more examples from elsewhere in his corpus, see *ep. Jo.* 9.10, *ep. Jo.* 10.2, *ench.* 56, *ep.* 55.10 and *ep.* 187.16.
[22] *en. Ps.* 93.6.
[23] *civ. Dei* x.19.

These two systems of worship, then, are not merely two parallel ways of honoring God, with Augustine championing the superior mode, since that view of Augustine's apologetic would impose the same understanding of worship-as-technology which the theurgists espouse. Magic is a technology, it is the "pastime of demons"[24] and invented by them.[25] Magic confines worship to the learning of a skill which can be acquired by those of like mind to quantify their religious power. It can then in turn be used to enslave others. Magical skill is therefore the ultimate parody of the praise of God.[26] The very origin of the name "demon," Augustine explains, comes from the Greek word for knowledge.[27] The demons have that kind of knowledge which puffs up, that is, "knowledge without charity" and this gives rise to their insane appetite for the "divine honours and religious services that they know to be due to the true God."[28] They employ their knowledge about the natural world to work wonders and gain adherents. The good angels also have a knowledge of the material and transitory, of course, in fact they possess it even more securely than the demons because they see these things in the Word, but they hold this knowledge cheaply compared to its source.[29] The good angels do not use this knowledge to shock and amaze, nor to subject human beings to their own will, but rather to turn our eyes toward God. So these two systems of worship are not of two types of the same, but rather are the product of two completely different communities, one pointing only to itself as the source of meaning, the other always pointing beyond itself. The one community is divided in its quest for praise, where one person's prayer prevents the purgation of another, for example,[30] whereas the other community is united in its worship of God, both sojourners and those already at rest working together to bring about the beatific vision for all.

Having established how these two objects of worship – God and the self – generate two completely different systems of worship, let us turn to discuss the content of that worship, which is sacrifice. At first glance,

---

[24] Ibid., X.12.
[25] Ibid., XXI.6.
[26] Augustine's view of magic is discussed at length in chapter 4.
[27] *civ. Dei* IX.20.
[28] Ibid.
[29] Ibid., IX.22.
[30] Ibid., X.9. Note the consistency between Augustine's view of angelic knowledge here and in book XI, as well as in *Literal Meaning of Genesis*. The angels have both evening and morning knowledge of God (knowledge of things in the Word and things in themselves) and they seek to incorporate human beings into this cycle of knowing, whereby their knowledge prompts them to praise God.

it might seem that the pagans simply offer an inferior form of sacrifice
to their gods (visible things), whereas the Christians have progressed to
offer superior sacrifices (invisible things). Augustine explicitly resists this
idea, arguing that "visible sacrifices are signs of the invisible, as the words
we utter are signs of things."[31] He offers the example of prayer, which is
the visible sacrifice (spoken words) of the invisible heart.[32] By holding visible and invisible sacrifice closely together, Augustine is able to maintain
two other important positions.

　First, he is able to dismiss the claim of those who think that they
can suitably offer visible sacrifice to the gods (the demons or even good
angels), while reserving invisible sacrifice to the one true God.[33] Augustine
does not want to mitigate the perniciousness of offering visible sacrifices
to the pagan gods, since the demons "who arrogate themselves divinity
are delighted not with the smoke of carcasses, but with the suppliant
spirit which they deceive and hold in subjection."[34] In other words, those
who merely offer burnt sacrifices to the demons unknowingly offer themselves in subjection as well, which is the devil's true aim.[35] Conversely,
good angels refuse all forms of sacrifice, "either in figure or in the reality,
which the mysteries of sacrifice symbolized."[36]

　Secondly, it allows Augustine to uphold the importance of both physical and spiritual sacrifices which are offered to the one true God. As in
the example of prayer, the sacrifice of the whole person is due to God
and no one else. That Augustine views sacrifice as intrinsically visible and
invisible should give us further pause when considering the arguments
of Phillip Cary, mentioned previously, who holds all exterior signs are
ultimately useless for Augustine. Cary avers that "the inferiority of the
body is tantamount to the powerlessness of external things over the inner
self."[37] With regard to participation in pagan rites, however, the signs are
anything but powerless in spiritual matters. The pagans' external sign
(their sacrifice) effects what it signifies (subjection to demons) even if
that is not at all the intent of the supplicant. Likewise, one is not able
to offer merely a symbolic gesture to a good angel, because the sign is
bound up with the actual sacrifice. Augustine insists on the importance

[31] *civ. Dei* x.19.
[32] Ibid.
[33] Ibid.
[34] Ibid.
[35] Ibid.
[36] Ibid., x.26.
[37] Cary, *Outward Signs*, ix.

of visible and actual worship of Christians, not merely a spiritualized worship wherein someone can do one thing and worship another – this is in fact the hypocrisy of the philosophers. In short, to God alone is due all worship "whether we render it outwardly or inwardly, for we are all his temple, each of us severally and all of us together."[38]

The sacrifices of the pagans, then, are truly offered both visibly and invisibly, and the church is not the only place where so-called spiritual sacrifice occurs. However, there are two ways in which the sacrifice of the Christian church stands in stark contrast to Roman sacrifice. The first is that Christian worship demands the sacrifice of the entire self,

Accordingly, when the apostle had exhorted us to present our bodies as a living sacrifice, holy and acceptable to God, our reasonable service [i.e. worship], and not to be conformed to the world but to be transformed in the renewing of our mind, it was so that we might prove what is the good and acceptable and perfect will of God, that is to say, the true sacrifice of ourselves.[39]

This self-sacrifice is done primarily in a spiritual way, but Augustine's refusal to neatly divide spiritual and physical sacrifice is perhaps what allows the martyrs to be most properly called Christian heroes, and what leads him to list martyrdom as the first way in which we can offer sacrifice to God;[40] one could say that martyrs sacrifice themselves in full (and certainly in a visible way). In any case, to sacrifice oneself is precisely the sacrifice which is impossible in the model of Roman imperial worship, since that system is designed to attract praise to its adherents, as we have already seen. For Augustine, on the other hand, any true sacrifice must entail service to both God and neighbor.[41] Augustine contends, "a true sacrifice is every work which is done that we may be united to God in holy fellowship ... therefore even the mercy we show to men, if it is not

---

[38] *civ. Dei* x.3. Likewise, both the words and visible rites of the law enjoin the worship of one God, not just the prescriptions of the law or its enactment alone, but both together (*civ. Dei* x.15).

[39] Ibid., x.6, cf. Rom. 12:1.

[40] Ibid., x.21; x.3 "Our heart when it rises to him is his altar; the priest who intercedes for us is his only-begotten; we sacrifice to him bleeding victims when we contend for his truth even unto blood; to him we offer the sweetest incense when we come before him burning with holy and pious love; to him we devote and surrender ourselves and his gifts in us ... (and so on) ... to him we offer on the altar of our heart the sacrifice of humility and praise kindled by the fire of burning love." Here Augustine lists a series of spiritual sacrifices which are often tied to, or embodied in, physical worship (e.g. incense). The first thing we place on the altar is ourselves literally (in martyrdom). Spiritually, this complete gift is the offering of our whole heart (the last thing listed).

[41] See, for example, his interpretation of sacrifices made in the temple in *civ. Dei* x.5.

shown for God's sake, is not a sacrifice."[42] All true sacrifice must be done selflessly, it must be done for the sake of God and the neighbor and not for the sake of oneself.

The second, but inseparable, character of Christian worship which sets it apart from that of the pagans is the source of its sacrifice. Where pagan sacrifice is determined by human beings, like theurgists, who have a technical understanding of what to sacrifice and how to purify oneself (magical or theurgical skill), Christian sacrifice is provided by God. The sacrifice of the Christian faith comes from Christ. Christ is both the archetypal pattern for understanding what it means to sacrifice oneself, and the very way in which Christians are able to sacrifice. Augustine explains,

> Hence that true mediator, in so far as, by assuming the form of a servant, he became the mediator between God and men, the man Christ Jesus, though in the form of God he received sacrifice together with the Father, with whom he is one God, yet in the form of a servant he chose rather to be than to receive a sacrifice.[43]

In offering himself, Christ is the perfect example of self-emptying. Echoing Phil. 2, Augustine explains that Christ did not covet his ability to receive sacrifice, but gave himself up. Thus, Christ is the antithesis of the demons in two ways: he both does not seek sacrifice for his own sake, and yet is the only true God to whom sacrifice is due. Augustine shows that Christ, unlike the pagan gods, does not need any sacrifice to complete himself, but rather allows sacrifice for our sake. After all, "who is so foolish as to suppose that things offered to God are needed by him for some uses of his own?"[44] Christ also opens the way for our own self-sacrifice. Augustine maintains that Christ "is both the priest who offers and the sacrifice offered. And he deigned that there should be a daily sign of this in the sacrifice of the church, which, being his body, learns to offer herself through him."[45] Christ, then, provided a perfect sacrifice on the cross, became the priest through whom this sacrifice might be offered and instituted a way for us to continually participate in that sacrifice: the Eucharist. The Eucharist is, for Augustine, both the recapitulation of Christ's sacrifice and simultaneously the self-sacrifice of each Christian, since they are the body of Christ, the church.

> This is the sacrifice of Christians: we, being many, are one body in Christ. And this also is the sacrifice which the Church continually celebrates in the sacrament

[42] Ibid., x.6.
[43] Ibid., x.20.
[44] Ibid., x.5.
[45] Ibid., x.20.

of the altar, known to the faithful, in which she teaches that she herself is offered in the offering she makes to God.[46]

In providing the substance and the means of sacrifice, Christ is the deconstruction of all systems of Roman worship. Such a sacrifice cannot be learned by skill, cannot be obtained by merit. The participation in Christ's self-sacrifice happens at an altar just like pagan sacrifice, but it is the eucharistic altar, Christ's own altar at which he presides. It is not only the thing signified in Christian sacrifice which is superior, but both the sign and the act of signifying are completely transformed.

The dispositions proper to the two cities and their worship have already been implicit throughout our discussion, as they permeate book x of *City of God*: the attitudes of humility and pride. The refusal of the philosophers to conform to the true system of worship is not the result of faulty logic, Augustine explains. Just like the demons, the philosophers recognize that there is only one true God. And, as in the case of the demons, what prevents these philosophers from converting to worship of Christ is what Augustine calls pride. This pride binds the philosophers to the system of pagan worship and prevents them from adopting Christian worship, which would demand that they give up their privileged position as intellectuals and "the pride of vain science."[47] Augustine, with polemical edge, suggests that the so-called intellectually superior philosophers may never be able to stoop in humility to the way of Christ,

I know it is useless to speak to a dead man – useless, at least so far as regards to you [i.e. the philosophers], but perhaps not in vain for those who esteem you highly and love you ... and these persons I address in your name. The grace of God could not have more graciously commended to us than this, that the only Son of God, remaining unchangeable in himself should assume humanity and give us hope of his love.[48]

Ironically, it is not the esteemed philosophers who will find it in themselves to accept the humility of Christ, but only the lowly ones who follow them, the very ones whom the philosophers would misdirect to keep their own position secure. But, without a doubt, it is in humility alone where Augustine locates the true worship of God, "it is lowliness that is requisite, and to this it is extremely difficult to bend you [i.e. the philosophers]."[49] Without humility, after all, it would hardly be possible

[46] Ibid., x.6.
[47] Ibid., x.28.
[48] Ibid., x.29.
[49] Ibid.

to refer the praise of yourself to God, nor to sacrifice yourself on the altar of love.

Nevertheless, Augustine contends that the philosophers actually do acknowledge the philosophical concept of grace, arguing that

> you believe in grace, for you say it is granted to a few to reach God by virtue of intelligence. For you do not say "few have thought fit or have wished" but "it has been granted" – distinctly acknowledging God's grace, not human sufficiency.[50]

For Augustine, then, the philosophers are not so unwilling to relinquish themselves as the source of their own salvation as we might first suspect. This argument may be apologetically motivated, in an attempt to attribute to the philosophers ideas with which they may not have been comfortable, but Augustine clearly locates the resistance of the philosophers in their rejection of Christ rather than the notion of grace. This refusal to accept Christ is strictly a matter of pride,

> Why is it then, that when the Christian faith is pressed upon you, you forget, or pretend to ignore, what you habitually discuss or teach? Why is it that you refuse to be Christian, on the ground that you hold opinions which in fact, you yourself demolish? Is it not because Christ came in lowliness and you are proud?[51]

Since Augustine has argued that the philosophers concede the necessity of grace, he is able to take this rhetorical turn. If grace is requisite, and the Christian faith has successfully explained the means of grace by which God has called all people to himself, what else could stand in the way of belief other than the philosopher's pride? Augustine aims to show that it is a particular form of divine intercession, that is, the incarnation, which the philosophers find detestable, and that there is no good reason apart from pride for them to do so. The philosophers, who think they are close to the vision of God, are actually quite distant:

> The incarnation of the unchangeable Son of God, whereby we are saved, this is what you refuse to recognize. You see in a fashion, although at a distance with filmy eye, the country in which we should abide by, *the way* to it you know not.[52]

The way to God, which is Christ's lowliness, defies the philosopher's inflated sense of the height of purity needed to reach God because God bends all the way down to the human condition. Christ is "the principle by whose incarnation we are purified," for which the philosophers have

---

[50] Ibid.
[51] Ibid.
[52] Ibid., emphasis mine.

been searching. Such passages in Augustine's corpus which pertain to the philosopher's knowledge of God are well known, and have led some scholars to question how central Christian teaching even is, for Augustine, in coming to a knowledge of God. To ask John Rist's question: Is the incarnation merely a "supplement" to philosophy, or a "missing link" which the philosophers can see and accept as a matter of rational discourse?[53] The analysis presented here suggests that the incarnation is not merely the missing piece of an intellectual puzzle which the philosophers had nearly solved by their own powers. That the philosophers know something about God is not, in the end, construed positively by Augustine, but is used against them. They know much and yet are still so far from God! The focus of book X is not the knowledge of God abstractly conceived but about love of God concretely realized in worship (embodied by the angels, parodied by the demons). It is in this regard that the philosophers fail.

The disposition of the two communities – one prideful and turned inward, the other humble and longing for God – also gives rise to Augustine's characterization of these two cities as private and public.[54] The privacy of the demonic system has already been intimated in the discussion of theurgy and magic above. Augustine refers to theurgic rites as "secret"[55] and associates their power and prestige with their exclusivity. The devil, who sometimes masquerades as an angel of light, does so in private and to a few.[56] These few become "addicted"[57] to their furtive rites because it inflates their own pride, and so the devil makes of them

---

[53] John Rist, "On the Nature and Worth of Christian Philosophy," 218 and 222. As Cavadini argues, rejecting the incarnation means, for Augustine, to have an entirely distorted view of God. It is not that the Platonists have merely misjudged God's economy, but the failure to understand God's economy and the refusal to accept it is a failure to accept God as Trinity. Their mistake is thus fundamental. See "Trinity and Apologetics," 61–62.

[54] On the importance of the concept of private and public in Augustine's social thought more broadly speaking, see Miikka Ruokanen, *Theology of Social Life in Augustine's De civitate Dei* (Göttingen: Vandenhoeck & Ruprecht, 1993), 79–81.

[55] E.g. *civ. Dei* X.26–27 and XXI.6. See also *civ. Dei* II.26 and footnote directly below.

[56] *civ. Dei* II.26. Here, with reference to the mysteries of Coelestis, the dynamic is spelled out in full; those who would be righteous are deceived in secret by seemingly virtuous sayings, but the masses are deceived on a public scale by those in possession of the secret teachings; "in public, a bold impurity fills the ear of the people with noisy clamour; in private, a feigned chastity speaks in scarcely audible whispers to a few." See also *civ. Dei* X.10; the so-called purified ones who claim angelic visions for themselves are in fact seeing demons.

[57] *civ. Dei* X.9. The demons themselves are also described as addicted (*dediti*) to magic (*civ. Dei* X.7–8). Their addiction to their own system of praise is consistent with Augustine's description in *civ. Dei* XII.1 of the demons as having "lapsed to this private good of their own (*ad propria defluxerunt*)." They are addicted to themselves.

his own angels,[58] who then go out and entrap the unlearned masses. The exclusivity of the devil's feigned virtue therefore serves to recruit the so-called righteous to his cause, because they are tempted to pride by the possession of these secrets and the appearance of goodness. The secretive nature of demonic religion also reflects the true intent of the devil, which is to privatize and thus fragment praise, as we have seen. Good angels, on the other hand, both publicly perform miracles and publicly refuse worship.[59] The two cities are defined by two loves, "one social, the other private."[60]

In his second sermon on Ps. 103, Augustine images the privacy and openness of the two cities when expounding verses 8–10. These verses speak of God's work in the mountains and the valleys, and declare that "streams shall flow midway between the mountains."[61] In an earlier passage, Augustine had already established that the mountains are the angels (i.e. preachers) of God, both the celestial spirits and others such as apostles who announce the gospel.[62] That the river flows in the middle of these mountains signifies the public and common nature of God's salvation,

> What is in the middle belongs to all. It is common property, on which everyone depends equally for life. It is centrally placed; it does not belong to me, but not you either: it is not the private possession of any of us. This is why we say of certain people "they have peace among themselves" … what do we mean by "among themselves"? Midway, centrally placed among them.[63]

The mountains surround and proclaim the common river of God's redemption, but none of the mountains have it for their own. The devil, however, is in the business of privatization, and it is against the devil that

---

[58] *civ. Dei* X.27. See also *s.* 376A.4 for another reference to human beings as angels of the devil.

[59] See, for example, *civ. Dei* X.16.

[60] *Gn. litt.* XI.20 (*alter socialis, alter priuatus*). See also *civ. Dei* XIV.27; all salvation history is brought about by the victory of the creator's protection over private presumption.

[61] *en. Ps.* 103.2.11.

[62] Ibid., 103.2.7 and again in 103.2.11. Elsewhere in the *Expositions of the Psalms* Augustine interprets mountains to be angels (angels in the sense of anyone who announces God, including celestial spirits); see *en. Ps.* 89.3 and 124.4.

[63] Ibid., 103.2.11. The idea of private property or possession suggested by the translation is not quite as strong in the Latin (see bolded passage): *quod medium dicitur, commune est. res communis, unde omnes aequaliter uiuunt, media est, nec adtinet ad me; sed nec adtinet ad te, nec ad me. propterea loquimur et sic de aliquibus ominibus: habent inter se pacem, habent inter se fidem, habent inter se caritatem; sic certe dicimus. quid est, inter se? in medio sui. quid est, in medio sui? commune est illis.*

Paul warns us when he mentions an angel coming to preach a gospel other than the one already received.[64] Remember, Augustine says, "if an angel who flowed in his own private stream in paradise had not been hearkened to, we should not have been flung into death."[65] The devil, claiming his own source of salvation (his own stream), caused Adam and Eve to fall by tempting them to claim for themselves the rivers of paradise.

The public nature of the beatific possession perhaps helps to illuminate a seemingly odd element of Augustine's demonology. When explaining why demons can foretell the future, Augustine has recourse to the idea that demons can overhear what God is saying to the good angels, or what good angels and human heralds proclaim to the world; "the proud and deceitful airy powers may well have been found to have uttered through soothsayers things they overheard from holy angels and prophets."[66] One might ask why God could not lower the sound of his voice! But of course, not all angelic exchanges are done with audible words. Perhaps demons can catch snatches of the will of God because it is open, as love is.[67] It is perfectly fitting with the foregoing discussion that demons should take what is accessible to all creation (God's decrees), claim it for their own and use it for their own glory in the form of demonic prophecies.

In book x of *City of God*, then, Augustine presents us with two distinctly different communities of worship. These two communities offer reverences to different objects by means of different sacrifices in different dispositions. One is a secret society, the other of common love and worship. The demons point to themselves in deceit, the philosophers follow them to gain praise, and augurs follow in turn for possession of

[64] Ibid.; Gal. 1:8–9.

[65] Ibid. *Si angelus de proprio fluens in paradiso non esset auditus, non praecipitaremur in mortem.*

[66] *trin.* IV.23. See also *divin. daem.* 10, *Dulc. qu.* 6.4 and *Jo. ev. tr.* 7.6. Demons can also predict the future by foretelling what they themselves plan to do or by means of their subtler awareness of body language and their speed. Augustine shares these common ideas about demonic activity with many others in antiquity. Jean Pépin, for example, demonstrates that Augustine is influenced by Platonic ideas about demonic bodies (see Pépin, "Les Influences Païennes sur L'angelologie et Demonologie de Saint Augustin" in *Ex Platonicorum Persona: Études sur les Lectures Philosophique de Saint Augustin*, [Amsterdam: Adolf M. Hakkert, 1977] 34–35), but similar ideas about how demonic prophecy works are found in many early Christian texts (for example, see *Life of Anthony* 31, where demons can predict the visit of some monks by speeding ahead and announcing their arrival). Nevertheless, the idea of demons overhearing angels is consonant with Augustine's angelology in the ways mentioned.

[67] The demons do not hear by mistake, of course, but can only hear what is ordained in God's providence for them to hear (*trin.* IV.22). In general, it would seem pride and anger can prevent us from hearing angels (*adn. Job* 5).

their own type of power. This order is completely inverted in the heavenly city, where good angels point to God, and Christians use the miraculous for the same ends; theirs is an outward and upward turn.[68] How is this reordering of worship achieved? It is achieved through humility, in particular, through the humility exemplified in the incarnation. It is this humility which is the philosophers' greatest lack, for although they can recognize the concept of grace, they cannot accept it when faced with it in the flesh.

Human–Angelic Community in This Life

In light of his depiction of the two communities of worship in book x, Augustine's view of human–angelic relations can be considered more broadly (both in *City of God* and elsewhere in his corpus). What kind of relationship can we be said to have with angels in the present age, given his understanding of our common goal and object of worship? At the beginning of book xii, before Augustine moves from the celestial history to the terrestrial, he shows an awareness of precisely this problem,

> Before I speak of the creation of man and show how the cities took their rise, so far as regards the race of rational mortals, I see that I must first, so far as I can, adduce what may demonstrate that it is not incongruous and unsuitable to speak of a society composed of angels and men together; so that there are not four cities or societies, but rather two in all, one composed of the good and the other of the wicked, angels and men indifferently.[69]

Augustine reminds his reader that although he intends now to speak of Adam and Eve, the fall and the course of human history, this story is contiguous with the heavenly narrative which has occupied his attention for books viii–xi. Note that he does not speak merely of a future reality of two cities – as if, in the end, only two cities will persist when human beings and angels are finally united according to their moral orientation. Even if it is inscrutable to human wisdom who belongs to each city, it is proper to speak about only two cities or societies (*sed duae potius ciuitates, hoc est societates, merito esse dicantur*), both now and then.

   That angels and human beings have a certain familiarity is characteristic of book x, as we saw in passages concerning angelic aid and

[68] As abundantly evidenced in *Confessions*, Christian conversion also requires an inward turn, but in the context of *City of God* Augustine emphasizes the openness and outwardness required for the worship of the Christian community.
[69] *civ. Dei* xii.1.

their common worship with us, and we should not pass this over. It is a consistent feature of Augustine's angelology, but it is certainly not self-evident that we should be considered, as creatures of God, to have so much in common with the angels as to be often numbered together with them, and to be capable of relationship with them.[70] The commonest way in which Augustine indicates our fellowship with angels is by calling them our fellow-citizens (*cives*).[71] This description of the angels fits especially well, of course, in *City of God*, as it designates their relation to us in the terms which Augustine has set for himself in that work. The angels await us in the heavenly Jerusalem, that city to which we journey, but that city to which we somehow already belong. But Augustine also uses even more intimate terms, to describe our relationship with angels. In *On Christian Teaching*, he asserts that angels are also our neighbors (*proximi*) and that they are included in the dual commandment which governs the entire interpretation of scripture; to love both God and neighbor means to love all human beings and all angels.[72] The scriptures, after all, tell us clearly of the "many courtesies and kindnesses" that the good angels have shown to human beings, proving that they have been a good neighbor to us.[73] And, of course, if Christ himself has become our neighbor, how could we exclude the angels from this all-encompassing fellowship? The two cities are cities composed of neighbors, defined by their love (or lack thereof) for the neighbor,

one of them wanting for its neighbour what it wants for itself, the other wanting to subject its neighbour to itself, one of them exercising authority over its neighbour for its neighbour's good, the other for its own good – these two loves were first manifest in the angels...[74]

Augustine also follows an interpretive tradition that sees the good angels as the neighbors who rejoice over the recovery of the lost drachma in the

---

[70] As Ruokanen notes, we are so often counted alongside the angels as heavenly citizens that Augustine sometimes does not bother to name us separately from them, see *Theology of the Social Life*, 79.
[71] This usage is common in *City of God*, see *civ. Dei* X.25–26, XIII.24, XV.26, XIX.23 and XXII.29. See also *symb. cat.* 2, *en. Ps.* 90.2.1, 121.2, 125.1, *s.* 157.6, 378 and *s. Dolbeau* 22.19. The word *socius* is also used to describe the angels as our companions, but much less frequently; see *ep.* 102.19 and *s.* 389.3. It is, however, extremely common for Augustine to speak of us as being in the *societas* of angels.
[72] *doc. Chr.* 1.30–33; see also 1.36.
[73] Ibid., 1.33; *a quibus tanta nobis misericordiae impenduntur officia.*
[74] *Gn. litt.* XI.20.

Lukan parable,[75] and he interprets the good angels to be those nearby Job (the *propinqui*) who have turned away from him in his miserable state.[76]

To return to *City of God* we find more intimate language still. The holy angels love us,[77] and in their works they prove their love for us.[78] We, in our turn, also "venerate and love" them while on our pilgrimage.[79] In book XIX Augustine speaks of the nature of the happy life, and notes that both pagans and Christians agree that the blessed life is a social one in which friendship plays a critical role.[80] The Romans consider themselves to have a relationship with celestial spirits and that this higher tier of friendship embraces all of heaven.[81] Augustine concurs that we too fancy angels for our friends, but he is somewhat reticent to say how these friendships are manifested.[82] Unlike human friendship, angelic friendship does not grieve us because we never have to mourn its loss, for the angels do not get sick and die.[83] But, as in human friendships, our ability to perceive the good in another being is limited, and so in seeking friendship with a good angel we may instead become associated with a demon. This error has already been made by the pagans, and consequently we cannot yet be on the same terms with an angel as we can with another human being. The level of familiarity must necessarily be less because of our state.[84] Nevertheless, the good angels are also described as the friends of the bridegroom (another widespread exegetical tradition, as noted by Daniélou),[85] and Augustine interprets Job's cry "have mercy on me my friends" (Job 19:21) as being directed to saints and holy angels.[86] The martyr Crispina is also said to long for angelic friendship.[87] Perhaps the just, with their more perfect configuration to charity, are better suited to

---

[75] *en. Ps.* 103.4.2.
[76] *adn. Job* 5.
[77] *civ. Dei* X.1, X.12, X.26.
[78] Ibid., X.17, particularly by not allowing us to worship them.
[79] Ibid., XIX.23; *ueneramur et amamus.*
[80] Augustine's speaks of the Roman view in *civ. Dei* XIX.3. For a summary of the importance of friendship throughout Augustine's life and the development of his conception of Christian friendship over time, see James McEvoy, "Anima et Cor Unum: Friendship and Spiritual Unity in Augustine," *Recherches de théologie ancienne et médiévale* 53 (1986): 40–92.
[81] *civ. Dei* XIX.9. See also XIX.3.
[82] Ibid.
[83] Ibid.
[84] Ibid., XIX.8–9.
[85] *Jo. ev. tr.* 13.15.
[86] *adn. Job* 19.
[87] *en. Ps.* 137.7.

address angels on the more familiar terms of friendship, rather than just as fellow citizen and neighbor.[88]

That we are one city with the good angels is not described only in positive terms, that is, by way of emphasis on their common citizenship, their friendship and their love. Augustine, both in *City of God* and elsewhere, also makes clear what angels cannot do. The angels have no dominion over us.[89] They are not our mediators strictly speaking, since Christ alone is mediator.[90] Likewise, when speaking of our protection against demons, Augustine almost never speaks of the good angels as coming to our aid, but it is Christ who defeats the devil.[91] Augustine insists that angels are in need of divine assistance and cannot do anything apart from God.[92] In his exposition of Ps. 117, Augustine explains that the words "it is good to trust in the Lord, better than to trust in mortals. It is good to trust in the Lord, better than to trust in princes" means we ought not to trust in any human being or in any angel.[93] An angel may be good, or a human being may be called a good angel, but "it is God who made them good in their measure."[94] No angel is good in itself, no one is good save God alone.[95] Angels are like us in origin, in end and so in our object of worship, as we saw clearly in *City of God*. It is this common bond which puts them squarely on the created side of the ontological divide, and it is in our worship of God that our fellowship is constituted. We are friends of the good angels, and so we are all creatures of God dependent on him.

That our communion with the angels is grounded in our common worship has already been demonstrated from book x of *City of God*. It is in joining the good angels' worship that we come to be part of the city of God, and it is always to this end that holy angels direct us, so we can be happy as they are, through the same source of blessedness that they

---

[88] In the future life, when we are saints, we are assured friendship with angels, patriarchs, apostles, prophets and martyrs. See *s. Denis* 16.7.

[89] *civ. Dei* x.26. On a related note, Augustine never makes direct reference to the tradition that there exist some "angels of the nations" who are assigned to the earth prior to the coming of Christ. He perhaps alludes to it once (*en. Ps.* 88.1.3), but his meaning is unclear. On the "angels of the nations" tradition elsewhere in patristic literature, see Daniélou, *Angels and their Mission*, 14–23.

[90] See *civ. Dei* ix.14–15.

[91] The role of good and evil angels in spiritual warfare is discussed at length in chapter 4.

[92] See, for example, *civ. Dei* xii.9 and *en. Ps.* 70.2.5. Angels, however, are not in need of mercy (see, for example, *en. Ps.* 56.17).

[93] *en. Ps.* 117.5. He interprets "princes" to refer to angels (such as Michael).

[94] Ibid.

[95] Ibid., 117.5 and 134.4.

have.[96] But what creates any horizontal fellowship, we might say, if all our energies are directed toward praise of God? What need have angels of us? Or, in the end, what notice ought we to take of angels, since they are always self-effacing and pointing to God? The answer, for Augustine, lies in God's providence and respect for creaturely freedom. God allows for us all, angels and human beings, to participate in the unfolding of salvation because it is good for us to do so, not because God needs us. In short, it is good for the holy angels to serve God in serving us, and good for us to accept their aid and learn from them; and is it not always upon the goodness of such mutual acts that even human friendships are built?

Augustine speaks of this human–angelic cooperation in a number of ways. One of the biblical examples of a human being and an angel working in tandem which he employs is the story of Cornelius the centurion in Acts 10. The Lord sends an angel to Cornelius to tell him that God has seen his good works and altruism, and also instructs him to contact Peter.[97] Cornelius does so without delay. Augustine points out that Cornelius is an example to all of us that we should never despise human ministry, since Cornelius thought nothing of submitting to Peter even after he had been in direct contact with an angel.[98] In other words, the angel and Peter are on equal footing as emissaries of God, but if Cornelius had been instructed and baptized entirely by an angel, as certainly he could have been, "no respect would have been shown to our human status (*condicio*)."[99] So, by showing respect for Peter's status, we also see an image of the angelic and human working together as colleagues. Both Peter and the angel are friends of Cornelius and ministers of God, or, as Augustine puts it, the angel is "Peter's fellow-servant" (*conseruus Petri*) and, indeed, it is "because he [the angel] worshipped God that he sent Cornelius to Peter."[100] From our mutual worship of God arises mutual consideration, that is, the good angel is concerned for our status and ministry because God is concerned with these things. The angel does not covet Cornelius' affection nor does the angel resist yielding authority to Peter, but the angel's love for God facilitates cooperation. We can see that if human friendship were patterned after the angelic, our friendship with other people would be more perfect and even more perfectly horizontal, because it would be mindful of God's mercy. For a contrary example,

---

[96] See, for example, *civ. Dei* X.7.

[97] See Acts 10:1–7.

[98] *en. Ps.* 96.3. See also *doc. Chr.* 6 (prologue).

[99] *doc. Chr.* 6 (prologue); *sed abiecta esset humana condicio*

[100] *en. Ps.* 96.12; *nam eum* [God] *adorans, Cornelium misit ad Petrum.*

we might look to Augustine's failure in friendship when he mocks the deathbed baptism of his unnamed friend in *Confessions* IV.4.7. Augustine remembers his own actions harshly because, to use James McEvoy's words, he "had not been sufficiently disinterested" to be capable of seeing what was truly good for his friend.[101] True friendship is not self-serving; thus true angelic friendship is possible because the holy angels are capable of mercy, but not mercy for some gain of their own, as was also clear from book x of *City of God*.[102]

Augustine exhibits a similar logic of human–angelic cooperation to that deployed in the Cornelius pericope with regard to baptism in his anti-Donatist writings. In the course of this controversy, Augustine famously defends the idea that Christ is the true minister of baptism, and that the moral degeneracy of any given minister does not nullify the effects of baptism. The Augustinian phrase passed on to posterity is *ex opere operatum*, used to express the inherent efficacy of sacramental action. If the effectiveness of baptism is dependent on human purity, Augustine contends, we would have no way to determine which baptisms have been performed correctly. According to Augustine, the Donatists resolve this problem by arguing that in the case of a minister who is undetected in his evil, God or an angel would be the hidden presider at the baptism. Augustine rejects this view, noting that a person who is baptized by a wicked Christian would, strangely enough, be promoted to receive some kind of divine or angelic baptism; "those then are justified with greater holiness who are baptized by undetected evil men, so as to be cleansed by God or by an angel, than those who are baptized by men who are genuinely and manifestly good."[103] The good angels cannot simply take over the baptism when a human being is found wanting, since this would show no respect for the properly human rite, and it would ignore all particularly

---

[101] See McEvoy, "Anima et Cor," 69. McEvoy follows the interpretation of J. B. Lotz, "Augustinus über die Freundschaft" in *Die Drei-Enheit der Liebe: Eros – Philia – Agape* (Frankfurt: 1979), 264–282.

[102] Angelic friendship is also perfect because it is unending (angels do not get sick and die, as we saw above in *civ. Dei* XIX.9, but see also *s.* 252.9). As McEvoy points out, the bitterness of human friendships, for Augustine, comes about in large part because they must be terminated by death. This is abundantly clear in the episode of *conf.* IV.4.7 where Augustine recounts his profound grief over the death of an unnamed friend (see McEvoy, "Anima et Cor," 50–52, although the relationship between friendship and mortality is featured throughout his article). True friendship, then, as Augustine comes to understand later in life, can only be found in God and be formed between believers.

[103] *c. litt. Pet.* 3.58. See also *cresc.* 2.22.

human striving for virtue, since the unvirtuous would actually provide a superior baptism.

Another image of human–angelic collaboration comes from Augustine's exposition of Ps. 128. He is expounding a passage which refers to those "who become like grass on the rooftops that has withered before it is plucked," as well as to those who do not greet the grass, and "pass by along the way." Augustine explains it is common to say a blessing when you see workers in the field; he claims it is a common practice among the Jews.[104] So who is the one in the field, who is the grass on the rooftop, and who the passer-by? The reapers are angels, collecting sheaves. Those on the rooftops are the arrogant who harvest what is not destined for storage in the barn, and these are the ones whom the passers-by ignore.[105] But who are the passers-by?

> Those who have passed along this way: in other words, those who have passed through this life to their homeland. The apostles were passers-by in this life, the prophets too were passers-by. On whom did the prophets and apostles call down a blessing? On those in whom they discerned a root of charity, but when they saw others waving high up on the rooftops … they predicted the outcome for such people but invoked no blessing upon them.[106]

Augustine has transformed the image of holy angels as reapers in the coming judgment[107] and imagined them as working away in the fields as human prophets and apostles come and go. The good angels are even working in the same space as the wicked, although these arrogant fools comically wave like grass in self-appointed heights. The apostles and prophets do greet their true fellow workers who have a root of charity (good angels and other passers-by, presumably). Angels and human beings toiling together in the field of the Lord is a biblical image, of course, and it is consonant with the imagery Augustine uses more generally for angelic work, which is that of the farmer who cultivates but does not cause to grow (an image discussed at more length in chapter 1). But the interpretation of these passers-by as prophets and apostles resonates with Augustine's description of the angels beckoning home the church on pilgrimage, seen in *City of God*.[108] Although the angels are not *in*

---

[104] *en. Ps.* 128.13.
[105] Ibid.
[106] Ibid. As an aside, the apostles and prophets are here called friends of the bridegroom, not the angels. But one could say the role of these friends is shared; they prepare for the groom and do not "seduce the bride" for their own gain.
[107] In other places, of course, Augustine does make use of the biblical texts that describe angels as reapers in the coming judgment, and these are discussed in chapter 4.
[108] *civ. Dei* x.7.

via, here they are still pictured working out in the field, a homely vision of condescending angelic aid. It gives the impression of a different kind of *corpus permixtum* on earth, not just a church where wheat and chaff are mixed indiscernibly, but a church where the just, both human and angel, are mixed in an equally invisible but real manner. In Augustine's tenth homily on 1 John he speaks of our pilgrimage in a way which has a similar character. We should rejoice and embrace other Christians when we encounter them on our journey, since "you have found a Christian, found a citizen of Jerusalem, found a fellow citizen of angels, found a traveler who is yearning on his journey; join yourself to him, he is your companion (*inuenisti christianum, inuenisti ciuem Ierusalem, inuenisti ciuem angelorum, inuenisti in uia suspirantem peregrinum; adiunge te illi, comes tuus est*)."[109] Being able to recognize that a fellow pilgrim is also already a fellow citizen of the angels is to have an awareness of the presence of angels in the midst of the church. Such an understanding of angelic communion which is definitely present but not perfected echoes the oft-described "now, but not yet" character of Jesus' preaching about the kingdom of God.[110] Our fellowship with angels thus has an eschatological orientation, which is intrinsic to the concept of pilgrimage in Augustine's thought. Our friendship with good angels is not a private good, and we cannot claim it for our own any more than we could claim a fellow traveler, but both forms of friendship reach out toward a future perfected communion, even as that communion is truly experienced in this life.

The immanence of the angelic community about which we have been speaking depends on God's own self-emptying love, especially in the example of Cornelius' angel. It naturally follows, therefore, that Augustine relates the vocation of the angels to the incarnation:

The church is both here below and on high: the church below consists of all the faithful, the church above of all the angels. Yet the Lord of the angels came down to the church below and on earth angels served him who had to come serve us,

---

[109] *ep. Jo.* 10.2.
[110] See, for example, the description of the use of "kingdom of God" in Matthew's Gospel found in the *Anchor Bible Dictionary*, ed. David Noel Freedman et al. (New York: Doubleday, 1992), vol. 4, 57–58. The kingdom has many features in the Gospel, as it is both the teaching of Jesus and the teaching about Jesus, both present now but coming in the eschaton, both temporal but also spatial. For more on this character of the kingdom in Augustine's writing in particular, see Emile Perreau Saussine, "Heaven as a political theme in *the City of God*" in *Paradise in Antiquity*, ed. M. Bockmuehl and G. Stroumsa (Cambridge: Cambridge University Press, 2010), 179–192.

as he himself said: "I did not come to be served but to serve" (Matt. 20:28). And what did he serve us if not what we eat and drink today? If, then, the Lord of the angels has made himself our servant, we should not give up hope of one day being equal to angels. He who is greater than the angels came down to the human level, the creator of the angels took upon himself our humanity and the Lord of angels died for us humans.[111]

God's free and loving choice to bend all the way to the human condition means Christ made himself lower even than the good angels, and Christ's condescension results therefore in the condescension of the angels too, in service to Christ. Augustine tempers his own statement that there are two parts of the church (one above, one below) by immediately pointing to the incarnation as the definitive bridge between these two communities. In Christ, the high is brought low, and the two parts of the church meet in him. This idea is echoed in *City of God*, when Augustine explains the reference to "their angels" in Matt. 18:10: "see that you do not despise one of these littles ones, for I say unto you that in heaven their angels always see the face of my Father in heaven."[112] He does not understand the verse to imply personal guardianship of angels as other interpreters before him had.[113] The angels do not belong to the little ones in any exclusive manner. Resistance to the idea of personal angelic patronage would seem fitting, given our previous discussion of private love as one of the characteristic of demons and their city, as well as the eschatological orientation of friendship. But how, then, are the angels said to belong to us? "The angels of God are our angels, as Christ is God's and also ours. They are God's because they have not abandoned him; they are ours because we are their fellow-citizens (*cives*)."[114] The

---

[111] *en. Ps.* 137.4.

[112] *civ. Dei* XXII.29

[113] Madec likewise notes Augustine's lack of interest in guardian angels, see "Angelus," 311. Muehlberger discusses the guardian angel tradition leading up to the "Evagrian school" at length, for example in the writings of Origen, Gregory Thaumaturgus and Evagrius himself. She also argues that vestiges of this tradition can be found in Athanasius' *Life of Anthony* and Gregory of Nyssa's *Life of Moses*; in general, it was widespread in the East. See Muehlberger, *Angels in Late Ancient Christianity*, 89–148. Daniélou also presents evidence for a pervasive belief in guardian angels in the East, from Clement of Alexandria to the Cappadocians and beyond. Perhaps more relevant for a consideration of Augustine, he notes the presence of the tradition in the West as well, from Hermas, Tertullian and Hilary of Poitiers. See Daniélou, *Angels and their Mission*, 68–83. Augustine can hardly have been ignorant of the tradition, and in citing the very verse that was most often used to support the idea of guardian angels, he makes a marked departure from it.

[114] *civ. Dei* XXII.29.

analog for understanding how the good angels belong to us is Christ, and this suggests an incarnational model for imagining how the angels come to be ours. They are ours because they give themselves to us, they join in our community without ever abandoning God, just like Christ.[115] The love with which they cleave to God and because of which they do not abandon him is the same love which forms our communion with them. In book X of *City of God*, Augustine repeatedly states that the good angels do not wish us to love them but to love God. Upon further reflection, however, in both *City of God* and the *Expositions of the Psalms* we come to see that, for Augustine, it is in loving God that true mutual regard is also born.[116] The angels' companionship, moreover, is part God's incarnational economy.[117]

So far, perhaps, we have succeeded in saying little more than that the holy angels love human beings and are truly present in our midst, and that this view of angels is consistent with other aspects of Augustine's theology, particularly his theology of worship. But his understanding of our familiarity with angels also reflects back and sheds further light on other aspects of his thought. First, it serves to reinforce one of the main arguments of chapter 1, which was to demonstrate that Augustine's view of angels is anti-mythological. We find in *City of God* that Augustine's angels are not imperious, exacting and enigmatic creatures. Their aim is clear – to worship God, and to have us join them – and their love is open. Throughout *City of God* and his other works, Augustine remarks on the angels' closeness to us. This fact alone serves to highlight their creaturely status and to resist a view of them as being independently powerful, even more so because he ties their friendship and patronage to the incarnation. Magical skill or theurgy will not attract their attention, but their love is properly ordered to us in God's own self-giving charity.

---

[115] In a number of places Augustine notes specifically that Christ came to us in the incarnation without abandoning heaven or the angels; "when he clothed himself in the weakness of flesh, he was received, but not locked up in, the virgin's womb; thus the food of wisdom was not withdrawn from the angels, while at the same time we were able to taste and see how good the Lord is" (s. 187.1). More generally, Christ was enclosed in the womb of Mary but remained present throughout the world. For more examples, see s. 28.4 and s. 225.2–3.

[116] This is, of course, a feature of Augustine's thought more broadly. Although it may seem odd to modern ears to hear Augustine advise us "to use" (*uti*) both material things and other people in order "to enjoy" (*frui*) God alone, this proper ordering of desire actually brings all forms of love to their fruition. The distinction is most clearly laid out in book I of *On Christian Teaching*.

[117] For more on the angel's office and their role in salvation history, see chapter 3.

Secondly, Augustine's insistence on angelic immanence invites us to reflect on the pastoral basis for his theology. The foregoing discussion has cited passages from many of his works, even if *City of God* has remained a touchstone. The drawing together of disparate material is necessary, as Augustine often refers to the angels in passing. But it is striking that it is with such frequency and such ease that he speaks about our relationship with the good angels, and that their part in the Christian journey is assumed.[118] It would not be unexpected if Augustine were to pass them over, especially given his concern to avoid the need for elaborate cosmologies to explain the biblical text. Perhaps it is a modern tendency to assume that speculations about angels are born out of an overactive intellectual imagination and that they are ultimately irrelevant, but angelic worship touches a common denominator in ancient religion and was a day-to-day spiritual concern.[119] As Robert Markus puts it, "Christians shared with almost all their contemporaries in Antiquity a sense of living in a world surrounded by invisible powers."[120] Augustine makes reference to these kinds of issues; there are those who are afraid angels will be angry if they are not worshiped.[121] There are others who seek to propitiate angels and demons in addition to God,[122] and still others who attribute good or bad fortune to the machinations of angels.[123] Many people were attracted to any form of religious protection possible. Providing a proper vision of angelic–human relations then, is itself needed for Augustine to orient the worship of his congregation and urge them to avoid what he saw as dangerous spiritual practices. It is no coincidence that many of his reflections on angels are found in his sermons.

[118] See *en. Ps.* 103.1.15 cited in full below; the scriptures proclaim that angels exist, and it would be therefore wrong to doubt it. In other words, because they are often part of the biblical narrative, angels are also a natural part of Augustine's exegesis. Madec, in fact, calls Augustine's angelology simply "une commentaire de l'angélologie biblique," see "Angelus," 303.

[119] See, for example, Rangar Cline's *Ancient Angels: Conceptualizing Angeloi in The Roman Empire* (Leiden: Brill, 2011), which is a study of angelic worship and veneration in late antiquity across traditions (pagan, Jewish and Christian). He investigates archaeological evidence which points to the popularity of devotion to angels, especially in the East. He does, however, mention one inscription from Ostia among his examples to show that a vocabulary for speaking about angels was shared across traditions and locations (see 73).

[120] R. A. Markus "Augustine on Magic: A Neglected Semiotic Theory," *Revue des Études Augustiniennes* 40 (1994): 378. Markus points us further to N. Brox, "Magie und Aberglaube an den Anfängen des Christentums," *Trierer theologische Zeitschrift* 83 (1974): 157–180 for a survey of such beliefs in antiquity.

[121] *civ. Dei* x.26, *en. Ps.* 96.12 and *s. Dolbeau* 26.47.

[122] *civ. Dei* x.19.

[123] *en. Ps.* 66.2.

Not only do these commentaries help Augustine to clarify the angels' role (both good and evil) for those who may be confused, or perhaps drawn to various rites in the culture around them, but they serve as a great comfort. The good angels are spectators on our journey;[124] they see our progress and mourn our relapses, and they always urge us homeward. St. Crispina, when she rejoiced over her martyrdom, was in fact singing in the court of the angels.[125] And, although we are miserable in our exile, although "we go on sighing in our wretchedness and toil until we make our way to that city where we shall be at home," still "our fellow-citizens, the angels, have not forsaken us during our exile, for they announced our king would come in person."[126] The holy angels do not abandon us, but like God, they serve us and wait for our return home. All of the language of closeness which Augustine employs to describe the angels shows us that they are not simply *up there* in heaven, but come *down here* in imitation of Christ. This pastoral element of his angelology should serve to remind us that even when Augustine is seeming to take up a most abstract topic, it may turn out to be surprisingly concrete for the spiritual life of his congregation.[127]

Augustine's angels, however, are not to be thought of in a sentimental way. To fully understand their companionship is also to contemplate what is better and more perfect; their mode of friendship is a model of beatific friendship. But the immanence of the good angels means that God's promises (i.e. salvation, eternal life, and the resurrection of the body) are real and tangible, if invisible.

We do not see the angels as present; this is something hidden from our eyes, something that belongs to the mighty commonwealth of God, our supreme ruler. But we

---

[124] See *civ. Dei* XIV.19, *en. Ps.* 38.15 and 39.9. We are a spectacle to both angels and human beings (cf. 1 Cor. 4:9), since both our spiritual acts and bodily acts have their proper witness. Those who see the martyrs carnally, in a human way, see a body mangled and destroyed, but "a splendid spectacle" is presented to the eyes of those who see like angels, "a spirit whole and unbroken while the body is torn to pieces" (*s.* 51.2). See also *s.* 356.1, where the clergy are described as a spectacle for those who want to criticize (human beings) and also those who want to love (angels).

[125] *en. Ps.* 137.7.

[126] Ibid., 125.1. *Nec ciues nostri angeli dimiserunt nos in peregrinatione, sed annuntiauerunt nobis ipsum regem uenturum ad nos.* Note here again that angels serve within the economy of the incarnation, as its heralds.

[127] Frederick van der Meer's biography of Augustine's later life also serves to remind of this: Augustine's "desire was to belong in an especial manner to the church at Hippo and it was the daily cure of souls in that locality that he conceived his first duty to lie." See *Augustine the Bishop* (London: Sheed and Ward, 1961), xvii.

know from our faith that angels exist, and we read of their having appeared to many people. We hold this firmly, and it would be wrong for us to doubt it.[128]

Belief in angels is concrete; it is verifiable by scripture. And therefore angels make the life to come truly present even in our midst, although we cannot see them. It is clear from *City of God* book x that the good angels have a perfected relationship with God in their steadfast adherence to him and in their desire for all creation to praise God as they do. To capture both the immanence and transcendence of angels, that is, to capture both their nearness in love and yet their perfection in charity, it is perhaps helpful to think of them as icons of worship, although by nature invisible. They both represent perfect worship as well as bring it about. They represent it aesthetically, as they are more beautiful[129] and their bodies are sometimes an object of our contemplation, but they also represent it morally by being a perfect example.[130] Moreover, they bring about perfect worship by means of their miracles,[131] their prophecies and their general efforts to teach us to praise God. The angelic presence not only comforts us but invites us to imitation.[132] Our fellowship with holy angels is good and leads us to do good, since we take "thought for the common good because of the companionship in the upper regions."[133] Likewise, in *City of God*, Augustine comments that the heroic acts of which pagans were capable for the glory of Rome should pale in comparison with that which a Christian can accomplish when mindful of the glory of heaven and the company of angels.[134] In all, then, gazing upon the angels encourages and

---

[128] *en. Ps.* 103.1.15.

[129] See *retr.* 1.11.4, Angels both administer and adorn the world – *decorandum atque administrandum*, and *s.* 19.5, "I imagine you would be absolutely stunned if you could see the beauty of angels." In *ep.* 189.3, Augustine's discussion of the beatific vision includes a hierarchy of beauty: we are beautiful to some degree, then the angels even more so, but God surpasses all these. This beauty is made by love. A similar ascending scale of beauty is found in *ep. Jo.* 4,5, *en. Ps.* 44.3–4 and *s.* 137.10. On the whole, Augustine recommends angelic beauty as a matter worthy of reflection, especially as a means to consider how surpassingly beautiful God is by comparison, but it is not an angelic quality he mentions very frequently.

[130] As they are a precedent for Paul and Barnabas, see *civ. Dei* x.19.

[131] On angelic miracles see *civ. Dei* x.12–13.

[132] In *civ. Dei* x.26, we primarily imitate angels by worshiping God instead of worshiping them – i.e. we do the same thing they are doing. The same idea is found in *en. Ps.* 96.12. In *s. Dom. mon.* 2.20–21 and elsewhere, the petition "thy will be done" in the Lord's prayer is a request to imitate the angels. For more on our call to imitate angels, see *s. Dolbeau* 25.21, *s. Dolbeau* 26.48 and *s. Casin.* 2.114.1.

[133] *Gn. litt.* xi.20.

[134] See, for example, *civ. Dei* ii.19 and v.17.

comforts us in moral struggles, provides a foretaste of the life to come and sparks the theological imagination.

Equal to the Angels; Human–Angelic Community in the Beatific Vision

The observation regarding the benefit of angelic companionship in this life, that is, that it makes God's promises concrete, is the aspect of Augustine's angelology on which Ellen Muehlberger focuses. She argues that in *City of God* Augustine's angels perform the role of a heavenly assurance. The good angels are stable, eternally blessed and therefore provide a tangible counter-example to the unreliable and unappealing promises of pagan religion. There can be no question that Augustine believes the angels to be infinitely superior to the demons (i.e. the patrons of Roman cult), and that he believes our fellowship with the good angels entails entrance to eternal life and secure blessedness. It is true also that Augustine associates the angels with stability and peace. Muehlberger's primary aim is to contrast this view with the more fluid spiritual state of angels found in the thought of the Eastern fathers, particularly Origen and Evagrius.[135] But this discussion raises a broader question, which is to say, what exactly is the promise that the angels embody? What sort of life do we anticipate when we think of being in the city of angels? Muehlberger has only begun to answer these questions, because the angels are more than a heavenly placeholder or a guarantor. Augustine speaks of the beatific vision in many places, but to approach this theme with particular attention to the angels' representation of the future life, his repeated use of the term "equal to the angels" (Luke 20:36) to describe the promise of heaven deserves attention.[136] Augustine uses this phrase so frequently

---

[135] This is the central point of discussion in Muehlberger's first chapter, *Angels in late Ancient Christianity*, 29–58. Ruokanen has a similar thesis regarding the angels in *City of God*, but it is expanded to include some of the ideas with which we are presently interested. Like Muehlberger, he notes that through the angels Augustine attempts to demonstrate both the state of humankind before the fall and also in the future, i.e. the angels are in some way a concrete guarantor of blessedness. But, he says, the angels are also proof of the eternal law by which we are all made happy, that is, proof of the original and future goodness of creation (as I argued in chapter 1). Going further, he notes that Augustine's celestial city is not an alien or abstract ideal, but his contemplation of angelic society also entails a concrete visualization of the possibilities for human society (as I argue in this chapter). See Ruokanen, *Theology of the Social Life*, 83–84.

[136] Augustine is not alone in his love of this phrase, and ἰσάγγελος is an epithet commonly employed by early Christian writers of the East. It is used both to speak about the future life as well as the achievement of holy people in this life (see, for example, Clement

that it would be gratuitous to cite them all. This equality with angels is not simply a cipher for one single concept, but encompasses a number of meanings, as will become clear. That we will be equal to the angels ultimately means we will be conformed to angelic society and fit for their company. It is the promise of a whole way of life, which is not merely an abstraction, but is already embodied by the good angels.

Augustine associates our future equality to angels with myriad ideas about the beatific life. The commonest is immortality and its accompanying incorruption; the "citizens of the city of God" will be "in that immortal condition in which they are equal to angels."[137] But Augustine also links our equality to angels with "justice,"[138] "perfection,"[139] "peace"[140] and the "vision of perfect beauty."[141] Equality to angels, moreover, is sometimes imaged using light, which is fitting given Augustine's interpretation of the *fiat lux* of Gen. 1.[142] He says, for example, that when we equal the angels we will also be in the "daylight in which angels live"[143] and that we will "shine like the sun."[144] This life is also expressed in the language of healing or the attainment of perfect health.[145] In addition, equality with the good angels entails the privilege of sharing angelic activity; we will see God face to face,[146] we will do God's will and praise him,[147] we

---

Paed. 1.6, Athanasius *exp. Psa.* 8:8, Cyril of Jerusalem *catech.* 4.1, Cyril of Alexandria *hom. Pasch.* 1, Basil of Caesarea *virg.* 68 and Evagrius *or.* 113). It is unclear, of course, whether or not Augustine was influenced directly by any of these authors, but the idea that human beings are or will be "equal to the angels" clearly has a hold on the imagination of early Christian writers.

[137] *civ. Dei* XV.26. See also *c. Faust.* 22.27–28, *Jo. ev. tr.* XIX.10, *civ. Dei* XV.26, XX.21, *ep.* 55.26, *en. Ps.* 33.2.9, 51.14 and 109.3. Augustine interprets the promise of incorruption to be the primary meaning of Jesus' explanation to the Sadducees. We do not die, and so we do not need to produce replacements, and therefore there is no need to marry. Augustine does not often speak, as other patristic authors do, of the angelic life as one of celibacy. In fact, he more often mentions that we will not have to sleep in heaven than the fact that we will not have sex (see, for example, *s.* 221.3 and *s. Dolbeau* 21.15).

[138] *trin.* IV.5. See also *en. Ps.* 36.1.10–11.

[139] *civ. Dei* XV.26.

[140] *en. Ps.* 136.6.

[141] Ibid., 136.6.

[142] This point is discussed at length in chapter 1. Augustine understands the creation of light on day 1 to be the creation of spiritual beings, i.e. angels. They live therefore in eternal day.

[143] *en. Ps.* 76.4

[144] Ibid., 51.14.

[145] See *en. Ps.* 36.2.8, 70.1.8, 102.6, *s.* 277.4 and 278.5.

[146] This is Augustine's favorite image for angelic contemplation, and is often paired with 1 Cor. 13:12 and/or Matt. 18:10. See, for example, *Jo. ev. tr.* 19.10, *civ. Dei* XI.32–33, *ep.* 55.26, *en. Ps.* 33.2.9 and 36.2.8.

[147] *c. Faust.* 22.27–28.

will experience eternal joy.[148] And, as Muehlberger emphasized, we will possess these things without fear of losing them and in permanent stability.[149] This plethora of benefits and images which Augustine associates with equality with angels suggests it is not simply a synonym for any one beatific security. Moreover, he often makes these promises about the heavenly life in the style of a list, on which "equality with angels" appears as its own item, not simply in apposition to happiness or immortality, etc. One such example comes from his second exposition of Ps. 36, where he consoles his congregation about the struggles of this life. After we have labored in the vineyard, when

all this toil is over the eternal kingdom will come, happiness without end will come, equality with the angels will come, Christ's inheritance will come, and Christ, our fellow-heir, will come. What did the toil amount to, if we receive so great a reward?[150]

Equality with angels, here, is not equated with the kingdom or with our inheritance or with happiness. All these rewards are somehow distinct, but fully realized in Christ himself.

The angelic life, then, carries with it its own ineffable hope, and it works well as such since it is a biblical assurance and therefore not reducible to any one explanation about its content. As Augustine says in *Sermon* 362: "if you ask what sort of life it will be, what human being can possibly explain it, who can explain it? It will be the life of angels (*vita angelorum*). Anyone who can show you the life of angels, will show you the life they will have, because 'they will be equal to the angels.'"[151] The phrase *vita angelorum* is used elsewhere in this same sermon, where Augustine explicitly identifies this life as a biblical promise, citing 1 Cor. 15:50 and Jesus' own resurrection body as evidence.[152] Miikka Ruokanen likewise argues that it is precisely in Augustine's vision of a "transcendental society" among the angels in a biblical idiom that makes his societal vision peculiarly Christian:

Augustine's eudaimonistic concept of the social life, expressed in his idea of the transcendental-eschatological city of God, is thus a theological construction

---

[148] *civ. Dei* XX.20–21, *en. Ps.* 33.2.9 and 36.2.16.
[149] *civ. Dei* XI.13 and XI.32–33.
[150] *en. Ps.* 36.2.16.
[151] *s.* 362.27. Augustine goes on to affirm our inability to speak about the life of angels except in an apophatic mode; "You will say 'how do angels live?' It's enough for you to know they don't live a life subject to decay. You can be told more easily, you see, what there will not be in that life than what there will be" (*s.* 362.28).
[152] *s.* 362.19.

reflecting the full realism of the biblical images. We have again illustrated that Augustine's concept of the social life is, in spite of its formal agreement with many of the main features of classical philosophy, in its essence, is a theological composition.[153]

The phrase "equality with angels," therefore, is a biblical idea that evokes all the life hereafter. In particular, it is the third step of our redemption. First death is destroyed, then we are raised and finally we are made like the angels. Augustine reminds us of Paul's words which warn that not all will participate in this third and final event of salvation, the angelic trans-formation.[154] Moreover, we should not think we will be merely raised back to this life. Rather,

we persevere steadily in this faith, and then we too shall rise to eternal life, when we are put "on a level with the angels" (Luke 20:36). So let him distinguish then, let him explain what we have dared to say; how there can be a resurrection before the resurrection, not of different people, but of the same one both times, and not like the one of Lazarus, but into eternal life.[155]

When we are made equal to angels (or, as Hill renders it, put on their level), we are not returned again to our present life, but to a new life as the same person. Equality with angels is not like the resurrection of Lazarus simply because we will live again and not die, but the angelic life represents something new for humankind. Similarly, although we are said to be restored in the resurrection, we will not become like Adam again. We will be restored to the original righteousness of Eden, but also changed to achieve angelic status; "we will not receive what we lost in him [Adam], but something altogether better to the extent that spirit surpasses soul, when we shall be equal to the angels of God."[156]

Augustine's resistance to the idea that we return to a recognizable human life (Lazarus), or even a perfected one (Adam) is not only an issue of the flesh, that is, he is not merely saying we will possess a body far superior to that of Adam or of Lazarus when we are equal to the angels. The promise of the angelic life, as some of our images have already indicated, goes beyond the reception of an angelic body.

In the first place, Augustine is ambiguous on the question of whether angels have bodies or not, an uncertainty which is not shared by the later

---

[153] Ruokanen, *Theology of the Social Life*, 90.
[154] *ep.* 50.26.
[155] *Jo. ev. tr.* 19.10.
[156] *Gn. litt.* 6.19.30.

tradition.[157] In *City of God* xv.22–23, *Letter* 95.7–8 and throughout *On the Trinity* III (especially in III.24), he is manifestly undecided about the nature of angelic bodies and often expresses doubt that we can have any sure knowledge about the question. He seems to favor the idea that angels have a subtle body of air, and demons a slightly heavier body (a common supposition in antiquity, particularly among the Platonists).[158] That the angels have some kind of body helps Augustine to explain angelophanies more easily, especially in the cases where angels are said to engage in physical activities.

Whether angels have bodies or not, our bodies will not be the same as theirs even in the resurrection. Augustine makes this clear in *City of God*.[159] He cautions us not to understand Jesus' rejection of marriage among the angels as a rejection of gender in heaven. God "who created both sexes will restore them both,"[160] and so equality with angels does not necessitate that our bodies become genderless. Our way of relating based on bodies (i.e. marriage) is changed to be suited to the angelic life, but our bodies do not simply become like those of the angels. When we are raised we will have

no deformity, no infirmity, no languor, no corruption – nothing of any kind which would ill become the kingdom (*quid aliud illud non decet regnum*) in which the

[157] See also Madec, "Angelus," 312–314.
[158] See Gregory A. Smith "How Thin is a Demon?" *Journal of Early Christian Studies* 16 (2008): 479–512. Smith sees Augustine's view of demonic bodies as very much in line with the tradition of the philosophers and of late antique thought.
[159] Other places where this question is discussed include *Gn. litt.* XII.68, where Augustine says that we need a body (unlike the angels) to see God. Occasionally, Augustine does speak of our gaining an angelic body (*corpus angelicum*); see *div. qu.* 47, *retr.* 1.26 (commenting on *div. qu.* 47), *en. Ps.* 145.3 and *s. Dolbeau* 21.15. This phrase is best understood in a general sense, i.e. we gain a spiritual body fit for heaven, and not a body exactly like the one that angels have. This basic idea is already implied in some of the usages cited (such as *en. Ps.* 145.3), but is also the case in *Gn. litt.* IX.17, where Augustine says that we receive a body with angelic form and with a heavenly quality (*angelicam formam caelestemque qualitatem*), *en. Ps.* 85.17, where we receive the sort of bodies angels have (*qualia sunt angelorum corpora*), and *s.* 362.30, where our bodies are changed to a celestial and angelic state (*in caelestem et angelicum statum*). Hill suggests that Augustine thinks of our bodies as being transformed into the same celestial material as the angels' (see footnote to *s. Dolbeau* 21.5, n. 39). At any rate, Augustine is not at all settled on the question of what type of bodies angels have, nor the ones we will have in the resurrection. It is a matter of some interest to Augustine, but it is only a secondary question when considering the whole transformation that happens in the beatific life. He ultimately considers the question moot and urges us to trust in God with regard to our resurrected bodies; our bodies are not what primarily separate us from the angelic state.
[160] *civ. Dei* XXII.17.

children of the resurrection and of the promise shall be equal to the angels of God, if not in body and age, at least in happiness.[161]

The promise of equality with angels means we will have nothing unsuitable for life in the kingdom, and we will be happy, but a difference of age and body persists between us and the angels (even if our new bodies are equally as good, so to speak).[162]

The ambivalence of Augustine regarding the promise of angelic bodies comes into sharper relief when we reflect on how he speaks of demonic bodies. Although immortality and incorruption of the body are a fundamental promise of the angelic life, they are not actually goods in and of themselves. Demons are immortal, but this leads to eternal punishment.[163] And, although being incorruptible is clearly better than being corruptible, the demons put their superior immortal bodies to evil use. For example, they aim to seduce humankind "by their boast of immortality" since "the immortality of the demons, which is miserable, might have some charm for man."[164] Augustine similarly bemoans that Apuleius writes a great deal about the superior aerial bodies of demons, but not about their virtue. Therefore, according to Augustine, Apuleius does not prove that there can be good demons just because they have more subtle bodies, as the pagans wish to maintain, but rather these creatures "resemble in character, if not in bodily appearance, wicked and foolish men."[165] Conversely, suffering itself is not something definitively connected to bodies. Augustine argues that demons do not need to gain a body in order to experience the interminable pain of hell, but will somehow be tortured according to their kind.[166] Neither are other vices – such as lust – excluded from the demonic life simply because demons do not have a body, or, because they have an aerial body better than our own.[167] In

---

[161] Ibid., XXII.20.

[162] Cf. 1 Cor. 15:35–58.

[163] See *civ. Dei* XIII.24; demons are not mortal but still die the second death, whereas the righteous are incorruptible without losing the nature of flesh. See also *civ. Dei* XI.11; the evil angels are eternal, but this means only eternal punishment; "everything eternal is not therefore blessed."

[164] *civ. Dei* IX.15. See also *civ. Dei* X.27.

[165] Ibid., IX.3.

[166] Ibid., XXI.10. Augustine remains undecided about the question of whether demons have an ethereal body or no body at all, but either way there is no hindrance to God being able to punish them with actual pain. See a slightly different approach to this question in *Gn. litt.* III.14–15, where he argues that the demon's airy bodies are part of their punishment. For the Platonic influences on some of Augustine's notions about demonic bodies, see Pépin, "Les Influences," 36–38.

[167] Demons can suffer all kinds of emotional perturbations, "a hurricane of passions" (*civ. Dei* IX.6), but good angels do not. Good angels do not feel angry when they judge, for example (*civ. Dei* IX.5).

explaining the story of the Nephilim, Augustine entertains the idea that demons could possibly have sex, and adduces the endless stories about satyrs and incubi as evidence. He concludes that demons can make themselves able to be touched, whatever their body, and so may be "capable of lust and of mingling sensibly with women."[168] The demons, however, cannot beget offspring, and they did not produce a race of giants from their intercourse with women (the Nephilim are, according to Augustine, men who are called angels).[169] Since demons have lust but none of the chance of producing offspring or marrying, one could say they represent the absolute perversion of sex, ironically without a fleshly body.[170]

Augustine thereby establishes that demons can both possess a good which is turned to evil (immortality) and can also suffer evils even without a body (lust, eternal damnation). Although a perfected body is a reward of the life everlasting, God's promise does not terminate in a body, since a body (or lack thereof) is by itself morally neutral. These observations regarding angelic bodies, both good and evil, are consonant with Augustine's concern to establish the nature of the risen body in *City of God*, his affirmation that saints do have a body,[171] and his constant reminder that bodies do not hinder God.[172] But our flesh, in the end, is not what stands in greatest need of transformation, for

it is not in locality we are distanced from them [good angels], but in merit of life, caused by our miserable unlikeness to them in will, and by the weakness of our character; for the mere fact of our dwelling on earth under the conditions of life in the flesh (*enim quia in terra condicione carnis habitamus*) does not prevent our fellowship with them. It is only prevented when we, in the impurity of our hearts, mind earthly things.[173]

---

[168] *civ. Dei* xv.23.

[169] Ibid.

[170] We might say demons lack the possibility of attaining any of the goods of marriage (offspring, chastity or the sacramental bond) which Augustine outlines in his work *On the Good of Marriage*. This surprisingly comes about, in part, because they are not embodied, or do not have bodies capable of the true physicality of human relations. In *civ. Dei* xiv.3, Augustine denies the devil has any "sensual indulgence" (*ad carnis pertinent uoluptates, non potest dici*), and yet even without flesh, vice has complete dominion over the devil (*quorum omnium malorum caput atque origo superbia est, quae sine carne regnat in diabolo*). Moreover, even without a body, he works these vices in the flesh (i.e. in human beings).

[171] The final books of *City of God* deal extensively with questions about the resurrection and the resurrected body, particularly books xxi–xxii. Augustine affirms that the saints have bodies in the resurrection in many places throughout the work, for example, in *civ. Dei* x.29.

[172] See, for example, *civ. Dei* xiii.18.

[173] Ibid., viii.25. In *civ. Dei* x.22, we are likewise said to be separated from the angels by sin only.

We can conclude that our equality with angels and our fellowship with them is not primarily based on the quality of our bodies nor embodiment more generally speaking.[174]

The meaning of our future equality with the angels is a life wherein we are suited to angelic company, which is not primarily related to what sort of bodies we will obtain, but about our love and moral orientation. Such a life encompasses all of the elements associated with the equality with angels; for this life we need healing, illumination, attainment of perfect justice and the possession of all these wholly and forever. These things are not necessarily a prerequisite for seeing God face to face, but rather seeing God face to face and clinging to God in charity are inextricably linked with the attainment of all aspects of the angelic life. Love is the occupation of the holy angels, and of us when are in heaven,

> What will be there? What will be our occupation? Our activity? Or will there be no activity at all, but simply rest? Shall we sit about lazily, doing nothing? Well, if our love grows cold, then indeed our activity will cool down too. But if we long for God even now, sigh for him even now, with what a fire will quiet love in God's presence consume us when we reach him?[175]

The promise of equality with angels is the promise of a perfected city of human beings and angels together, and this is intimated by Augustine in a number of places. At the beginning of his exposition of Ps. 65, he reflects on resurrection in general. The Sadducees, he explains, did not understand Jesus' promise of the resurrection because they thought that they would merely be raised to possess "the same kind of good things that had afforded them pleasure in the present life."[176] It is this mistake which led them to be perplexed by the question of the woman with seven husbands, since they assumed marriage and the goods it brings in this life would remain the same, but the "Lord was not promising the corruptible life of the flesh, but equality with angels."[177] This equality with angels is much wider in scope than simply the absence of corruption, "the hope itself is our consolation. But the reality will come when we too rise again and become equal to angels, for we shall be transformed, to live the life of heaven."[178] It is this hope of a new way of life that is incomprehensible to a carnal worldview and is described by the phrase "equal to angels."

---

[174] Wiebe reaches a similar conclusion, see "Demons in the Theology of Augustine," 27.
[175] *en. Ps.* 85.23. See also *en. Ps.* 83.8.
[176] Ibid., 65.1.
[177] Ibid.
[178] Ibid. *Res enim erit cum et nos resurrexerimus, et in caelestem habitum commutati, aequales angelis facti fuerimus.*

In a passage from *Literal Meaning of Genesis* the promise of communion is even more explicit. Augustine speaks of how the mystery of God's kingdom was revealed to the angels in the beginning, which is due at least in part to that fact that the promise exists fulfilled in them. The divine plan was hidden in God from the ages, but

in such a way nonetheless that the manifold wisdom of God would be made known to the principalities and the powers in the heavenly places through the church, because that is where the original church is, into which this church too is to be gathered after the resurrection so that we may be equal to the angels of God.[179]

In order to be equal to the angels, we must be gathered into their company. According to this passage, the primary benefit of equality with angels is in fact communion with the good angels, the rejoining of the church into one body, beholding the manifold wisdom of God. In his *Tractates on John*, Augustine likewise suggests that the unity of the whole church is related to the equality with angels, since the church in "its universal character is understood as including those two sons, the elder and the younger, along with all the holy angels whose equals we shall be in the kingdom of God."[180] The church is wholly complete when all parts of the church reunite, and it is then when we are equal to the angels.

The fact of our future equality with angels also leads Augustine to propound the doctrine of substitution, that is, the belief that the number of the saints in heaven will make up the lost number of fallen angels.[181] Perhaps this doctrine represents his most concrete expression of the meaning of angelic equality. It is in the *Handbook on Faith, Hope and Love* where he puts forth the idea most clearly,

But that, on the other hand, humankind, who constituted the remainder of the intelligent creation, having perished without exception under sin, both original and actual, and the consequent punishments, should be in part restored, and should fill up the gap which the rebellion and fall of the devils had left in the company of the angels. For this is the promise to the saints, that at the resurrection they shall be equal to the angels of God. And thus the Jerusalem which is

---

[179] *Gn. litt.* v.38.

[180] *Jo. ev. tr.* 107.2. In this case, Augustine's reference to the two sons is a reference to the prodigal son (the younger) and the faithful son (the elder).

[181] On the history of the doctrine of substitution, see Émilien Lamirande, *L'église celeste selon st. Augustin* (Paris: Études Augustiniennes, 1963), 146. Following B. Lohse, he notes that although there is precedence for this doctrine in Ambrose and Hilary, Augustine's formulation of it is original. For an Eastern parallel, we can look to Gregory of Nyssa (*de hom. op.* XVII.4), who shares the idea that providence has arranged a set heavenly population.

above, which is the mother of us all, the city of God, shall not be spoiled of any of the number of her citizens, shall perhaps reign over even a more abundant population. We do not know the number either of the saints or of the devils; but we know that the children of the holy mother who was called barren on earth shall succeed to the place of the fallen angels, and shall dwell forever in that peaceful abode from which they fell.[182]

As we have been discussing, after the human race has been made perfect and has been elevated to equality with angels, we will therefore be fit to complete the angelic company. This perfection is again understood primarily as a moral perfection and not a corporeal one, and we will substitute for fallen angels when "the enmity which sin had put between men and the holy angels is removed, and friendship is restored between them."[183] The idea of being equal to the angels in this passage, however, also means that we will be not merely be added to the angelic company, but we will form one whole with them. Human beings make up a lack in heaven, and so our place in the company of the angels is not one of superficial attachment, rather we are integrated completely and can truly be said to join them. As Augustine says elsewhere in the *Handbook on Faith, Hope and Love*, the angels already know the number of human beings who will once again make their city sound (*angeli sancti ... quanti numeri supplementum de genere humano integritas illius ciuitatis exspectat*).[184] Through the doctrine of substitution, Augustine unambiguously expresses our equality with angels in terms of our community with them. He also explicitly suggests that although Christ did not die for the sin of angels, the angels do in a way gain from the death and resurrection of Christ in the restoration of their number,

Now it was not for the angels that Christ died. Yet what was done for the redemption of men through His death was in a sense done for the angels, because the enmity which sin had put between men and the holy angels is removed, and friendship is restored between them, and by the redemption of man the gaps which the great apostasy left in the angelic host are filled up.[185]

As we saw in our discussion of human–angelic relations on earth, the good angels do in fact benefit from our company: their company is made complete by ours, as ours is made complete by them. Both holy angels and human

---

[182] *ench.* 29.
[183] Ibid., 61.
[184] Ibid., 62. In the citation of *ench.* 29 above, Augustine does think it is possible that we will not only fill the number of angels, but even exceed it, which would fit with God's gracious character. Presumably the good angels know the outcome in any case.
[185] Ibid., 61.

beings form one church, and, knowing that the demons would fall, this eschatological ecclesial structure forms part of God's plan of salvation from the first moment of creation.[186] As Augustine tells us in both *City of God* and *Literal Meaning of Genesis*, even if humankind had not sinned they would have gone on reproducing until they reached the requisite number.[187]

To move beyond the restriction of speaking only of those passages where we are said to be equal to the angels, we find more evidence still to support the claim that Augustine imagines the angelic life to be the whole community of angels and human beings together in Christ, that is, the reunification of the church. He speaks of the hope of the life hereafter as joining the society of angels (their *societas*) on many occasions. In Ps. 33, "we are promised the joy of immortality and fellowship with angels" (*gaudium immortalitatis, societas angelorum promittitur*).[188] Psalm 119 reminds us that we cannot escape the clutches of evil people except "by returning to the society of angels, to be at home" (*nisi cum redierit ad societatem angelorum, ut ibi sit unde peregrinatur*).[189] Likewise, in *Literal Meaning of Genesis*, the day created by God, that is, the spiritual day of rest, is "the harmonious unity of angels" (*in societate unitatis angelicae*)[190] and "the fellowship and unity of the supercelestial angels and powers" (*ille societas atque unitas supercaelestium angelorum atque uirtutum*).[191] When our will is conformed to God's, we gain "the reward of eternal life and companionship with angels (*angelorum societatis*)"[192] At her martyrdom, Crispina was "longing for what was best," and in giving up her earthly family, she was not cruel, but rather was already in the "presence of God's angels, and knew how to long for their friendship, for a holy pure society, where she would never die again" (*desiderare consortium, amicitiam sanctam et puram, ubi ulterius non moreretur*).[193] Likewise, *City of God* unsurprisingly yields a number of references to the future community of angels and human beings. God who makes both men and martyrs has "associated (*sociauit*) them with the holy angels in celestial honour."[194] We are also instructed to eschew association with demons "so as to be associated with the uncontaminated angels (*societatem incontaminatorum*

---

[186] See Lamirande, *L'église celeste*, 145.
[187] *civ. Dei* XIV.23 and *Gn. litt.* III.33.
[188] *en. Ps.* 33.2.19.
[189] Ibid., 119.6.
[190] *Gn. litt.* V.4.
[191] Ibid., V.10.
[192] Ibid., VII.36.
[193] *en. Ps.* 137.7.
[194] *civ. Dei* VIII.27.

angelorum)."[195] In short, the glorious city of God is full of the praises
of the angels "who invite us to their society (*societatem*), and desire us
to become fellow-citizens (*cives*) with them in this city."[196] In perhaps
the most provocative passage, Augustine imagines the heavenly court in
terms of Roman society; heaven is a new curia in a new republic with a
new law. When we forsake the disordered and prideful system of Roman
glory and yield to Christ, we win "an eminent place in that most holy city
and august assembly of angels (*curia angelorum*) and republic of heaven
(*re publica caelesti*), in which the will of God is the law."[197]

To go on citing references to the *societas angelorum* as the promise
of the hereafter would belabor the point,[198] but beyond these disparate
examples, the idea that the angelic life holds out for us the expectation of
a communion encompasses Augustine's entire attitude toward the beatific
life.[199] We are not going just to a place, but also to a people, the holy angels
are the city of God, not just *in* the city of God. The holy city "is above
among the holy angels ... it is, it sees, it loves."[200] In his exposition of Ps.
119 and elsewhere, when Augustine speaks of the life hereafter, he readily
changes his image from going to a place to being in a communion: "I have
not yet arrived in that homeland where I shall live untroubled by evil. Not
yet have I attained to the fellowship of angels (*societatem angelorum*)

---

[195] Ibid., IX.18.
[196] Ibid., X.25.
[197] Ibid., II.19. This fits with Augustine's overall polemic in book II, which is to show that
the republic of Rome really never was a true republic at all. Such a true republic now
exists only among the angels.
[198] References to the *societas angelorum* in Augustine's corpus beyond what has been
cited are legion. In *civ. Dei* it appears at XI.12, XI.19, XI.31–33 (toward their society
and assembly we sigh), XII.28, XIV.28 (a mention of the society of saints and angels),
XVIII.18 (the demons and evil men as a society), XXI.17–18 (will the devil ever rejoin
the society?). For some examples from his sermons, see *Jo. ev. tr.* 30.7, *en. Ps.* 68.2.16,
121.1–2, *s. Dolbeau* 4.5 (where it is treated as a synonym for paradise, heaven, kingdom
of God, etc.) and *s. Dolbeau* 17.6 (there is another life, that is, the society of angels).
In his letters, see *ep.* 102.15 and 19 (being a *socius* of angels is the opposite of being
in *societas* with demons). These are merely a few interesting uses; this list is far from
exhaustive.
[199] Brian Daley, commenting on Augustine's eschatology, writes "the *societas angelorum*,
in fact, is one of the 'eternal rewards' he [Augustine] frequently lists when depicting the
details of Christian fulfillment ... this emphasis on eternal fellowship with the angels as
a central feature of human beatitude reveals the essentially ecclesial, social character of
salvation as Augustine conceives it." Daley, *The Hope of the Early Church: A Handbook
of Patristic Eschatology* (Cambridge: Cambridge University Press, 1991), 146.
[200] *civ. Dei* XI.24. *Inde est ciuitatis sanctae, quae in sanctis angelis sursum est ... est,
uidet, amat.*

where I shall have no scandals to dread."[201] Eugene TeSelle notes that in Augustine's very use of *civitas* instead of *urbs* for his denotation of the two cities, Augustine proves himself "more civic than urban, emphasizing the people rather than the physical setting."[202] Indeed, Augustine proves that this is the case not only in his thinking about the future city, but in the actuality of the city now, since "the original city is not one of bricks and mortar but of lucid mind and fervent love,"[203] as TeSelle puts it, that is, the community of the good angels. Moreover, the primordial angelic city "is not a mere ideal or a hypostatization of an ideal, or a structure. It is an 'event' enacted freely by God and by created spirits."[204] And so, likewise, when we come together with the good angels in the event of the resurrection, we will not just occupy the same space but together constitute the place.

> In the whole city of Jerusalem, in which all believers from the beginning even to the end shall be enrolled, together with the legion and armies of angels, so that there may be one city under one king, or one province under one emperor ... the body of Christ, the church, is like a single human being...[205]

The city of God is built on love and humility, and so the good angels are the church and the church exists in them. In *Literal Meaning of Genesis*, Augustine explains that Eden signifies "both this life of the saints which is now being lived in the church and the eternal life that is coming after this one," just as Jerusalem is an earthly city but its heavenly type is "realized in those who have been saved by hope, and while hoping for what they do not see wait for in patience ... or realized in the holy angels themselves through the church of the manifold wisdom of God."[206] That communion itself is the foremost promise of our equality with angels is also consonant with our previous discussion about the benefit of angelic companionship now, because the value of angels in this life and the next turns out to be the same. The benefit of angelic love is love for love's sake, and so the promise made present in our midst (both in angels and saints too) is a glimpse of the very communion we will have in heaven.

---

[201] *en. Ps.* 119.6.
[202] Eugene TeSelle. "The Civic Vision in Augustine's *City of God*," *Thought* 62.3 (1987): 271.
[203] Ibid., 274.
[204] Ibid.
[205] *en. Ps.* 36.3.4.
[206] *Gn. litt.* XII.56.

Angels and the Eucharist

In the course of this chapter, the Augustinian features of human–angelic relations both in this life and in the future life have been laid out, with special focus on *City of God*. The loves which orient the two cities both constitute and define them, and, in the city of God, love of God is the constant activity of all the blessed. There is yet another question pertaining to angelic communion raised by a consideration of book x of the *City of God*, which is, to what extent does Augustine imagine the angelic life to have a sacramental or eucharistic character? Can this give us a further glimpse into his vision of the life of the angels? To this question we now turn, beginning again with *City of God*, and then surveying other evidence from throughout Augustine's corpus.

The inquiry is prompted by a number of passages in *City of God* which speak of the angels as offering common sacrifice with us. Augustine writes that

regarding the true religion from the ever-blessed spirits, who do not seek for themselves that honour which they know to be due to their God and ours, and who do not command us to sacrifice save only to him, whose sacrifice, as I have often said already, and must often say again, we and they ought together to be, offered through that priest who offered himself to death a sacrifice for us, in that human nature which he assumed, and according to which he desired to be our priest.[207]

The holy angels, as Augustine never tires of reiterating throughout *City of God*, offer sacrifice to God with us and do not want sacrifice to be offered to them. His description of the sacrifice of angels, however, contains language that is similar to the way in which he speaks of the Eucharist in book x. Near the beginning of the book, when Augustine is still explaining the meaning of worship and what the content of true sacrifice to God entails, he describes the role of the Eucharist in Christian worship.[208] All sacrifice, he explains, is done so that we may draw near to God, not for God's sake.[209] This sacrifice "is offered to God as our sacrifice through the great high priest, who offered himself to God in his passion for us."[210] This sacrifice which is offered by and in Christ is the

---

[207] *civ. Dei* x.31.

[208] Gerald Bonner suggests that it is here, in book x of *City of God*, that we find Augustine's most important discussion of the Eucharist. See Bonner, "The Church and the Eucharist in the Theology of St. Augustine," *Sobornost* ser. 7, no. 6 (1978): 454.

[209] *civ. Dei* x.6.

[210] Ibid.

sacrifice of the whole self, both the whole individual as well as the whole church together as one body:

> This is the sacrifice of Christians: we being many, are one body in Christ. And this is also the sacrifice which the church continually celebrates in the sacrament of the altar, known to the faithful, in which she teaches that she herself is offered in the offering she makes to God.[211]

The sacrifice of Christ on the cross, the sacrifice of all Christians of their whole hearts and the sacrifice of the altar are here described as one and the same.[212] The angels are also mentioned in the very next breath, as having a sacrifice they "know to be in common with us."[213]

In these two passages from book x of *City of God*, Augustine employs very similar language when describing the angels' sacrifice and our sacrifice (which is also the Eucharist). Firstly, he says outright that we share the same sacrifice, even in close proximity to describing that sacrifice specifically as the Eucharist, as we have just mentioned. Secondly, he describes both angelic and human sacrifices as being mediated by Christ. In both cases, he draws special attention to the fact that Christ himself is both victim and priest, and it is for our sake that he both became a sacrifice and allows us to offer sacrifice.[214] Thirdly, the general role of sacrifice – which is to draw near to God – is even more typical of sacrifice in the life of angels than it is here on earth, since they draw close to God perfectly and always. Augustine often cites this verse (Ps. 73:28) in connection with the holy angels, and in book xii of *City of God* he says that the verse applies especially to them.[215]

At first blush, then, we see that sacrifice is integral to all worship, including angelic worship, and that even angelic worship can be described in eucharistic terms. Is it possible, however, to say more about the commonality of angelic sacrifice with our own? Clearly all creation must

---

[211] Ibid.
[212] For a more expanded reflection on Augustine's view of the sacrifice of the Eucharist, see Bonner, "Church and Eucharist," 454–458.
[213] *civ. Dei* x.7.
[214] Bonner notes that the priesthood of Christ is a central tenet of Augustine's eucharistic theology. He summarizes Augustine's view of the Eucharist as follows; "Christ is both priest and oblation; the Church also offers herself as the oblation through Christ, because he is the head and she is the body," see "Church and Eucharist," 457. We may therefore find the parallel language in Augustine's discussion of angelic sacrifice all the more striking.
[215] *civ. Dei* xii.9. See also *civ. Dei* xix.23; "the whole city of God constitutes the sacrifice made to God, and this is what is celebrated in all our sacrifices."

sacrifice its own pride, or more generally speaking, its own illusion of self-sufficiency to draw near to God. Augustine sometimes uses the *sursum corda* of the liturgy to make this point; we must lift up our hearts to God, and not ourselves, an interpretation fitting for the Eucharist itself.[216] It is easy to see the spiritual parallels between angelic and human sacrifice (i.e. as a sacrifice of pride), but Augustine's use of eucharistic language in reference to the angelic sacrifice resists a strictly spiritual interpretation. In other words, we should not be so quick to dismiss any notion that he conceives of a worship in heaven which involves signs or sacraments (although they would be necessarily transformed).[217] Augustine not infrequently uses the language of eating when speaking about the angelic life.[218] Christ the eternal Word "is eternal food. The angels eat it, the celestial powers eat it, the blessed spirits eat it, and in eating it they are totally satisfied, yet this food that fills them and gives them joy remains undiminished."[219] The Word of God both fed the angels (as the Word

[216] See, for example, *civ. Dei* XIV.13. On a related note, in *en. Ps.* 148.5, Augustine understands the *sursum corda* to be an invitation to praise as the angels do.

[217] Pamela Jackson (following Bonner) points out there is some slippage in the usage of this terminology, since for Augustine a sign or *sacramentum* is by definition that which points to the *res* and so is not also the *res*, as it is in later theology. This creates a seeming inconsistency between Augustine's use of highly symbolic language to speak of the Eucharist, and also highly realistic language. Jackson suggests that when Augustine speaks of the Eucharist as sign, he tends to emphasize its symbolism and the spiritual reality to which it points, but when Augustine speaks of the performance of the Eucharist and what it effects, he tends to use realistic language. See Jackson, "Eucharist," 330–334. This problem is related to one we have noted in the first chapter (in conversation with Rist), that is, Augustine develops a theory of signs which cannot be directly applied to liturgical acts.

[218] The most common Latin word Augustine uses to speak of angelic eating is *pascere* – the angels feed on the Word, on Christ or on God. However, he also uses the word *manducare* (eat, chew, devour), both when speaking of angelic appearances (for example, of the angels at Mamre and of Raphael in *s.* 362.10–11) – perhaps in order to emphasize their real bodily appearance – but also when speaking of the angels consuming the eternal word (as in *en. Ps.* 33.1.6). *Manducare* is always the word he associates with the consumption of the bread of angels (following the biblical text). Augustine does not seem to use *manducare* to denote everyday eating, although his version of the New Testament does, and so does Augustine therefore when he cites it. *Manducare* perhaps then has eucharistic overtones, as in *s.* 130.2 (cited in full below) and the aforementioned *en. Ps.* 33.1.6, but the actual words of the eucharistic prayer from his liturgy have not been transmitted to us, nor the words used for eating therein. On that question, see Patout Burns and Robin Jensen, *Christianity in Roman Africa* (Grand Rapids: Eerdmans, 2014), 266–267. Ambrose, however, does use *manducare* in his institution narrative, as does the vulgate text of Mark and Luke. On Ambrose, see Paul Bradshaw and Max Johnson, *The Eucharistic Liturgies* (Collegeville: Liturgical Press, 2012), 102–109.

[219] *en. Ps.* 33.1.6. *Ecce cibus sempiternus; sed manducant angeli, manducant supernae uirtutes, manducant caelestes spiritus, et manducantes saginantur, et integrum manet quod eos satiat et laetificat.*

from the beginning of time) and feeds them now (even after the incarnation).²²⁰ Christ is the "true bread of angels (*vere cibus est angelorum*),
for as the Word of God he feeds those incorruptible creatures in a way
immune to all corruption."²²¹

One of Augustine's preferred images for the incarnation depends on
this phrase, "the bread of angels" (Ps. 78:25), and is that of a mother pro-
cessing solid food through her body so that her infant may feed upon it.
He explains that the faith we have in this life is

babies' milk adapted to our age; for it is bread processed through his flesh. That
"in the beginning was the Word" is the bread of angels; but to make it possible
for humans to eat the bread of angels, the creator of angels was made man. Thus
the incarnate Word became assimilable to us. We would not have had the strength
to feed on him if the Son who is the Father's equal had not emptied himself.²²²

The Lord of John 1:1 is made palatable by his actions in John 1:14.²²³
Although certainly the image is one of eating, it would be an overstatement to say it is strictly Eucharist. In speaking of the bread of angels,
Augustine often imagines our mind gaining the ability to comprehend
Christ in some measure because he became visible, and later to see God
face to face. This is imaged in our ability to eat him because he made
himself edible (or, in the case of milk, potable). Augustine sometimes
even mixes these metaphors; for example, he once calls the meat eaten by
angels the "food of sight (*cibum speciei*)."²²⁴

Nevertheless, the gustatory nature of the imagery is striking, and it is
difficult to think he did not in any respect have the Eucharist in mind,
especially given that the illustration is popular in his homilies. In at least
one place, the condescension of Christ and the bread of angels is linked
explicitly with the eucharistic meal:

Let us turn back to the one who performed these miracles. He himself is the bread
of angels which came down from heaven; but bread which nourishes and never
diminishes; bread which can be eaten but cannot be eaten up. This bread was
signified by manna of which it was said "He gave them the bread of heaven, man
ate the bread of angels" (Ps. 78:24–25). Who can the bread be, but Christ? But

---

²²⁰ *ep. Jo. tr.* 6.13. See also *en. Ps.* 127.10; the angels are fed on the Word.
²²¹ *en. Ps.* 77.17.
²²² Ibid., 109.12. See also *en. Ps.* 30.2.9, 33.1.6, 77.17, *Jo. ev. tr.* 98.6 and *ep. Jo.* 1.1. As
Maria Boulding notes, the image comes from combining the "spiritual milk" of 1 Pet.
2:2 and Paul's reference to milk needed for the immature in 1 Cor. 3:1–2. See her footnote to *en. Ps.* 109.12.
²²³ See also *Jo. ev. tr.* 13.4–5.
²²⁴ *Jo. ev. tr.* 18.7. The expression is used in the context of contrasting the meat of the
mature, the angels (sight) and milk of immature, human beings (faith).

for man to eat the bread of angels, the Lord of angels became man. Because if he hadn't become this, we would not have his flesh; if we didn't have his flesh, we would not eat the bread of the altar.[225]

Here, Augustine says not only that Christ became edible in the sense of being apprehensible by human reason or visible to human eyes, but that his flesh also provided the Eucharist. Without Christ's flesh the bread of the altar, which is the bread of angels, would not be available. Eating the bread in this way, therefore, is also communion with the angels who feast on the same meal.

Even without explicit eucharistic references, at the base of its meaning, the image of meat-into-milk informs us that whatever it is that the angels eat, it is still this very thing upon which we feed in the incarnation. The primary point Augustine is trying to convey is that we should marvel at the fact that we eat the bread of angels, and nothing other, even though Christ has made that bread suitable to our stomachs.[226] Both angels and human beings feed on Christ. The mere fact that we are fed is not an accommodation to our state, since even the perfected angels feast upon Christ, but rather it is the form of the food that has been adapted. A good example of this congruity of milk and meat comes from Augustine's 98th tractate on the Gospel of John. He is responding to those who think that Paul's contrast between milk and solid food means that some doctrines ought to be withheld from the simple. Augustine warns that such thinking is dangerous, as it promotes the necessity of special knowledge and an elite group within the church.[227] He asserts instead that milk and meat are of the same type, they contain the same doctrines and truths, even if we must adapt our teaching to suit babes in Christ.[228] But, he explains, unlike in human beings, where a mother's milk is eventually left behind in favor of solid food, Christ is both milk and meat to all who need it, and so we pass to the higher without ever leaving the lower; the "milk of babes is, when rightly understood, found to be the Lord of angels."[229]

---

[225] s. 130.2. The most critical section reads: *Quis est panis caeli, nisi Christus? sed ut panem angelorum manducaret homo, dominus angelorum factus est homo. si enim hoc non factus esset, carnem ipsius non haberemus: si carnem ipsius non haberemus, panem altaris non manducaremus.*

[226] This is clearly the point, for example, in *en. Ps.* 33.1.6.

[227] Augustine's resistance to an elite within the church possessing secret knowledge is surely anti-gnostic (and so anti-Manichean), but it also fits well with our previous discussion about secrecy as a feature of demonic religion.

[228] See *Jo. ev. tr.* 98.6.

[229] Ibid. Likewise, in his second exposition of Ps. 30, Augustine speaks of milk as the food which strengthens us to eat meat so that the one food (human) leads directly to the other

To add to these observations regarding angelic eucharistic imagery, we may note that Augustine does not preclude the possibility that the angels and the saints in heaven actually eat, since "we read that the angels also have partaken of food [i.e. in angelic visitations] of the same kind and in the same way; not, however, under the pressure of necessity, but in the free exercise of their power."[230] He also suggests, even more strongly, that our resurrection would be "imperfect in its felicity if it be incapable of taking food."[231] In *City of God* Augustine reiterates that we can eat in heaven, and that the angels truly ate when they visited earth, such as when they sampled Sarah's cooking at Mamre.[232] If anyone thinks the question of angelic eating is in doubt, he argues, they should remember that Christ himself certainly ate, even after his resurrection.[233] Augustine, however, in one place rejects the notion that angels eat by tearing with their teeth,[234] and, in another, that they have feasts and banquets just as we do in this life for pleasure (we may presume then, perhaps, a transformed way of eating).[235]

There could be any number of reasons why Augustine keeps open the possibility of heavenly eating. For one, he is unsure whether angels have actual bodies, and he must help explain angelic apparitions and the actions of angels in the body. He wants to affirm that these appearances were real, whatever the angelic body might be like. What Abraham and Tobiah saw was not an illusion but the angels who appeared truly ate, in order to become relatable to us.[236] Secondly, he does not want to dismiss the gravity of the incarnation and its associated resurrection; when Christ is said to eat after he had risen (Luke 24:42–43), he did eat.[237]

(angelic); see *en. Ps.* 30.2.9. Or, as elsewhere he puts it, "suck on what he became to draw near to what he is" (*en. Ps.* 119.2).

[230] *ep.* 102.6. See also *ep.* 95.7; here Augustine simply states that angels can consume food although they do not need it.

[231] *ep.* 102.6. It is "imperfect also, if, on the other hand, it be dependent on food."

[232] *civ. Dei* XIII.22.

[233] Ibid.

[234] *Jo. ev. tr.* 13.4. The Word of God is "that which daily the angels eat," given to humankind, but God cannot be torn to bits. God nourishes while remaining whole.

[235] *en. Ps.* 65.1.

[236] See *s.* 362.10–11; "human beings eat in order not to die; angels eat in order to adopt themselves to mortals" (*manducat homo, ne moriatur: manducat angelus, ut mortalibus congruat*). See also *civ. Dei* XIII.22.

[237] In *s. Denis* 25.4 the reality of angelic bodies is used to affirm the reality of Christ's body (if angels can truly appear in a body, how much more the Lord of angels?). In *ep.* 95.7–8, Augustine likewise assures us of the reality of Christ's resurrected body, which, although it is not like Lazarus' body, can truly consume food. See also *ep.* 102.6.

Nevertheless, the fact that Augustine attends to this question also allows for the possibility of a sacramentality in heaven which more closely parallels that of earth. Angels are said to eat only when they want to, and not out of necessity, but this freedom is the defining feature of the angelic life in general (and of Edenic life, for that matter). That perfectly free and uncoerced eating is eucharistic or an image of the Eucharist is at least a possibility, especially given the nature of this meal even in its earthly context; it is completely free, provided and prepared by Christ. Our reception is a free response to it and a sacrifice of the heart. It is fitting that Augustine interprets the tree of life, which is likewise unneeded food, as a representation of the angels feeding upon Wisdom.[238]

Augustine also occasionally employs what we might call anti-eucharistic imagery in the life of demons, which by juxtaposition serves to highlight further the use of such language in descriptions of the angelic life. In his fourth exposition of Ps. 103, he interprets the psalmist's praise of God for feeding all creatures to include God's proper feeding of the devil. The devil wants to devour anyone he can, since "the dragon is hungry too, but he does not get everyone he wants to eat."[239] God, in his justice, feeds the dragon only dirt, which is the snake's food, but we must not turn our back on the Word if we want to avoid Satan's jaws; "you have your food, and the dragon has his. If you live as you should, you have Christ as your food. If you forsake Christ, you will be food for the dragon."[240] As in *City of God* book x, the devil completely inverts the worship of the kingdom. Where Christ becomes food for everyone to redeem them, the devil wants to consume all he can, in order to obstruct us from receiving God's nourishment. The devil eats, Christ provides. In a different homily on the same psalm, the lion cubs who seek their food by night (mentioned in the psalm) are interpreted as demons. Those who do not have the light of Christ are in danger of being devoured and "as Christ becomes known throughout the world and his name is glorified, the lion cubs gather together more and more hungrily."[241] Augustine refers to these lion cubs again in his exposition of Ps. 100, when commenting on how Christ can light up a darkened place. Again, these lion cubs who "hunt for food at night" are the "lackeys of the rulers and powers of the air, the demons and angels who serve the devil."[242] Despite the prowling demons,

[238] See *Gn. litt.* XI.42.
[239] *en. Ps.* 103.4.11.
[240] Ibid.
[241] Ibid., 103.3.23.
[242] Ibid., 100.12.

however, Christians should have nothing to fear. When the devil went hunting for Job, who was "rich, succulent fare," he was not successful.[243] In the same context, Augustine speaks of those who will be cast out from the city of God, as those who "enjoy the sinful feasts of people who ministered to themselves instead of to the Lord, by furthering their own interests."[244] The angelic eating of the *City of God* is done in humility, by being fed on Christ; the eating of that other city is defined by the *libido dominandi*, the desire to consume others to satisfy hunger, and the prideful offering of feasts to oneself. In short, Augustine describes both the worship of the city of God and the city of earth with visceral imagery, and eating is an activity that forms both communities.[245]

Since Augustine has left us no treatise on the Eucharist, and since the scholarly debate on Augustine's view of the nature of Christ's eucharistic presence continues, it is difficult to assess with precision this eucharistic imagery in the angelic life. Does Augustine think the angels have some exchange with God which is like the Eucharist in heaven? Let us review the evidence here presented. First, Augustine speaks of angelic sacrifice using similar vocabulary and concepts as he does when speaking of the Eucharist. Angels participate in common sacrifice with us, and when we reach heaven we will have God himself as our "common food and nourishment."[246] Moreover, he tells us that the angels feed on Christ, the very Christ who became milk in the incarnation and no other. Angels and human beings are also capable of eating in heaven, although their eating is completely free and does not diminish God by cutting him into chunks. Lastly, the devil inverts the economy of heavenly eating. The evidence is suggestive, but Augustine rarely links angelic eating with the Eucharist in an explicit way. Nor does he, as some writers of the Christian East, speak of our being swept up into the liturgy of heaven or the angels coming to attend the eucharistic celebration.[247] Augustine once comes

---

[243] Ibid.
[244] Ibid.
[245] Although one can only guess how Augustine would have developed the idea, another (rather grotesque) example comes from *adn. Job* 5. Here he understands a reference to the "offspring of the vulture who flies very high" (a phrase found in Augustine's text of Job 5:7 according to the LXX) to mean the demons of the air. They are called vultures because they feed (*pascere*) on corpses, that is, on those having sinned. Presumably he is evoking the image of being dead in sin (cf. Eph. 2:5; Col. 2:13).
[246] *civ. Dei* XXII.1.
[247] On this, see Muehlberger's excellent chapter on the angels in the liturgy in *Angels in Ancient Christianity*, 176–203. Her main sources for this discussion are John Chrysostom, Cyril of Jerusalem and Theodore of Mopsuestia. Daniélou also discusses traditions pertaining to the angels and the liturgy, see *Angels and their Mission*, 55–68.

close to answering our question, and I will cite the passage in full, despite its length. He is expounding the petition to "give us this day our daily bread." He writes,

I agree, there are two ways of understanding this petition about daily bread, either with reference to our need for bodily victuals, or our need for spiritual nourishment. We obviously need material goods for our daily victuals, and without it we can't live. Our needs include clothing, but we are to understand the whole from the part. When we ask for bread, we receive everything with it. The faithful know a spiritual sustenance, which you are going to know, and to receive from the altar of God. That too will be a daily bread, necessary for this life. I mean, are we going to go on receiving the Eucharist when we have come to Christ himself, and when we have begun to reign with him forever? So the Eucharist is our daily bread, but we should receive it in such a way that our minds and not just our bellies find refreshment. You see, the special property to be understood in it is unity, so that by being digested into his body and turned into his members we may be what we receive. Then it will really be our daily bread. And the fact that I am dealing with this subject for you, and that you hear reading in church every day, is daily bread; that you hear and sing hymns is daily bread. These are things we need on our pilgrimage. But when we finally get there do you imagine we shall be listening to a book? We shall be seeing the Word itself, listening to the Word itself, eating it, drinking it, as the angels do now (*ipsum uerbum uisuri, ipsum uerbum audituri, ipsum manducaturi, ipsum bibituri, quomodo angeli modo*). Do angels need books, or lectures, or readers? Of course not. They read by seeing, since they see Truth itself, and drink their fill from that fountain, spray from which sprinkles us.[248]

Although Augustine seems to come at our question head on, his answer here contains many of the same ambiguities which we have already noted. As we saw above, he readily changes his metaphor from eating to seeing and then back again. Clearly, we will not eat the Eucharist in the bodily way in which it is consumed now, with the stomach, because when our minds are refreshed and our body is made into Christ, then the Eucharist approximates the true daily bread. This true bread will become, as Augustine says earlier in the sermon, not daily bread but simply the bread of "one eternal day."[249] Becoming one with Christ, which is the principal effect of the Eucharist, does not pass away in the hereafter but is brought to completion. Moreover, as soon as he rejects the concept of a bodily Eucharist in heaven, he returns again to the vivid imagery of the angels seeing, hearing and consuming the Word always (using both

[248] *s.* 57.7.
[249] Ibid. A fitting image for sharing eternal life with the angels who are created light (discussed at length in chapter 1).

manducare and *bibere*). Likewise, although the angels do not read with books, they still read.[250]

We may say at the very least that Augustine imagines that eucharistic eating is a foretaste of heaven, and of the unity with God that the angels experience. In the Eucharist, moreover, our complete dependence on God, that is, our being fed and satisfied by the Word, is both imaged and anticipated. In a slightly different reading of the Lord's prayer, Augustine explains that when we ask the Father to give us our daily bread we are asking both for everyday food, which our body needs for this life, and the Eucharist, which we need for eternity.[251] Perhaps this discussion of the relationship of angelic eating to the Eucharist can help to further dismantle the symbolic/realistic dichotomy which is sometimes used to analyze Augustine's thought, but is in fact foreign to his eucharistic theology. Whatever the Eucharist is for us on earth, it is the same thing which is received in heaven; although milk passes to meat, it does not give way to meat. Moreover, the "special property" of the Eucharist, as Hill translates, is unity, which is also the special property of the beatific life and is the promise of our equality with angels.

Conclusion

The organizing principle around which Augustine centers his conception of human–angelic relations is worship. When we worship God and not ourselves, we behave like the good angels instead of like the demons. The acts of worship performed in public cult, however, are not just the external expression of an internal desire or attitude, because these external acts of holy angels, demons and human beings also create the communities in which they reside, either the city of God, or the city of the devil. Therefore, when we ask what sort of communion the angels have with human beings both now and in the future, we find that our fellowship is based on humility, which is realized in public and communal worship of God. This communion does not wrest from good angels and human beings the qualities that make them properly created, and thus individuated, but rather when angels and human beings come to accept their created status and in that knowledge to worship God, they are also most perfectly themselves and most perfectly united with their

[250] Another example of Augustine's imagery of eternal reading comes from *conf.* XIII.15.18, which is discussed at more length in chapter 1.
[251] *ep.* 130.21.

neighbor. In this life, our fellowship with angels is hindered by sin, but still grounded in common worship and love. In the future, when we will be equal to the angels of God, we will be morally perfect, but perhaps more importantly, we will be united to the company of angels and suited to life in heaven. We thus have real communion with angels on earth, but this fellowship has a definite eschatological orientation, and in both cases – either here or there – the city of God is defined by its worship, or put otherwise, by what it loves.

The Eucharist, for Augustine, is the primary sacrament of unity, of unity with Christ, of unity with other Christians and also of unity with the angels, because the angels eat the very same Word which was made flesh and which is presented on the altar. Eucharistic imagery in the angelic life certainly reinforces the idea that worship (i.e. sacrifice) is the central activity of the beatific state and that we are made perfect when we wholly depend on God, but it also suggests that Augustine may have had some conception of an angelic sacramental life.

Augustine's view of the angelic community here discussed also has significant implications for what one might call his political theology. Augustine has been appropriated by many theologians and philosophers of the twentieth and twenty-first centuries in their efforts to understand Christianity's proper relationship to the modern state. The scope of the present study does not permit a full discussion of so-called political Augustinianism, nor of the position advanced by Robert Markus, who maintains that Augustine's theology leads to the necessary existence of a *saeculum*,[252] that is, a neutral territory where both the city of God and the earthly city co-exist. It is striking, however, that very few of the authors who take Augustine as their patron even mention angels and demons, despite their prominent place in the oft-cited *City of God*.

The analysis in this chapter raises several important questions for political theologians, particularly for anyone who wishes to claim the legacy of Augustine in all its complexity. What does our political theology look like when we recognize that the two cities are not primarily made up of human beings? That is, what does a non-anthropocentric politics look like? This challenge does not merely pertain to the orientation of politics toward a final eschatological consummation of the cities in the future. The two cities, for Augustine, were founded by angels and demons, and are currently populated by them. For this reason, as has been shown

---

[252] R. A. Markus, *Saeculum: History and Society in the Theology of St. Augustine* (Cambridge: Cambridge University Press, 1970).

above, Augustine speaks of angels as our fellow-citizens, not just in the future, but now. It is also why he describes the demons as inventors of magic and patrons of Rome.[253] The city of God and the visible church are not identical, but the city of God subsists there. Rome is not the city of the devil, but it is truly encountered there. The two cities exist now, we belong to them even as we journey toward them, or in a more biblical idiom, the kingdom is both now and not yet. The prevailing sentiment that Augustine domesticates the apocalyptic spirit results in part from a lack of appreciation for this dimension of *City of God*. For Augustine the eschaton is palpable, because the two cities which are now mixed are only mixed from a human, temporal perspective; a tare is never a stalk of wheat, it is only indistinguishable from one. This illusion could be removed at any moment and the true cosmic reality revealed – and is that not the heart of the apocalyptic? Only, for Augustine, that apocalyptic vision is already breaking into and being experienced in the liturgical life of the visible church, and that cosmic reality has been always just a hair's breadth away from history as we know it. He expends great energy demonstrating this in his history of the two cities (books XII–XVII), a discussion which begins, as already noted, with the foundation of the two cities in the first chapter of Genesis.

Therefore, if the idea of a *tertium quid* (or *saeculum*) is to be attributed to Augustine, the role of angels and demons in that "third" space must be taken into account. In Augustine's worldview two distinct, opposing communities are both present in and being built by two separate economies, one of humility and the other of pride. These communities are also formed by the sacraments of the church and by a prideful parody of the sacraments (magic, theurgy). It would seem that in light of this vision of the immanence of both good and evil angelic actors, true neutral space would be hard to come by.

253 For more on demons and magic, see chapter 4.

3

Angels in Salvation History

Having examined Augustine's vision of the human–angelic community found in *City of God* and elsewhere, we move on to a more concrete question in the same vein: how, for Augustine, have angels participated in the unfolding of salvation history? His view of the character of angelic ministry has already been outlined in a general sense. The good angels love God, and all human beings in God, and they direct all worship to God instead of themselves. But at what particular stages in human history have angels intervened, and what is the significance of these angelophanies? The aim of this chapter, then, is to examine Augustine's view of angelic mediation with specific reference to their participation in the story of salvation. First, the role of the angels before the coming of Christ, in their ministrations to the patriarchs, prophets and kings of the Old Testament will be considered. The major text for consideration is *On the Trinity*, since he argues in the opening books of this work that angels are intimately involved in the administration of the old covenant. This angelic ministry will be compared to that of the prophets, the group with which the angels are most often paired in Augustine's writings. Second, the angels' subsequent role in the New Testament will be discussed, with particular attention being paid to Augustine's understanding of the vocation of "angel" as one which is ordered toward the incarnation. Third, Augustine's brief comments on the role of the angels in the last judgment will be considered. Lastly, the overall import of Augustine's understanding of the role of angels in salvation history will be assessed. The good angels, like good human beings, participate in salvation history in a significant way, because it is good for them to do so and fitting to their created nature. As their name implies, the particular duty of the angels is "announcing," and this duty is especially suited to them due to their createdness, their beauty and the authority of their superior knowledge.

Angels and Prophets: Angels in the Old Testament

In the first three books of *On the Trinity*, Augustine makes a marked departure from patristic tradition (and his own earlier views) about Old Testament theophanies by arguing that they are not to be understood as appearances of the Son, the second person of the Trinity.[1] He revisits major biblical stories which were interpreted in this mode, and suggests that the whole Trinity is involved in the theophanies; no one member of the Trinity should be considered to have appeared exclusively. Two of the most important narratives which he discusses both in *On the Trinity* and elsewhere are the stories of the three men at the Oak of Mamre (Gen. 18:1–15) and that of Moses and the burning bush (Exod. 3).[2] Augustine mentions that other authors have understood these events to be Christophanies, but he distances himself from this interpretive strategy for a number of reasons. His primary objection to such a reading is that it disrupts the narrative of scripture, which, for Augustine, culminates in the incarnation. If Christ is said to be sent in the New Testament, and the Holy Spirit after him, surely this sending loses both its force and its distinctiveness if Christ had been sent at any number of times in the Old Testament to speak with the patriarchs.[3] Augustine is also concerned that interpretations which depict these theophanies as appearances of Christ could lead to an incorrect understanding of the Trinity, one wherein the three are not always working together,[4] or a Homoian understanding of the Son, wherein he is the visible and therefore created member of the

---

[1] For a detailed account of theophany traditions, and the shift in Augustine's own thinking on the matter, see Kari Kloos, *Christ, Creation and the Vision of God: Augustine's Transformation of Early Christian Theophany Interpretation* (Leiden: Brill, 2011). She notes that Augustine interprets the theophany narratives in accordance with earlier traditions in only one work (*c. Adim.* c. 394/5), but that he rarely outright disavows literal Christological readings (see her comment, 175). See also Basil Studer, *Zur Theophanie-Exegese Augustins: Untersuchungen zu einem Ambrosius-Zitat in der Schrift* De videndo Deo *(ep. 147)*, Studia Anselmiana 58 (Rome: Herder, 1971).

[2] The giving of the law at Sinai and Jacob wrestling with the angel are also frequently described as angelophanies. For some examples, see *Jo. ev. tr.* 38.8, *c. Max.* 2.26.5–2.26.11, *civ. Dei* VIII.11, XVI.29–31, *s.* 6.1–3 and 7.1–7.

[3] See *trin.* II.12, II.20 and III.3. See Kloos, *Christ, Creation and the Vision of God*, 154–160.

[4] See *trin.* II.7–8, and II.12–13.

three.[5] Augustine also avers that there is no clear textual support for the position that Christ in particular revealed himself either at Mamre or in the burning bush. At Mamre, the three who appear as men are called angels, and although Abraham does refer to three as Lord, this should be taken as an intimation of the Trinity rather than an indication of the presence of Christ alone, since God the Father can also be called Lord. Moreover, although some earlier commentators held that at Mamre Christ appeared (the one referred to as "Lord") accompanied by two angels, Augustine notes that these two angels who go on from Mamre to Sodom are also called "Lord" by Lot.[6] Augustine carefully parses the Mamre story, in *On the Trinity* and elsewhere, in order to demonstrate that the text does not suggest that one or all three of these angels should be seen as Christ.[7] Likewise, in the story of the burning bush when the name of God is proclaimed – I am who I am – it is not the Son alone who speaks, since the name obviously applies to all three persons of the Trinity.[8] The text itself describes the voice speaking both as "an angel of the Lord" and "the Lord" (Exod. 3:1).[9]

Augustine concludes that although Old Testament theophanies adumbrate the Trinity or the incarnation, these appearances were carried out by holy angels. No one of the three divine persons is visible, and none yet had been sent into the world, and therefore God is revealed in the Old Testament through created things, the good angels first and chief among them. Although Augustine does maintain that God can appear in many ways, the good angels are the primary agents in all Old Testament theophanies, either appearing themselves in various forms, or enlisting created things for the task, both mundane objects and other things which are made manifest but then dissolved.[10] Augustine tends, in particular,

---

[5] See *trin.* II.15, *c. Max.* 2.26.7 and *s.* 7.4. On the anti-Homoian polemic in *On the Trinity*, see Michel Barnes "The Visible Christ and the Invisible Trinity: Mt. 5:8 in Augustine's Trinitarian Theology of 400," *Modern Theology* 19.3 (July 2003): 329–355 and "Exegesis and Polemic in Augustine's *De Trinitate*," *Augustinian Studies* 30.1 (1999): 43–59. Marie-Odile Boulnois offers a similar analysis to my own on the shift in Augustine's thinking about the theophanies. She argues that Augustine is concerned primarily to safeguard the invisibility and immutability of God and to clarify the difference between the theophanies and Christ's mission. See "L'éxègese de la théophanie de Mambré dans le *De Trinitate* d'Augustin: enjeux et ruptures" in *Le De Trinitate de Saint Augustine: Exégèse, logique et noétique*, ed. Emmanuel Bermon and Gerard O'Daly (Paris: Institut d'Études Augustiniennes, 2012): 35–67.
[6] *trin.* II.21. See also Kloos, *Christ, Creation and the Vision of God*, 149.
[7] *trin.* II.19–22. See also *c. Max.* 2.26.5–2.26.9, *civ. Dei* XVI.29 and *s.* 7.6.
[8] *trin.* II.23.
[9] Ibid.
[10] Ibid., III.19.

to describe biblical encounters with the divine (such as Mamre, the burning bush, the giving of the law and Jacob wrestling with God), not as instances of any of the persons of the Trinity being made visible, but as the work of angels,

> Whatever it was that the Old Testament fathers saw whenever God showed himself to them, unfolding his plan of salvation in a manner suited to the times, it is clear that it was always achieved through created objects. It may escape us how he did these things with angels to assist him but that they were done through angels is not something we put forward as our own idea ... No, in this matter we have the authority of God's scriptures, which our minds should not stray from.[11]

In short, there is no reason to understand the many biblical allusions to angelic participation as referring to Christ and not to celestial spirits. The scriptures frequently mention that angels were involved in theophanic events, and this is corroborated by New Testament texts, in particular, by the first chapter of Hebrews.[12] In the course of a discussion concerning the giving of the law in his commentary on Galatians, Augustine goes so far as to say "it was through angels that the whole dispensation of the Old Testament was administered."[13] In his departure from the traditional interpretation of the theophany narratives, then, he has given a surprisingly prominent role to the holy angels in the management of the economy of salvation.

Augustine has not so easily done away with the interpretive problems to which these theophany stories give rise, however. As he himself notes in one of his sermons on this issue, anyone who argues that angels appeared at Mamre must explain why the angels are referred to as "Lord" and seem to be unequivocally aligned with the divine presence.[14] He dedicates a significant portion of book III of *On the Trinity* to addressing questions about angelic visions and the way in which angels can represent God. Just as he is agnostic about how angelic bodies function, he is equally undecided as to how they bring about theophanies. Angels may use "bodily guise for the performance of their service" or perhaps they are able to change their bodies at will, because "they dominate and are not dominated by"[15] their bodies. But how exactly do angels work through these "constant and stable spiritual qualities of their bodies?"[16] Augustine soon gives up this line of

---

[11] Ibid., III.22.
[12] Ibid.
[13] *exp. Gal.* 24.15 9 (*per angelos autem ministrata est omnis dispensatio ueteris testament agente*). He makes a similar statement in *s.* 7.6.
[14] *s.* 7.5.
[15] *trin.* III.4.
[16] Ibid., III.5.

inquiry. He himself is not an angel, he reminds us, and he has no firsthand experience of their corporeal abilities, nor the way in which they interact with the physical world. Attempting to determine why and how an angel appears in a certain way, or how it makes an impression on our mind is a task which he deems practically impossible.[17] But he does not abandon the pressing issue. He asks whether one can maintain that Old Testament apparitions are in fact the work of angels, and if one can explain the fact that the Bible states that God himself appeared. Augustine answers in the affirmative, and holds that angels act *in persona Dei*, representing God to us. He compares this angelic role to that of the prophets. In the scriptures the prophetic voice is often portrayed as God's voice, which is why the words of a prophet can be qualified by such statements as "the Lord spoke."[18] When prophets speak in this manner it is not a marvel or a miracle, it is normal human speech, so also when the angels act *in persona Dei* (or employ something in the created order to relay divine communication), they are doing nothing out of the ordinary, nothing miraculous, but they are working according to their proper nature, even if it seems amazing to us. From the perspective of the angels, however, since these deeds are "their own actions, they are quite straightforward."[19]

Augustine parallels the vocation of prophet and angel frequently throughout his corpus, and it is the primary way in which he seeks to establish a point of reference for human comprehension of the angelic office.[20] The law was given by and administered "through angels (who, like the prophets, sometimes represented themselves and sometimes represented God)."[21] As for the angels who appeared at Sodom, "there was about them something so excellent" that there was no doubt "God was in them as he was wont to be in the prophets."[22] Again, in the burning bush, the angel who speaks is referred to as Lord,

Just as a prophet speaks in the scriptures and it is said the Lord speaks, but not because the prophet is the Lord, but because the Lord is in the prophet, so too when the Lord is prepared to speak through an angel, in the same way as

---

[17] *Gn. litt.* XII.48. Here he describes the question of angelic visions as "extremely difficult" to answer. Even if he himself could sort out the problems, he laments, "to analyze and explain them would be a task unimaginably laborious."

[18] *trin.* III.19 and *c. Adim.* 9.

[19] *trin.* III.20. *itaque illa quae per angelos fiunt quo difficiliora et ignotiora eo mirabiliora sunt nobis, illis autem tamquam suae actiones notae atque faciles.*

[20] Boulnois, although thinking primarily of *On the Trinity*, also notes Augustine's frequent use of this parallel; see "L'éxègese de la théophanie de Mambré," 60.

[21] *exp. Gal.* 24.15–16.

[22] *civ. Dei* XVI.29.

an apostle, in the same way through a prophet, it is rightly said to be an angel because it is, and to be the Lord because of God dwelling in him.[23]

There are myriad examples of Augustine pairing the prophets with the angels in terms of their general vocation of announcing God, and in the particular act of speaking *in persona Dei*.[24]

Augustine also mentions the work of specific prophets in order to elucidate incidents of angelic intervention into human history. For example, he uses the angel–prophet analogy to help explain the difference in Gabriel's response to Zechariah and Mary in their respective annunciation narratives. When the angel announces that Elizabeth will give birth to a son, Zechariah asks "how will I know that this is so? For I am an old man, and my wife is getting on in years" (Luke 1:18). When the angel likewise informs Mary that she will conceive, she answers "how can this be, since I am a virgin?" (Luke 1:34). Augustine notes that these two responses, which are situated closely together in Luke's Gospel, are almost identical.[25] Both Zechariah and Mary ask how the promise which the angel has made can possibly take place, but the angel's response to each is quite different. Zechariah is charged with disbelief, and struck mute until the birth of John. Mary, however, is given a full explanation not only of what will happen to her, but also to her cousin Elizabeth. Augustine explains that the angel is able to see the intent of Zechariah and Mary, just as Nathan was able to discern that David was truly repentant (whereas Samuel knew that Saul was not).[26] Gabriel, then, knew that Zechariah's question was prompted by a lack of trust, but Mary's was prompted by her faith and wonder, so he cursed one and instructed the other; "in the words of each the thoughts of each were hidden; hidden though from human beings, not from the angel, or rather, not hidden from the one speaking through the angel."[27] In another sermon, Augustine likens the role of the prophet Isaiah to that of the angel in the burning bush. By once again using a particular prophet as a point of comparison, he makes the parallel especially vivid,

If he [God] is prepared to dwell in a man and speak, so that when the prophet speaks it says "God said," how much more through an angel? And when it says "God said

---

[23] *s.* 7.5.
[24] For some examples of the pairing of angels and prophets (and their vocation) see *Jo. ev. tr.* 24.7, *Gn. litt.* VIII.50, *c. adv. leg.* 2.37, *c. Max* 2.26.5–6, *civ. Dei* X.24–25, X.30, X.32, *en. Ps.* 49.3, 66.1, 93.13, 124.4, *s.* 6.1–3, 232.3 and 369.1. Apostles are sometimes included in the group as well (as in *s.* 7.5).
[25] *s.* 291.5 and *s.* 293.1.
[26] *s.* 291.5.
[27] *s.* 293.1 *in utriusque uerbis cogitatio latebat; sed homines, non angelum latebat: imo non latebat eum qui loquebatur per angelum.*

116 *Angels in Salvation History*

through Isaiah" what was Isaiah? Wasn't he a man wearing flesh, born of a father and mother like all of us? And he speaks, and what do we say when reading his speeches? "Thus said God." If it was Isaiah then, how can it have been God, except by being God through Isaiah? So here, when the angel speaks, God is said to speak. How so, if not because it's God through an angel?[28]

If we can understand that it is possible for God to speak through a mere human being, and for that prophetic speech to be called God's own speech, we should have no qualms about attributing this ability to the angels.

Throughout the Old Testament, therefore, in theophany narratives and in other places where God is said to speak, Augustine understands that it is, for the most part, an angel speaking.[29] The fact that the speaker is sometimes called God and sometimes an angel is no mystery, since the Bible also refers to prophetic speech in the same way. Augustine, as we have already mentioned, does not attempt to explain fully how God inhabits the angel or the prophet, nor exactly how the angel is able to accomplish a theophany,[30] but angels can present God's revelation in any

---

[28] *s.* 6.3. It is unclear why Augustine chose Isaiah in particular as a point of reference for the angel in the burning bush; Isaiah is also compared to the angels of Jacob's ladder in *en. Ps.* 119.2. Perhaps there was a reading from the book of Isaiah on the day that this homily was preached which included a phrase such as "the Lord spoke," although there is scant evidence of Augustine's lectionary, see G. G. Willis. *St. Augustine's Lectionary* (London: SPCK, 1962). Speaking generally, Isaiah is a prophet of preeminent importance for Augustine. As Brian Dunkle notes, he is the only prophet cited in book one of *cons. eu.*, in which Augustine aims to show the Hebrew scriptures prophesy about Christ. See Brian Dunkle, "Humility, Prophecy and Augustine's Harmony of the Gospels," *Augustinian Studies* 44.2 (2013): 207–225. Dunkle points out that Isaiah is an unlikely prophet for Augustine to use in this work, as it is directed at pagans, and Isaiah does not unambiguously speak about Christ as divine. Augustine, however, uses Isaiah in particular because he prophesies a suffering Christ; "Augustine argues that it is precisely the prophecies of Christ's weakness, rather than his public shows of power, that reveal his divine identity" (Dunkle, 215). In short, the very fulfillment of prophecy proves that Christ is God, and the pagans would not deny that Christ suffered. Isaiah, therefore, may have been the prophet which most readily came to mind for Augustine, especially when speaking of angels as heralds of the incarnation.

[29] Augustine tends to assume angelic involvement in the theophanies, even if the biblical text does not explicitly mention an angel, but he does hold that it is possible for God to speak directly to our "inner ear" (see, for example, *civ. Dei* XVI.6).

[30] Augustine is, of course, interested in different types of vision (corporeal, spiritual and intellectual are the categories he uses) and discusses the ways in which a human being can be said to see God. The role of the angel in effecting these various types of visions, or how angelic bodies function in bringing them about, however, is never resolved, and it does not seem to be a matter which Augustine is overly concerned – or able – to sort out. For a discussion of how Augustine's different categories of vision applies to the theophanies, see Kloos, *Christ, Creation and the Vision of God,* 171–175 and 180–187. See also Pépin "Les Influences," 32–36, where he makes some helpful suggestions for understanding

number of ways; externally by an apparition, or internally by a vision or in a dream.[31] Augustine also describes both angels and prophets as temples in which God dwells.[32] When the biblical text refers to the speaker *qua* speaker it is evoking the temple, but when it refers to the speaker *in persona Dei* it is evoking the one who dwells in the temple. Although Augustine offers the image of temple to our imagination to help explain how God can speak through an angel, he does not employ temple language in a technical way, and he does not apply it exclusively to angels and prophets as a means to express their acting *in persona Dei*. Augustine is, after all, drawing the image from Paul (cf. 1 Cor. 3:16–17, 6:19 and 2 Cor. 6:16) and he speaks of God dwelling as in a temple in angels, saints, apostles and each Christian.[33] In one of his homilies, Augustine does give us a suggestion of how this cooperative action of God and angel might function. The example is not from a theophany, and it is not explicitly in an instance when an angel is acting *in persona Dei*, but it is helpful. When the psalmist asks "give me understanding" (Ps. 119:34), Augustine remarks,

Now on occasion an angel seems to have had the power to do this to someone. An angel said to Daniel. "I have come to give you understanding." (Dan. 10:14). The Greek expression here is συνετίσαί σε, the same idiom that we find in our Psalm ... God is light, and of himself he illuminates faithful souls, imparting to them understanding of what is divinely revealed or said to them. If he chooses to use an angel as his minister, the angel can produce an effect in the human mind, enabling it to receive God's light and so to understand. In this sense an angel is said to give understanding to a human being – to "intellectualize" him, so to say – as a person could be said to give light to a house – to illuminate it – when he makes a window. Yet the man who makes the window does not flood the house with light from himself; all he does is make an opening through which the house can be lighted up.[34]

When angels show something to a human being, they pull back a veil (or open up a window, as it were) and allow human beings to glimpse the divine. Augustine goes on to qualify his image, reminding his audience

how Augustine may have imagined spiritual bodies to make impressions on the physical world, or how angels enter the mind, in comparison with Platonic thought.

[31] *ench.* 58.
[32] For examples, see *en. Ps.* 137.4, *s.* 6.3 and *s.* 7.5.
[33] For some examples of Augustine using the temple metaphor in a variety of ways, see *vera rel.* 110, *c. adv. leg.* 1.2, *civ. Dei* XII.9, and *ep.* 187.6. *s.* 217.4 is a good example of Augustine speaking about the motif of the temple in a number of different ways in one passage – as the church, but also as Christ's body, as literal buildings, but also as the Christian.
[34] *en. Ps.* 118.18.4.

that in the case of his example the sun could not be said to be responsible for the house, the window nor even the light it emits, whereas in God's case, he is the creator of the man, the angel by which he illuminates as well as being the truth which illumines. This image of angels as window-makers is similar to Augustine's favorite image of angels as farmers, since angels cooperate with and reveal God's plan, but are never the authors of it.[35]

On the whole, Augustine is clearly using the angel–prophet parallel to help solve an exegetical problem, namely why the biblical text should call an angel "God" and why the patriarchs should address angels (such as at Mamre and Sodom) as "Lord." His answer in turn lends further credence to his claim that theophanies need not be understood as appearances of Christ. The prophets provide a biblical precedent for a created being who is referred to as God when acting as a divine messenger. Although Augustine further illustrates this indwelling with the image of temple and window-maker, his primary concern is not to describe how angelic agents operate, but to affirm that angelic ministry in the Old Testament is not only possible, but is the most plausible conclusion given the biblical evidence. His parallel between the angels and the prophets is not merely convenient, however, or a bit of clever biblical proof-texting. Augustine himself asserts that God does not need to work through the intervention of angels, and that God can (and still does) speak directly to human beings if he wishes.[36] It is not necessary that angels carry out theophanies. Rather, the Bible attests that God chose to make use of angels in this way, and that the role given to angels is consonant with the story of salvation which God has deigned to tell. Augustine therefore does assign meaning to the fact God chose the angels, as he chose the prophets, when he could have acted in any number of other ways.

There are two major implications of Augustine's choice to align angels with prophets, both of which have already been alluded to in the foregoing discussion. First, it emphasizes the personal character of angels. The angels, like the prophets, do not vanish when they become the temple of God and serve as his messenger. The biblical text often reminds us of this fact by mentioning the speaker *qua* speaker ("the angel of the Lord says") along with his or her role as God's representative

---

[35] On angels as farmers, see chapter 1.

[36] For example, see *en. Ps.* 49.3 and 104.9, where God is said to speak either by angels or directly, *Gn. litt.* XI.33.43, where he suggests that God may have spoken to Adam and Eve as he does to the angels, and *civ. Dei* 11.4 where God is described as speaking to the prophets without noise, as he does to his angels.

("thus says the Lord"). By proclaiming both that the angel speaks and that the Lord speaks, the scriptures do not dissolve the subject of the angel into God, even though the angel speaks on God's behalf with complete authority. Augustine further underscores the importance of angelic character by using certain angels and prophets to draw his parallels, as cited above: Gabriel is paired with Nathan/Samuel, and the angelic voice from the burning bush is compared to Isaiah. Simply put, an angel is no less personal than any one of the prophets. Augustine emphasizes the fact that the prophets are human beings when he describes Isaiah as "a man wearing flesh, born of a father and mother like all of us," precisely when Isaiah is speaking on behalf of God.[37] Although Augustine imagines that the angels act on God's behalf more completely than a human being can, he does not often draw attention to this fact, but rather emphasizes the ordinary characteristics of angelic heralding. His choice to pair prophets with angels, therefore, further corroborates our previous observations regarding angelic free will. Angels, in being completely united with God's will, do not lose their freedom, but rather come into full possession of it.[38] Although the angel can stand in God's place to such an extent as to be called God, this does not indicate that the angel is therefore bereft of character. When speaking *in persona Dei*, angels remain who they are.[39]

A further problem arises, however, from a consideration of this point, namely, that angels remain personal and individuated at theophanic events. If we understand, as Kari Kloos does, that "God truly appeared and was seen" in the theophanies, so that "the sign and reality were so conjoined that they cannot be separated into two discrete phenomena,"[40]

---

[37] *s.* 6.3.
[38] The nature of angelic freedom is discussed at more length in chapter 1.
[39] Boulnois also points out an interesting duality in the way that Augustine describes how Abraham sees and addresses the angels. She notes that, for Augustine, when the angels seem to be behaving as men (e.g. when they are eating), Abraham refers to them in the plural, but when they are speaking on God's behalf (e.g. announcing the promise of a son), he refers to them in the singular. This exegesis suggests that even the patriarch himself experiences and recognizes the simultaneous presence of actual angels and of God. See "L'éxègese de la théophanie de Mambré," 44 and 50. She cites *trin.* II.19 and *c. Max.* II.26.5, and finds a parallel in Philo's treatment of the passage.
[40] Kloos, *Christ, Creation and the Vision of God*, 156–157. I agree with Kloos about the importance Augustine assigns to the theophanies, and appreciate the nuanced way in which she understands that, for Augustine, mediation gives rise to the vision of God, but not everyone writing on Augustine's interpretation of the theophany narratives concurs. Barnes, for example, writes that "what was seen [in the theophanies] was not God; it was an instrument of God's presence. An encounter with such an instrument, such as experienced by the patriarchs and prophets, was an occasion for assent to be given to that which remained unseen and only symbolized: in short, an occasion for faith in God"

how can we also acknowledge that angels remain who they are during these encounters and are not merely "signs," behaving like mouthpieces or mannequins? The answer perhaps lies in Augustine's social vision of heaven. In *City of God*, he suggests that in heaven we will see God with the eyes of the heart, that is spiritually, and perhaps even corporeally with our bodily eyes, but we will also see God in each other person and in all creation,

> God will be so known by us and will be so much before us, that we will see him by the spirit in ourselves, in one another, in himself, in the new heavens and the new earth, in every created thing which will then exist; and also by the body we will see him in every body which the keen vision of the eye of the spiritual body will reach.[41]

Perhaps this understanding of the vision of God as including, and being constituted in, the true vision of the neighbor and of all created things can give us a framework for understanding the way in which angelophanies function. As the saints in the beatific life remain themselves, individuated, but are also the vision of God, so angels in theophanies are able to fully represent God while being themselves fully present. This interpretation would be fitting given Augustine's understanding of the angels' blessed state. It would also resonate with one of Kloos' principal theses with respect to theophanies: that mediation for Augustine does not interfere with an encounter with God but facilitates it. This type of mediation is perfected in the new heaven and the new earth (and presumably, is perfected now in the good angels) where an encounter with the neighbor or with creation is an encounter with God.

The second implication of Augustine's prophet–angel parallel, related to the first, is that he once again affirms God's concern for the creature's condition. When an angel becomes God's messenger, even though perhaps God is present "especially (*maxime*) when he speaks"[42] through them,

---

("The Visible Christ and the Invisible Trinity," 346). Kloos follows this line of reasoning generally – God, of course, cannot be seen corporeally for Augustine – but she goes further in explaining how the "vision of faith" experienced in the theophanies is a real and special encounter with God, and constitutes a true vision. Bogdan Bucur (writing earlier than Kloos), takes Barnes' observations in a much more negative direction in "Theophanies and Vision of God in Augustine's *de Trinitate*: An Eastern Orthodox Perspective," *St. Vladimir's Theological Quarterly* 52.1 (2008): 67–93. He harshly contrasts Augustine's interpretation of the theophany narratives with the Eastern tradition, arguing that Augustine does not see the theophanies as transformative experiences, nor does he value "seeing" God as essential to the present Christian life. Therefore, he argues, Augustine's *On the Trinity* marks a regrettable break with the East.

[41] *civ. Dei* XXII.29.
[42] *c. Max.* 2.26.9.

God does not act coercively, nor against the nature of either angelic or human heralds. When Augustine does attempt to understand how angels act, he always insists that these feats come naturally to angels. Since the symbolic actions and utterances of the prophets are evidently carried out by human beings, people "cannot regard them with amazement as marvels or miracles, though they may treat them with reverence as objects of religions. All things done by angels, on the other hand, seem marvelous to us the more difficult and mysterious they are."[43] As we have already seen, however, this attitude of utter amazement toward the workings of angels is a mistake. The actions of angels come easily to them, and here the prophet–angel parallel helps Augustine to reinforce the point, since the actions of the prophets are likewise normal human actions. Old Testament theophanies, although often engineered by angels, are achieved through created things even if we are at a loss to show how they were accomplished.[44] Elsewhere, Augustine speaks of angelic visions in a similar way. When explaining how angels can reveal their thoughts to us, he suggests that angels simply bring their thoughts out of hiding, as they can spiritually conceal their mind as we can conceal our bodies from sight.[45] In other words, spiritual acts are as natural to angels as physical ones are to us. Bringing angelic speech down to an even more mundane level, Augustine also suggests that when an angel speaks *in persona Dei*, it is like when a court herald speaks on behalf of the judge.[46] Angels need not be endowed with supernatural abilities to act as God's messengers, even when they are representative of God's very person.

Augustine's observations about the likeness of angels to the prophets, taken together, produce a vision of angelic cooperation that is consonant with other observations throughout this study. Angels remain always themselves, and God gives them tasks which are suited to their nature. The herald retains his or her personal character, and although messengers act on behalf of God, their actions fall squarely within the normal range of their natural creaturely abilities. We can reiterate therefore the point made at length in chapter 1 with regard to angelic creation, that is, angels do not lose free will or become automatons by being conformed to God's will, rather they are able to act as messengers because of their freedom and the original goodness of their nature.

---

[43] *trin.* III.20.
[44] Ibid., III.21.
[45] *Gn. litt.* XII.22.48.
[46] *s.* 12.7. Augustine uses this analogy in the context of explaining how Satan could have been said to speak with God in the book of Job. He suggests that although Satan is said to be in God's presence, he conversed with angels. See also *trin.* III.23.

The Meaning of Angel: Angels and the Incarnation

The angels have a preeminent responsibility in the administration of the old covenant, in the law and in the theophanies. In Augustine's view of salvation history, it is fitting, if not necessary, for the angels to have such a role rather than Christ, since he is sent only when the new covenant is introduced. So, although God uses the angels according to their proper nature and with respect for their created status before the incarnation, what relationship do they have to Christ's coming, and how do they continue their ministry after-wards, if at all? For Augustine, the angelic office from the very beginning is ordered to the incarnation and, in fact, the angels receive their vocation from Christ. There is nothing the angels do in the unfolding of the story of the Old Testament which is not in direct preparation for the completion of God's plan of salvation in Christ. They are not merely passing the time until Christ can come along and bring about the fullness of revelation, nor are they second-rate mediators standing in Christ's place, but all their ministry participates in and anticipates Christ's advent.

In general, we can say this is true for Augustine because the angels announce Christ; that is their specific mission.[47] When the Israelites received the law, for example, it was "proclaimed by angels, but the coming of our Lord Jesus Christ was being prepared and foretold by means of it; and he, as God's Word, was present in a wonderful and inexpressible way in the angels through whose proclamation the law was given."[48] Augustine likewise interprets "the seed ordained by angels" (Gal. 3:19) to be referring to Christ's future incarnation,

For we were men, but we were not righteous; whereas in his incarnation there was a human nature, but it was righteous and not sinful. This is the mediation whereby a hand is stretched out to the lapsed and fallen; this is the seed "ordained by angels" by whose ministry the law was given enjoining the worship of one God, and promising that this mediator would come.[49]

---

[47] Gregory Wiebe likewise notes that the incarnation is at the heart of the angelic vocation, but he argues that Augustine also therefore sees the angels as linked indelibly with the sacraments: "angels administer the signs serving the sign *par excellence*, the human-divine, sign-signified union that is the person of Christ, the sacrament by which God redeems the world." See Wiebe, "Demons in the Theology of Augustine," 189. Here Wiebe is speaking of sacraments in a general sense (as Augustine often does), and our present study also intends to emphasize the sacramental life of angels and their rela-tionship to human signs. Augustine, however, has little to say about the participation of angels in liturgical celebrations.

[48] *trin.* III.26.

[49] *civ. Dei* X.24 (an extremely similar passage appears in *trin.* III.26). Linking the "seed ordained by angels" with the incarnation also occurs in *exp. Gal.* 27.3, *Gn. litt.* 9.16.30

Angels therefore herald the coming of Christ through various means. In the case of the law, angels announce Christ by presenting a text which prophetically speaks about Christ, both in its words and in the actions it proscribes.[50] But, as Augustine notes, the angels at Sinai also prophesy Christ's person because the Word is especially present in them. Other major events in the lives of the patriarchs that were carried out by angels also powerfully foreshadow Christ. In the case of the sacrifice of Isaac, it was an angel's voice which both ordered and stayed the execution of Abraham's beloved son.[51] It was an angel who wrestled with Jacob, and by allowing himself to be overcome, symbolized the great mystery of Christ's passion, "the wrestler stands conquered and blesses his conqueror, conquered because he willed to be, weak in his flesh, powerful in his majesty."[52] Angels also appeared to Jacob in his vision of the ladder. This episode is replete with incarnational imagery, according to Augustine, both in the fact that Jacob rested his head on a rock, which he then anointed (symbolizing Christ), and in the contents of the vision itself. Angels are seen traveling up and down the ladder, because they "are charged with announcing the truth," that is, with announcing Christ.

Let them [angels] mount high and see that "in the beginning was the Word and the Word was with God and he was God" (John 1:1). Then let them come down and "see the Word was made flesh and dwelt among us" (John 1:14). Let them ascend and lift up the great, but let them descend to nourish the little ones ... And this is what happens all the time in the Church: God's angels ascend and descend upon the Son of Man (cf. John 1:51), because the Son of Man is enthroned on

and *en. Ps.* 88.2.9. Later, however, in *retr.* 2.24.2 (with respect to the passage in *Gn. litt.*) Augustine tells us that he discovered his text of this verse – "the seed, to which the promises had been made, which was disposed through angels in the hand of mediator" – was not the version in more reliable Greek manuscripts. He then realized the verse was about the law. Boulding notes the problem with Augustine's use of Gal. 3:19 in *en. Ps.* 88.2.9 "Augustine has considerably altered the bearing of the text, where Paul is contrasting the law, ministered by angels according to a Jewish tradition, through the mediation of Moses, with the primal, direct promise of God, which is fulfilled in Christ for those who believe him." But perhaps the way in which Augustine readily understood (the corrupt version of) Gal. 3:19 only serves to reinforce our conviction that Augustine is determined to see the angels' ministry as consonant with the incarnation. He assumes the seed referenced, which was entrusted to angels, is Christ.

[50] On Augustine's positive valuation of the law, not only in its statutes but in its enactment, see Paula Frederickson, *Augustine and the Jews* (New Haven: Yale University Press, 2010), 243–245.

[51] *trin.* III.25.

[52] *en. Ps.* 79.3. He offers the same interpretation of the story in several places. See *c. Adim.* 9, *c. Sec.* 23, *c. Faust.* 12.26, *c. Max.* 2.26.9, *civ. Dei* XVI.39 and *en. Ps.* 44.20.

high and to him we ascend in our hearts, in this respect he is our head. But the Son of Man is here below, inasmuch as his body is on earth.[53]

In expounding Jacob's vision, Augustine gives us a rich image of the angelic ministry. The angels are in fact performing their ministry in giving the vision, by displaying before Jacob a scene of Christ's advent. They are bearing witness to Christ both as enthroned in heaven and also showing that he will descend – even as they are descending to instruct Jacob. But this mission, which they are in the process of performing for Jacob's sake, is also the mission they continue even to this day. The angels hustle up and down the ladder, raising human hearts to Christ and ministering to Christ's body on earth, the church. In the vision of Jacob's ladder, the angels herald the incarnation, pay homage to the incarnation and reveal how they will continue to image the incarnation in their service to the human race. The use of the prologue of John punctuates Augustine's concern with the integrity of the scriptural narrative. In rejecting the view that the Old Testament theophanies are Christophanies, Augustine has refused to collapse the entire story of God's revelation into the incarnation. Although the incarnation is the critical event of salvation, it is an event which happens at a particular time and place. The incarnation is the climax of a story in which the angels have their proper part. God never violates the temporal rule upon which creation is founded, but he desires to weave the divine tale, including his angels, into its fabric.

The emphasis on the meaning of the word "angel" in Augustine's texts further demonstrates the indelible link between the angelic vocation and Christ's. One of the most common statements he makes when discussing the angels is to remind us that the word "angel" is from the Greek ἄγγελος, which is the equivalent of the Latin *nuntius*.[54] It is therefore the name of the angels' vocation and not their substance, as Augustine demonstrates at length in his exposition of Ps. 104:4 ("he makes spirits into his angels, and blazing fires into his servants"),

The angels are spirits. When they are simply spirits, they are not angels, but when they are sent, they become angels (*cum mittuntur, fiunt angeli*); for "angel" is the name of a function not a nature. If you inquire about the nature of such beings, you find that they are spirits, if you ask what their office is, the answer is that

---

[53] *en. Ps.* 44.20. See also *c. Faust.* 12.26 and *s.* 122.6.
[54] See *c. Faust.* 16.20, *Jo. ev. tr.* 24.7, 54.3, 121.1, *Gn. litt.* v.37, *trin.* 11.23, *civ. Dei* xv.23, xviii.35, *en. Ps.* 135.3, *s.* 7.3 and 125.3. Boulnois discusses the use of this explanation in Augustine's predecessors such as Novatian and Hilary of Poitiers; see "L'éxègese de la théophanie de Mambré," 60.

they are angels. In respect of what they are, such creatures are spirits; in respect of what they do, they are angels. Make a comparison of human affairs. The name of someone's nature is "human being," the name of his job is "soldier." The name of someone's nature is "man," the name of his office is "herald." A human being becomes a herald; in other words, one who was already a man becomes a herald. We cannot say the opposite, that one who was a herald becomes a man. Similarly some beings existed who were created by God as spirits, but he makes them angels by sending them to announce what he has ordered them.[55]

In this passage, Augustine makes clear his basic point about the word "angel," but he also describes the angelic ministry in a similar way to Christ's own. The Son does not become the Christ until he is sent, so also the angels receive their name when they enter into relationship with us as God's messengers. As in the narrative of the incarnation, the angels *become* something for us; they were spirits and become angels. We too can become angels, Augustine explains, when we announce the gospel to others, and the apostles have a similar name to the angels since they also are sent out (ἀποστέλλω).[56] He likewise calls John the Baptist an angel, in accordance with the scripture "I send my angel before your face" (Exod. 23:20; Matt. 11:10; Mark 1:2; Luke 7:27). John holds the angelic office because he is a herald of the incarnation. Christ's vocation as the one who is sent out and becomes man is shared by the angels, apostles and saints who are sent out and become his heralds.

The angelic vocation, therefore, is not simply connected to the incarnation because the incarnation is its goal, so to speak, but because it is also its means. Angels receive their vocation from Christ and carry it out in Christ. In the case of Jacob's ladder, the ladder not only begins and ends in Christ, but the ladder itself is Christ,

They [angels] ascend when they rise above the created universe to describe the supreme majesty of the divine nature of Christ as being in the beginning God with God, by whom all things were made. They descend to tell of his being made of a woman, made under the law, that he might redeem them that were under the

---

[55] *en. Ps.* 103.1.15.
[56] *Jo. ev. tr.* 54.3. For some more examples of Augustine grouping angels with apostles, see *c. mend.* 2, *c. Iul. imp.* 2.52, ep. 237.9, *en. Ps.* 49.3, *en. Ps.* 66.1, *en. Ps.* 124.4, *s.* 12.4, *s.* 303.2 and *s. Dolbeau* 19.6. Dunkle also argues that Augustine ties the prophets closely with the apostles in *cons. eu.*, as both primarily bear witness to Christ's humility (see Dunkle, "Humility, Prophecy and Augustine's Harmony of the Gospels," 218–219). This same observation is made here with regards to Augustine's linking of prophets, apostles and angels; all these bear witness to Christ's bending down in the incarnation, and they do so by pointing beyond themselves. They herald humility in a posture of humility.

law. Christ is the ladder reaching from earth to heaven, or from the carnal to the spiritual.[57]

Angels not only move up and down the ladder by preaching Christ's divine nature and his condescension in the incarnation, but Christ himself is the means by which they carry out their mission (that is, to bring human beings from a carnal state to a spiritual one). By being both God and man, Christ creates the ladder on which the good angels ascend and descend. Augustine further suggests that the angels receive their vocation from Christ in his *Tractates on John*, as he expounds the words of the five thousand concerning Christ: "this is indeed a prophet" (John 6:14). In a fairly lengthy discussion, he demonstrates that Christ is both prophet and Lord of prophets, and thereby perfectly embodies the vocation of angel and prophet alike.

They may have still been thinking of Christ as a prophet because they were reclining on the grass. But he was the Lord of prophets, the one who inspired the prophets, the one who sanctified the prophets; even so he was also a prophet ... The Lord is a prophet and the Lord is the Word of God and no prophet prophesies without the Word of God; the Word of God is with the prophets and the Word of God is a prophet. Previous ages were thought worthy of inspired prophets and prophets filled by the Word of God; we have been thought worthy of a prophet who is the very Word of God. Christ however is a prophet, the Lord of prophets, in the same way as Christ is an angel, the Lord of angels. For he was also called the "angel of great counsel" (Isa. 9:6 LXX). And yet what does the prophet Isaiah say in another place? "That not an ambassador nor an angel. But he himself will come and save them" (Isa. 63:9 LXX); that is, to save them he will not send an ambassador, will not send an angel, but will come in person. Who will come? The angel himself. Certainly not acting through an angel, except insofar as this one is an angel in such a way as to be also Lord of angels. In Latin, in fact, angels are heralds. If Christ had had nothing to announce, he would not be called an angel. He exhorted us to believe, and by faith to lay hold of eternal life; he announced something present, foretold something to come in the future. Insofar as he announced something present he was an angel; insofar as he foretold something to come, he was a prophet; insofar as "the Word made flesh" (John 1:14), he was, of both angels and prophets, Lord.[58]

Again, Augustine regards the office of prophet and angel as closely linked, because both announce God's will, although here he associates the prophetic office more closely with foretelling the future. But he also shows that without Christ, who is the Word of God, there would be neither

---

[57] *c. Faust.* 12.26. In this context, Augustine once again notes that "angels" means all those who preach Christ.
[58] *Jo. ev. tr.* 24.7.

prophecies nor angels, for the content of their message would be empty. Christ, since he is God come in person, is the angel *par excellence*. Christ does not only announce the future, but he does so by being present, and therefore by putting faith in his person, we are promised eternal life in the future. Christ embodies the message, that is, the will of God, and is therefore the foundation of all angelic mediations and all prophecy. This is encapsulated in the title "angel of great counsel" (Isa. 9:6), which fittingly is "the name the prophets gave him."[59] In short, the angelic (and prophetic) vocation is received from and perfected in Christ, and therefore completely ordered to the incarnation. Conversely, the incarnation, from its inception, is an angelic economy in which the role of heralds is constitutive. God intended from the first to come as a herald himself, but also for the rest of creation to participate in Christ's vocation and thus in his plan of salvation.

Moreover, as Augustine makes abundantly clear in *City of God*, angels themselves cannot be properly said to mediate, but only as they relate to Christ. Angels do not stand midway between God and man, but rather Christ does (because he is mortal like us but blessed like God) as well as the demons (because they are miserable like us but immortal like God). Christ places himself between us and God in order to bring us to blessed immortality, the demons interpose themselves in the same place to prevent it, but in both cases only someone who has one foot in this world and one in the next are able to effect mediations properly speaking. For Augustine, this means that good angels "cannot mediate between miserable mortals and blessed immortals, for they themselves are both blessed and immortal."[60] Since Christ is the sole mediator to blessedness, then, any mediation or heralding done by the angels must, by necessity, participate in Christ's mediation. The angels' place is always understood relative to Christ, who

does not lead us to the immortal and blessed angels, so that we should become immortal and blessed by participating in their nature, but he leads us straight to

---

[59] *en. Ps.* 33.2.11. Boulnois notes that Isa. 9:6 was always a key scriptural text for the Christian interpretation of the theophany narratives. Augustine, however, rejects the notion that this text from Isaiah implies that any reference to an angel is a reference to Christ, like a cipher, especially since many passages refer to angels in the plural. We may contend further, then, that Augustine has a more consistent application than his predecessors of the word "angel." When used by scripture this word is always indicative of the office, and could refer to Christ, human beings or celestial spirits depending on context. See "L'éxègese de la théophanie de Mambré," 60.

[60] *civ. Dei* IX.15.

that Trinity in which the angels themselves are blessed. Therefore, when he chose
to be in the form of a servant, and lower than the angels, that he might be our
mediator, he remained higher than the angels in the form of God.[61]

The angels do not change positions, rather Christ, in becoming a mediator, is both lower than the angels and higher. The angels then do not
mediate for us, properly speaking, since they do not stand between God
and man, nor to themselves, since they lead us to God. Rather, the angels
participate in Christ's mediation by heralding him (by ascending and
descending the ladder) in order to bring all people to the triune God.[62]
In chapter 2, we saw that Augustine portrays the angels in a similar way
with respect to how they come into communion with us. Christ makes
himself lower than the angels, but the angels in turn lower themselves
to serve him, even though Christ does not need their ministry. Angels
therefore come into communion with us because they give themselves
to us as Christ does, and their friendship is both modeled on Christ and
enabled by him. Likewise, as heralds the angels do not just participate in
the incarnation by knowing about it and telling about it, but by being
conformed to it. Angels can be said to mediate only in Christ.

Not only does angelic mediation depend entirely on God's self-
emptying action, but Augustine suggests that our knowledge of angels,
like our earthly knowledge of God, is also inextricably bound to God's
incarnational economy. As we have seen, he repeatedly mentions that
the name angel is the name of an office, not a nature, and so we know
the angels by their work. In book ix of *City of God*, he gives some consideration to how we ought to use the name "angel." He notes that the
Platonists prefer to call angels by the name "good demons." He allows
for the Platonists to speak about good angels in this way, as long as
they understand these angels to be "immortal and yet created by the
supreme God, blessed by cleaving to their creator and not by their own
power."[63] If this is the case, Augustine says, he will not bother to "spend
strength in fighting about words."[64] But this concession does not hold
for long. He criticizes the use of the term "demon" for the good angels
since it confuses the matter. As he explains, the word "demon" has come

---

[61] Ibid.
[62] One might expect to find more instances of Augustine speaking about the relationship
of the angels to the Trinity, but explicit references are few. Lewis Ayres suggests that *trin.*
III.4.9 speaks about the angels being bound together in love by the Spirit. See *Augustine
and the Trinity* (Cambridge: Cambridge University Press, 2010), 190–191.
[63] *civ. Dei* IX.23.
[64] Ibid.

to have a universally negative connotation.[65] Augustine insists that he
need not "laboriously contend about the name" since it is obvious that
these "good demons" are holy angels "who are sent to announce the
will of God to men."[66] But still, he goes on, although "it may seem mere
wrangling about a name, yet the name of demon is so detestable that we
cannot bear in any sense to apply it to holy angels."[67]

Augustine here makes a concerted effort to leave the subject of the
name, and allow the Platonists to use their own vocabulary; certainly
the best of them, Augustine tells us, understand "good demons" in the
proper way. But other people believe that the demons, not to mention the
good angels, are actually capable of mediating by their own power, and
the Platonists are guilty of perpetuating this system of demonolatry. The
name "angel," however, leaves no doubt as to their place, which is that
of herald. This discussion betrays the importance of the angelic name
for Augustine, since he is unable, in the end, to relinquish it despite his
best intention.[68] Although the name is not the name of their essence, and
therefore not strictly necessary, it is the name by which the good angels
are known to us, it is the name used in scripture to denote their relation
to us and in this name there can be no confusion about their part in salvation history. To call the angels by another name, therefore, obfuscates
their mission, and if they are called by the name "demon" it is an indig-
nity to them. Perhaps there is some analogy here to the way in which the
language we use applies to God, for Augustine. Although none of our
words describe God's essence, we must still use these words to speak
about God, especially the words of scripture.[69] The angels are creatures,
and therefore not ineffable as God is, but still we know them by the way
in which they are revealed to us.

Perhaps the most beautiful image of the relationship of the angelic
life to the incarnation comes from *The Literal Meaning of Genesis*.

---

[65] Ibid., IX.22. Augustine recognizes that this word has not always had a negative connotation, but maintains that the word "demon" is not used of good angels in his own time.

[66] Ibid., IX.23.

[67] Ibid.

[68] In *civ. Dei* X.23, in the course of discussing the term *principium*, Augustine sees himself
as being required to use words more carefully than the philosophers in any case: "for
philosophers speak as they have a mind to, and in the most difficult matters do not
scruple to offend religious ears; but we are bound to speak according to certain rule, lest
freedom of speech beget impiety of opinion." This comment could equally be applied to
Augustine's ultimate refusal to call angels by the name "demon," since it is offensive and
could give rise to false opinion.

[69] See, for example, *doc. Chr.* I.6.

Augustine is in the course of explaining the creation of Eve and the way in which God chose to form her. Surely God did not need to make Eve from Adam's rib, he explains. God could have made Eve fresh from the earth like Adam himself or chosen many other ways of creating. As in Gen. 1, God could have merely spoken her into existence. Angels need not have been involved, moreover, although the scriptures suggest that angels aided.[70] The creation of Eve, according to Augustine, therefore, proclaims a mystery, so that

> just as the seed for which the promise was made was disposed by angels in the hand of the mediator, so all things were done miraculously in the realm of nature, but against the usual course of nature, to predict or to proclaim the advent of that seed, [these things] were done through the ministry of angels.[71]

We discussed in chapter 1 the implications of angels as the first witnesses of creation, and here we return to the question, since Augustine implies that from the very first moment of angelic participation in God's work (that is, during creation itself), already the angels' role as heralds of Christ had begun. He sees the very participation of the angels in creation (since they are entrusted with the seed) as suggestive of the incarnation. The angels therefore helped to plant the seed of male and female that would grow into the mystery of Christ and the church. The sleep that overcame Adam, although unnecessary, was a kind of ecstasy which allowed Adam to see the true beauty of Eve's creation.

> So by the same token that ecstasy, which God cast on Adam, to put him into a deep sleep, may be rightly understood as cast upon him precisely in order that he too in his mind might through ecstasy become as it were a member of the angelic court (*per extasin particeps fieret tamquam angelicae curiae*), and "so enter into the sanctuary of God and understand the last things" (Ps. 73:17). Finally, on waking up, full of prophecy so to say, when he saw his wife brought to him he immediately burst out with what the apostle holds up to us as a great sacrament; "this is now bone out of my bones and flesh out from my flesh, this shall be called woman since she was taken out of her man; and for this reason a man shall leave his father and mother and shall stick to his wife, and they shall be two in one flesh" (Gen. 2:23–24).[72]

Although Adam was asleep during Eve's creation, he is able to recognize Eve immediately as his wife, and he is also able to proclaim the mystery of the church, and their union, therefore, as a great sacrament. The reason Adam is able to do this is because he spent time in the court of the angels.

[70] *Gn. litt.* IX.34. He also rejects God's need to use a rib in *Gn. litt.* IX.24.
[71] Ibid., IX.35.
[72] Ibid., IX.36.

It seems that by being present there he received a prophetic vocation and saw in some degree the mystery of the incarnation. Augustine therefore conjures an image of a heavenly court that is always occupied with the glorious vision of Christ's advent, since it was in this angelic company that Adam first glimpsed Christ's plan to unite himself with the church.

From the beginning, the angels have set before them both the vision of creation and the relationship of the incarnation to that creation; they see Adam and Eve, and indeed the creation of the whole cosmos, as begotten in the same love which will become incarnate. These connections may also lead us to return to a consideration of the *fiat lux* and ask in what way the angels received their vocation from the beginning. God who is light illuminates the angels on day one of creation at the same time as they receive their being, but this also means that the angels are always capable of shedding light on others. If we recall Augustine's image of angels as window-makers, we can reassert the suggestion made at the end of chapter 1 that the *fiat lux* is not merely the gift of life and knowledge to the angels, but it is also simultaneously a vocation, since to be light means to understand, (i.e. to be enlightened), but it also means to show or demonstrate (i.e. to enlighten).

However it is that the angels receive their vocation, one could say that the pivotal moment for the angels is the same as it is for God. It is not during the time of the old covenant when the angels are entrusted with the weighty (and prestigious) responsibility of communicating all of God's revelation to Israel and the world, but rather at the incarnation. Angelic activity, after all, reaches a fever pitch at the nativity. Gabriel visits Mary and Zechariah (Luke 1:5–38). An angel warns Joseph in a dream both to take Mary home as his wife and to flee for the land of Egypt (Matt. 2:13–23). Angels also announce to the shepherds (Luke 2:8–20) and warn the Magi in a dream not to return to Herod (Matt. 2:12). The flourish of angelic activity at the incarnation does not go unnoticed by Augustine, who mentions the angels' presence at the nativity in many of his homilies, especially his Christmas sermons; one can hardly avoid doing so.[73] The angels also appear often in Augustine's epiphany homilies.[74] On epiphany, Augustine contrasts the angels who were sent

---

[73] In the collection of Augustine's sermons, there is a set of Christmas homilies (185–196), and although his primary topic of discussion is often the virginity of Mary or the two natures of Christ, angels are mentioned in all but three (those being s. 186, 188 and 195). The angels' role in the nativity (and surrounding events) is also mentioned in s. 50.10,' 184.3, 291.1, 373.1–5, s. *Dolbeau* 23.13 and s. *Erfurt* 3.5.

[74] See s. 199, 201, 202 and 205.

to the shepherds with the star which was sent to the Magi, and hints at the symmetry between the angels' role before the incarnation and on the night of Christ's birth. Christmas day is the announcement of the incarnation to the Jews, whereas epiphany is for the Gentiles,

Therefore that he might be announced to the Jewish shepherds, angels came from heaven, that he might be worshipped by the Gentile Magi, as a star shone brilliantly from the sky. So whether by means of angels or of a star "the heavens declared the glory of the Lord" (Ps. 19:1).[75]

As the preeminent heralds of the incarnation to the people of Israel prior to Christ's coming, the angels fittingly announce the day of Christ's birth to the Jews. A star, however, beckons the Gentiles. God uses a star because the Magi are astrologers and therefore attracted to the strange sign (although Jesus' birth in fact deconstructs astrology, Augustine tells us, since the star bends down to him rather than his appearance being bound to the movement of stars).[76] In general, it is fitting that both angels and the star should have their proper role in announcing the incarnation in accordance with Ps. 19.[77] The use of both angels and the star is also consonant with God's mode of communication in the old covenant, as they cooperate with, rather than supplant, the human witness to the incarnation. The prophets, human beings who foretold Christ's advent, were suited to their task because Christ was going to become human, whereas the angels and the star bear witness to Christ's divine nature; "rightly therefore did the prophets foretell that he would be born, while the heavens and the angels announced that he had been."[78] When Augustine speaks more at length about the angels on Christmas day, he emphasizes their joy. The Christmas proclamation of the angels calls us to reflect on the "glorious divine praises" and "exultant joy of angels."[79] On that day "the song of angels" is "poured out exultantly"[80] and "the angels celebrate, the shepherds rejoice."[81] This joy is again reminiscent of the angel's

---

[75] *s.* 373.1. The same parallel (angels for the Jews, a star for the Gentiles) appears in a number of homilies: *en. Ps.* 101.1.1, *s.* 185.1, 199.1, 201.1, 203.1, 204.1 and *s. Dolbeau* 23.13.

[76] *s.* 199.3. In *s. Dolbeau* 23.13, Augustine also allows that the angels may have orchestrated the appearance of the star which led the Magi.

[77] In *s.* 373.1 quoted above, but also in *s.* 204.1. Augustine also sees the extraordinary heavenly activity surrounding Christ's birth as fulfilling Hag. 2:6, i.e., that God will shake the heavens as well as the Earth. See *s.* 50.10.

[78] *s.* 184.3.

[79] *s.* 193.1.

[80] *s.* 194.2.

[81] *s.* 373.3.

activity at creation itself, when they turn always in the morning to praise God. In one of his Christmas homilies Augustine suggests precisely this connection, making mention of how Christ is "great as the day of the angels," that is, in the eternal day described in Gen. 1, but becomes "little in the day of man."[82] The same angels who were made in the light that is Christ bear witness to that light coming into the world. The events are parallel, and the angels respond to both by turning in praise to God. In another image of angelic cooperation, Augustine suggests that the angels' joy substitutes for the normal superstitions surrounding birth, with the angels replacing the "pack of women with solemn human rites"[83] – and so Mary has the angels for her midwives.

In Augustine's vision of the nativity, then, we see a number of resonances with his view of angels presented elsewhere. The angels are the heralds of the incarnation and they are suited in their nature to announce Christ in their own way; for example, Augustine speaks of them as bearing witness to Christ's divine nature in particular. Yet, the angels cooperate with human heralds (i.e. the prophets), and God at all times uses forms of signification which are suited to the needs of particular times and places, for example, in using a star to summon the Magi to the newborn king. Augustine also speaks of the angels' joy and role in the incarnation in a similar way as he does the angels' joy at creation itself, linking the two as he did when he suggested Adam saw the incarnation in the heavenly court. It would be an overstatement to say that Augustine is systematic in assigning particular roles to angels, others to prophets and others to John the Baptist (for example), but a pattern emerges: whatever biblical passage Augustine finds himself commenting on, he is concerned to show how angels and human beings have a proper place in the plan of salvation, and how each group participates in preparing for the incarnation in a way fitting to their station and nature.

In addition to commenting on the angels at the nativity, Augustine also repeatedly notes the angels' presence at the ascension. Here too, the angels bear unfailing witness to the glory which Christ has displayed in his condescension. As Christ goes to sit at the Father's right hand, the disciples are struck with amazement, but the angels admonish them.[84]

---

[82] *s.* 187.1.
[83] *s.* 193.1.
[84] The general sense that the angels are admonishing the disciples, even though the disciples are happy, is present in a number of texts, but the phrase *admoniti sunt uoce angelica dicente* in particular, is used in *en. Ps.* 49.5.

Although the disciples are now joyful, their shock betrays a disbelief in
the fact that the one who is going into heaven is the same man Jesus,

The angels proclaimed the Lord's ascension, but they also had an eye on the
disciples, who, as the Lord ascended, lingered there amazed and marveling, saying
nothing but shouting with joy in their hearts. Then the clear voices of the angels
rang out like trumpets "Why stand there, men of Galilee? This is Jesus" (Acts
1:11). As though they did not know it was Jesus! Had they not seen him in their
company so short a time before? Had they not heard him talking to them? And
more: besides seeing him visibly present, they had even handled his limbs. Were
they likely to be in any doubt this was Jesus? But the angels were talking to men
almost out of their minds with wonder and shouting with joy, so they said "this is
Jesus" as if to say "if you believe in him, this is the one at whose crucifixion you
tottered, at whose murder and burial you thought you had lost your hope. This is
the same Jesus. He is ascending before your eyes, but he will come again, even as
you have seen him go to heaven" (Acts 1:11).[85]

The disciples lived with Jesus, touched him and spoke with him, but
many doubted him in his darkest hour and did not truly see Christ's
glory until the ascension. Now they, like Adam, experience some measure
of ecstasy when they see God's plan. The clarity and perspicacity of the
angels, however – for they truly see the incarnation, both its beginning
and end – is revealed in their continued ability to speak clearly (*uox
iam tubae in clara uoce angelorum*). As the angels praised the ascension, so also "a prophecy was trumpeted:"[86] that the same Christ who
ascended will return to judge the living and the dead. Augustine consist-
ently interprets the angels' speech found in Acts 1:11 ("Men of Galilee,
why do you stand looking up toward heaven? This Jesus, who has been
taken up from you into heaven, will come in the same way as you saw
him go into heaven") to mean that when Christ comes in judgment, he
will come again in the same human form in which he was mocked and
crucified, that is, the form in which he was incarnate.[87] As Christ ascends
into heaven, therefore, the angels continue to bear witness to his incarnation, in particular, to the lasting meaning of Christ's presence on earth
and its ultimate culmination on judgment day. In contradistinction to
the demons, who lord their incorporeality over human beings and use it
to deceive them, as we saw in chapter 2, the good angels, although spiritual, testify about and perfectly comprehend Christ's body, which the

[85] *en. Ps.* 46.7.
[86] *en. Ps.* 109.12.
[87] See *Jo. ev. tr.* 21.13, *ep.* 199.41 *en. Ps.* 109.12, *s.* 127.10, 214.9, 265.2, 277.16–17 and *s.
    Morin* 17.6.

apostles fail to understand. The fleshly disciples must be told how Christ will come in judgment by creatures who have no fleshly body, as if the apostles make the philosophers' mistake of seeking some higher – but ultimately prideful – spiritualized understanding of a surprisingly physical event, the upward movement of Christ's actual body.

Augustine, moreover, understands the angels' work at the ascension to be like their other actions. This means that the angelic proclamation to the awestruck Galileans is not merely a deed which illuminates the incarnation, but is also evidence of the angels' conformation to God's love. In his sermon on Ps. 91, while expounding verses 11–12 ("For he will command his angels concerning you to guard you in all your ways. On their hands they will bear you up, so that you will not dash your foot against a stone"), Augustine explains in what way the angels lifted Christ upward at the ascension. The angels carried Christ not because they were superior to him nor because Christ needed to be supported; rather, the angels bore Christ like a horse or a donkey bears its master.[88] At the ascension, then, as during Jesus' time on earth, the angels serve humankind in serving Christ. Christ does not need their ministry, but by means of their prophetic voice and by the visual spectacle of Christ's upward ascent, they reveal Christ's glory; "the psalm speaks of it as a sign not of weakness on the Lord's part, but of their [i.e. the angels'] desire to honor and serve him."[89] Again we see a consistency between the acts of the angels in the old covenant and the new. God has no need to use angels, but he allows the angels to participate as an act of service.[90]

---

[88] *en. Ps.* 90.2.8.

[89] Ibid. *non ad infirmitatem domini pertinet, sed ad illorum honorificentiam, ad illorum seruitutem.*

[90] Following ancient pagan and Christian tradition (on this tradition, see Daniélou, *Angels and their Mission*, 95–105), Augustine also occasionally speaks of the angels conveying human beings to heaven after death, our "ascension," so to speak. One such example is *trin.* xv.44: "thus freed from the power of the devil they [the dead] are taken up by holy angels, delivered by the 'mediator between God and men, the man Jesus Christ' (1 Tim. 2:5). For as the divine scriptures agree in declaring, both the old which foretell Christ and new which tell of him, 'there is no other name under heaven by which man can be saved' (Acts 4:12)." Here, Augustine has incorporated an ancient tradition concerning the angels into his overall angelic program; the angels serve us in carrying us upward into heaven, by the power of the incarnation, that is, by the same power to which they bore witness in the Old Testament. Moreover, Christ alone is mediator and conqueror of the devil, not the angels. Other references to angels conveying the dead to heaven are rare. In *cura mort.* 18, the angels are said to be present in the realms of both the living and the dead; this is proved by the example of Lazarus. One could perhaps adduce as evidence many more passages where Augustine cites Lazarus being carried by the hands of angels into the bosom of Abraham (Luke 16:22), but he rarely comments on the angels when citing this verse.

The activity of the angels, therefore, is heightened both at the commencement of the incarnation (the nativity) and, we might say, its finale (the ascension). Their presence, and Augustine's comments on their role at these two moments, serves to demonstrate further what we have been arguing, namely, that the angels' ministry is bound to the incarnation and fulfilled in it. The Old Testament and New Testament are two parts of the same; "the new is in harmony with the old, and the old with the new. The two seraphs sing to each other 'holy, holy, holy, is the Lord, the God of hosts' (Isa. 6:3). The two Testaments are in agreement, the two Testaments speak with one single voice."⁹¹

Angels at the Last Judgment

A survey of angelic activity in salvation history would not be complete without considering the future, that is, the angels' task in the coming judgment. We know from their actions at the ascension that the angels can prophesy about the eschaton and know how Christ, in the glory of his ascent, prefigures the Christ who will come again in glory to judge. Augustine, however, has surprisingly little to say about the angels during the second coming of Christ. This absence is certainly not due to his general lack of interest in the last judgment,⁹² and he frequently cites verses that feature the angels' eschatological presence in particular, although he rarely discusses their role. Some of his favorite verses pertaining to the judgment, in fact, mention angels, such as Matt. 25:41, "Then he will say to those at his left hand, 'You that are accursed, depart from me into the eternal fire prepared for the devil and his angels.' "⁹³ Another of Augustine's oft-cited eschatological texts is the story of the wheat and the tares. In this parable the angels play a dominant role, both as the eager farmers ready to tend the field attacked by the enemy and as the agents who will one day gather the scandals from out of the kingdom (see Matt. 13:24–30). One of the contexts in which Augustine frequently uses this story is in his anti-Donatist writings, where he argues that the parable proves the church is a mixed body (*corpus permixtum*) until judgment day. He sometimes accuses the Donatists of trying to usurp the angels' place, since it is the

---

⁹¹ *en. Ps.* 49.4
⁹² For an excellent summary of Augustine's eschatology including his consideration of the final judgment, see Daley, *The Hope of the Early Church*, 131–150.
⁹³ Augustine never tires of using this phrase, especially in his homilies; it is cited 139 times in his corpus. The only verse from Matthew's Gospel which he cites more frequently is Matt. 6:12 (part of the Lord's prayer).

angels alone who are commanded to weed the garden or sort the fish (depending on the metaphor he is using).⁹⁴ Christ tells us that "the reapers are angels," not "the reapers are the captains of the Circumcellions."⁹⁵

Augustine most frequently mentions the angels on judgment day in the context of this parable, but it is often only in passing that he refers to the angels as reapers or gatherers. He does occasionally make an effort to give the angels a particular role of their own, as he did when speaking about them at the nativity and ascension, but he remains vague. For example, in commenting on John 4:38 ("I sent you to reap that for which you did not labor. Others have labored, and you have entered into their labor"), he takes the privilege of the apostles and hands it to the angels. The apostles who reaped what they did not sow, that is, the work of the prophets, went on to sow what they will not reap, that is, the final harvest. At the end of the age it is the angels who are the reapers and not the apostles.⁹⁶ Augustine here make a distinction in time, then, between the work of the prophets, apostles and angels, seeing their sowing and reaping as successive (although, of course, elsewhere he speaks of angels doing seminal work in the Old Testament). In another sermon, he makes the same point even more plainly; we will be judged and the angels will help judge since, as Christ tells us in the parable, "we are men, the reapers are angels."⁹⁷ In *City of God*, moreover, Augustine suggests that only the angels are really fit for the task of separating the goats from the sheep and gathering the saints, since "certainly a matter so important must be accomplished by the ministry of angels."⁹⁸ Angels are also specially enabled by God to judge without flaw, as they "are able to make the separation and cannot make a mistake."⁹⁹ Augustine, therefore, as already stated, is not wholly consistent in the particular roles he

---

⁹⁴ Along with the wheat and the tares, Augustine likes to use the miraculous haul of fish (Luke 5:1–11; John 21:1–14) as an analogy or image of the *corpus permixtum*, since many fish are caught without discrimination and must therefore be sorted later. Tears in the nets represent schisms. For a good example see *ep.* 108.12, where Augustine draws on a plethora of biblical images for the judgment simultaneously. He urges the Donatists to wait until the end of the world when the Lord, either by himself or through his angels, will separate weeds from grain, tares from wheat, vessels of anger from vessels of mercy, goats from sheep and bad fish from good. For more examples of Augustine accusing the Donatists of assuming this angelic role, see *c. ep. Parm.* 3.28, *ep.* 76.2 and *s.* 47.16.

⁹⁵ *ep.* 76.2. See also footnote directly above.

⁹⁶ *Jo. ev. tr.* 15.32.

⁹⁷ *s.* 73.4. Augustine echoes Christ's terse explanation of the parable; *nos homines sumus, angeli messores sunt.*

⁹⁸ *civ. Dei* XX.24.

⁹⁹ *s.* 73.4.

assigns to prophets, apostles or angels, but he is constant in his attempt to both delineate and compare these groups in whatever biblical context he happens to encounter them, and he often suggests how their task is fitting for them, or for their place and time.

A de-emphasis on the angelic role of reaper could perhaps correspond to Augustine's anti-mythological concerns.[100] It is God alone who is judge, and the divine does not struggle against diverse powers in the final apocalypse; the triumph of good over evil is a forgone conclusion. It is in this light that we could perhaps read his attempts to dispel caricatures or oversimplified depictions of angels at the last judgment.[101] In his exposition of Ps. 94, which speaks of a pit being dug for sinners, for example, Augustine cautions his congregation not to understand this representation of judgment too literally, "when you are told God makes you gentle through days of misery, until a pit is dug for the sinner, you must not imagine even now angels are stationed somewhere, equipped with mattocks, busy digging a huge pit to hold the whole race of evildoers."[102] Rather, the pit represents the nadir sinners will reach when they have fallen from their pride. Augustine takes a similar tack when speaking about the episode described in Rev. 20:12, wherein a book is opened and each person is judged according to his or her deeds. Of this scene, he asks, "shall there be present as many angels as men, and shall each man hear his life recited by the angel assigned to him?"[103] Augustine rejects this notion, noting that the biblical texts speak of only one book, and, after all, if some such literal book existed, it would be unthinkably long. Rather, each person will recall his or her own works, and see the merit of these deeds with "marvelous rapidity" and "each shall be simultaneously judged."[104] We are not to think of ourselves as waiting in a long queue to hear our fate from angels reading solemnly from massive tomes. Augustine, in this passage, once again shows his resistance to accept the concept of a guardian angel, one who is assigned to each of us in particular, even after death. He also paints these caricatures of angelic activity at the judgment so vividly that their absurdity is apparent. To summarize, then, Augustine does not speak often about the angelic office

---

[100] This concern is laid out more thoroughly in chapter 1.
[101] Of course, Augustine's desire to excuse the angels from such "carnal" conceptions (*en. Ps.* 92.16) is not unique to this sermon nor to the subject of angels. He often urges his congregation to resist anthropomorphic depictions of God, for example.
[102] *en. Ps.* 93.16.
[103] *civ. Dei* XX.14.
[104] Ibid.

on the last day, but what he does say seems to confirm the particularity of the angelic ministry, to de-emphasize the importance of the angels in the act of judging (perhaps with anti-mythological concerns) and to curtail what he considers crude ideas about the angelic hosts.

The Merits of Angelic Mediation

Having discussed Augustine's comments on the angels' role at every stage of salvation history, and their presence at this or that biblical event, we may now ask a recapitulatory question, namely, what purpose does angelic mediation serve? Augustine considers angelic heralding to be an obvious fact of the biblical narrative, but what meaning does he ultimately assign to all of this angelic activity? God can surely speak himself through any means he wishes, and Augustine allows that sometimes God does speak directly to us as he does to the angels, "in an ineffable manner of his own."[105] We have already begun the task of answering this question. God uses angels, according to Augustine, both for the benefit of the angels themselves and for our benefit as creatures. This understanding reveals a more general respect for creation on his part, a concern which we have seen repeatedly throughout this study. He also suggests that the angels have a special aesthetic quality and that they provide an authoritative witness to God's work, both of which make their participation in the economy of salvation valuable.

First, Augustine sees the fact that angels are heralds as evidence of God's accommodation for the angels themselves. We have seen this suggestion of accommodation for the sake of angels already in chapters 1 and 2 in different contexts. In chapter 1, the spectacle of creation was performed for the benefit of the angels, in order that they might come to know themselves as creatures and creation as good; God has no inherent need to create in seven days. In chapter 2, it was shown that the relationship formed between good angels and human beings is not only for our benefit, but for the benefit of the angels. This point was proved, in part, by Augustine's doctrine of substitution. Here again, when we approach the question of why God might use angelic heralds instead of created matter, or the divine voice proper, or even human beings alone, Augustine suggests it is for the benefit of the angels themselves, in addition to the fittingness of angelic mediation to various situations. As we have seen, the angels carry Christ in the ascension because they want to, not because Christ needs

[105] Ibid., XVI.6.

it. Likewise, when Christ declares in the Psalms "he sent from heaven and you saved me,"[106] the Lord is not to be understood as asking for angelic aid. Angels do minister to Christ, "but not like merciful beings ministering to one in need: rather as subjects to the omnipotent" because "all the angels are creatures who serve Christ."[107]

There are a few passages in which Augustine makes this point more explicit. The first was already mentioned in chapter 1. It is found in *Literal Meaning of Genesis*, in the midst of a discussion regarding God's use of angelic heralds. God

certainly does not need a reporter to inform him about things lower down the scale, as if to keep him abreast of current affairs; but in that simple and wonderful way he has a steady and unchanging knowledge of all things. He does have reporters however, *both for our sake and for their own (propter nos et propter ipsos)*, because for them to wait upon God obediently in that manner ... is good for them in accordance with their proper nature and mode of being (*bonum est eis in ordine propriae naturae atque substantiae*)[108]

The angels announce to us but also to God, like a go-between. This is not because God needs angels to communicate with us, and certainly not because he needs to be told what happens on earth, but it is good for the angels to be heralds and such a task is "in accordance with their proper nature and mode of being." The angels are allowed to participate in God's inner life as perfected beings, but they are also permitted to participate in God's saving acts. The angels want to play a part, and it is good for them to do so. A similar idea appears in *en. Ps.* 78.1. Augustine is again contemplating the double duty of angels, since they speak both to God and to human beings,

When angels make announcements to mortals, these announcements are made to persons who are ignorant, but when they bring tidings to God, they are telling him what he already knows. This is what happens when they offer our prayers to him, or in some way beyond our understanding take counsel about their own actions with his eternal truth, as with an unchangeable law.[109]

As in the citation from *Literal Meaning of Genesis*, Augustine tells us that the angels report to God even though God already knows what they

---

[106] For Augustine, the words of the psalmist are always the words of Christ.
[107] *en. Ps.* 56.10. *Omnes enim angeli creatura seruiens Christo est*, which Boulding translates as "for all the angels form part of the creation that is at Christ's service." While this translation would suit my interpretation, it seems to me that *creatura* must refer to the angels and not to creation more generally.
[108] *Gn. litt.* v.37.
[109] *en. Ps.* 78.1.

have to tell him. As an example of such reporting, he offers the responsibility of the angels to present our prayers before God.[110] Perhaps even more importantly, he goes on to say that we can imagine the angels themselves taking counsel with God in a similar way to our prayer, even if it is incomprehensible to us. The role of the angelic herald, then, is extended to include the prayers of the angels themselves, which benefits them in helping them to determine their own actions. This image of a consultation taking place between angels and God goes further to dispel the notion of angels receiving rote marching orders from the divine throne; rather, the angels bring news to us, bring news to God, but most importantly, bring themselves to God. Augustine describes the role of angels as conveyors of prayer in a similar way in *ep.* 140, as he expounds Ps. 22:32 ("there will be announced to the Lord a generation to come"),

> This should not be interpreted as if something is announced to the Lord who does not know it in order that he may know it, but as the angels announce not only to us the gifts of God, but also our prayers to him. For scripture says where an angel speaks to human beings "I present a record of your prayer" (Tob. 12:12), not that God then came to know what we want or what we need – "for your Father," says the Lord, "knows what you need before you ask him" (Matt. 6:8) – but because a rational creature who obeys God must bring temporal concerns to the eternal truth, either asking that something be done for him or consulting him about what he should do. This pious disposition of the mind aims at the rational creatures being built up, not at God's being instructed (*ut ipsa construatur, non ut deus instruatur*). For it is a kind of proof of a rational creature that it is not for itself the good by which it becomes blessed; but that good is immutable by participating in which the rational creature is made wise.[111]

The heralding activity of the angels has, as we have seen, two directions: angels present good news to human beings, and they bring our prayers before God. And, once again, our own prayers are compared to the action by which the angels themselves consult with God about what to do, as any rational creature must. The angelic consultation with God is similar in its end to our own prayers, as our prayers are not intended

---

[110] That angels are involved in conveying prayers from earth to heaven is another long-standing patristic tradition (See Daniélou, *Angels and their Mission*, 73–74, 78–82). Unlike some of the other popular angelic traditions which Augustine uses rarely or with reservation, he accepts the conveyance of prayer as part of the angels' duties. There is biblical precedent, and the "angel of prayer" tradition is strong in the West; it derives from Tertullian, according to Daniélou (see *Angels and their Mission*, 73). See also *vera rel.* 112, where Augustine says that angels abide in God and therefore can hear our prayers, *cura mort.* 20, where angels enact the prayer of the martyrs, and *civ. Dei* X.12, where God is said to hear us in the angels. See also *ep.* 140.69 cited in full below.

[111] *ep.* 140.69

to inform God about a course of action which he had not considered, but rather prayer serves as an opportunity for the creature to be built up (construatur) and conformed to God's will. The angels, however, can pray the perfect prayer, we might say, because they are fully blessed and so have become immutable participants in God's wisdom by which they are made wise. The angels are conformed to God, but precisely by behaving as perfect rational creatures who know they must fully depend on God. The angelic office is therefore tied at its most basic level to the virtue of humility. The good angels find their meaning in being created and not in being God, the opposite of *superbia*, and this results in their desire for service. Augustine describes humility as the constant lesson of the angels and prophets.[112]

That Augustine believes the angels receive the office of herald for their own benefit reveals, once again, the importance of the doctrine of creation for him. The Genesis proclamation of goodness applies to the whole created order, even the lofty angels, and he considers what that goodness might entail in their case. God respects the angelic creation by acting for its benefit and in accordance with its own nature, which God himself laid down. God acts in this way so that his good creatures may come to possess their goodness – so that they may come into their own. The very fact that God uses angels to herald at all is proof of the point. God does not employ messengers made *ex nihilo* each time he needs to communicate, but works within the created order already in place and declared good.[113] Augustine maintains that God works through the created order,

---

[112] *s. Guelf.* 32.5; "[God is] the teacher of humility by speech and work: by speech, since always from the beginning of creation he has never been silent, but through angels and through prophets, he taught humility to humankind" (*doctor humilitatis sermone et opere: sermone enim semper ab initio creaturae numquam tacuit, per angelos, per prophetas, docere hominem humilitatem*).

[113] In *trin.* III.19 Augustine summarizes the ways in which God speaks: through an angel proper, or by the work of an angel who employs either a preexisting body, or one produced *ad hoc* and dissolved. This third category (*aliquando ad hoc exoritur et re peracta rursus absumitur*) is perhaps made *ex nihilo*. Augustine notes earlier in the book, however, that demons are also able to make things come forth *ad hoc* because of their intimate knowledge of nature, by seeing and manipulating "the hidden seeds lying dormant in the corporeal elements of the world" (III.13). The example he has in mind is that of Pharaoh's magi, who make snakes appear with demonic aid (III.13–15). These *ad hoc* things are probably best understood, therefore, not as being made *ex nihilo* but called forth (*exoritur* has just this sense) from the seeds of creation for a brief appearance. At the very least, a created being (i.e. the angel) is the primary agent in producing the miraculous sign, thus demonstrating God's intent to work always through the created order.

even in the case of angelic acts which seem quite miraculous, and he holds the same position on other kinds of miracles.[114] At the end of book IX of *Literal Meaning of Genesis*, he discusses the role of the angels in creating Eve, and then, more generally, the angelic cooperation with acts of divine grace. He uses metaphor of the farmer, but includes this comment on angelic activity:

> Since he said that it [God's intent] was hidden in God precisely "in order that the manifold wisdom of God might be made known to the princes and powers in the heavenly places" (Eph. 3:10), the most likely supposition is that just as "the seed for which the promise was made was disposed by angels in the hand of the mediator" (Gal. 3:19) so all the things that were done miraculously in the realm of nature, but against the usual course of nature (*in rerum natura praeter usitatum naturae cursum*), to predict or to proclaim the advent of that seed, were done through the ministry of angels.[115]

As in *On the Trinity*, here Augustine determines that angelic ministry is the most likely means by which God interacts regularly with the created order. Even though these acts of God are indeed miraculous (they were done *mirabiliter*) and are not reflective of the day-to-day cycles of nature (*cursum naturae*), still these things happened, as Hill translates, "in the realm of nature" (*in rerum natura*). God therefore undertakes even the most wondrous actions (i.e. the creation of Eve), by acting on creation through creation (i.e. the angels) in the realm of created natures (*in rerum natura*), albeit in an extraordinary way.[116] On a similar note, we saw that the plan for redemption from the very beginning of the world (glimpsed in the court of angels) involved the redemption of creation through creation, by means of the incarnation, and not from something else made anew by God.

---

[114] Augustine thinks miracles are produced within, and not against, the order of nature. For an overview of Augustine's reflections on miracles, see Serge Lancel, "Augustin et le miracle" in *Les miracles de St. Etienne* (Turnhout: Brepols, 2006), 69–77. In particular, Lancel discusses the way in which miracles are not supernatural for Augustine (73–75); it is an idea "frequemment exprimée par Augustin," but he cites in particular *ep.* 137.10 and *s.* 247.2.

[115] *Gn. litt.* IX.35.

[116] We must not think of Augustine's distinction that Eve's creation is natural but happens against the usual course of nature as being essentially a euphemism for something that is really supernatural in a modern sense. He speaks of extreme weather, comets, eclipses and so on in a similar way. These occurrences are natural, but they are not in the normal course of nature, i.e. commonplace (III.7 and III.19). These things are amazing to us, but can be explained by scientific inquiry. Scientific study, for Augustine, however, can only ever uncover the proximate cause, it cannot discern the will of God.

Augustine also suggests in *On the Trinity* that God uses angelic ministry because of its aesthetic quality. As an example, he explains that the rod which was turned into the serpent by the work of an angel (Exod. 4:3) signifies Christ, just like the stone upon which Jacob rested his head (Gen. 28:18), however "the first case was something both to wonder at and understand (*mirandum est et intellegendum*), the second only something to understand."[117] The two signs both point to the same thing, but "the quality of the two signs differs – rather as if you were to write the Lord's name both in ink and in letters of gold. The gold letters are more valuable and the letters of ink cheaper, but they both mean the same thing."[118] Augustine goes on to caution us that more miraculous signs do not always have more sublime meanings. Nevertheless, he assigns a value to the way of signifying which is a marvel (*mirandum est*), even if the information it conveys is not in itself superior. God's use of angels can therefore be linked to the role he gives to wonder more generally. In *City of God*, Augustine argues that God did not have any need to use miracles to accomplish his purpose (just as he has no need of angels *per se*), but he still rejects the position that God has worked no miracles. No miracle can be considered greater than creation itself, he reminds us, but God's miracles are consistent with the miracle that is creation: "God, who made the visible heaven and earth does not disdain to work visible miracles in heaven or earth, that he may thereby awaken the soul which is immersed in things visible to worship himself, the invisible."[119] This citation concerning the function of the miraculous actually appears in *City of God* book x, which, as we saw in chapter 2, is dedicated to a discussion of the good angels, and the miracles he is speaking of here are described as "wrought by angels or by other means."[120] We can see the value of the angels' role is therefore related to the value of miracles, which by their awesome character seek to stir the soul. Awe leads us to begin the ascent and to contemplate the divine. As agents of wonder, therefore, we can see again how the angels can be said primarily to preach humility, since wonder destroys pride. Angels by being wondrous and effecting the miraculous, turn human beings outwards toward something that is

---

[117] *trin.* III.20.
[118] Ibid.
[119] *civ. Dei* X.12. See also *util. cred.* 34, where Augustine describes a miracle as "whatever appears that is difficult or unusual above the hope or power of them who wonder." However, in his earlier works especially, he is more skeptical about the need of wondrous signs for the wise.
[120] *civ. Dei* X.12.

more powerful and more beautiful than themselves, the beginning of humility.[121] Indeed, in an early attempt to explain the reason for angelic creation, Augustine calls them "ornaments of his [God's] universe."[122]

Finally, Augustine suggests on a few occasions that there is an important quality to angelic witness or testimony. He sometimes confirms the significance or verity of certain statements by highlighting their angelic authority. At the ascension, for example, we are assured of Christ's second coming by the authoritative utterance of angels. As Jesus ascended into heaven, the disciples were given a promise, "they heard with eager ears a testimony, the voice of angels foretelling that Christ will come again."[123] Likewise, we should not doubt that Joseph is to be considered the true father of Jesus, since we know it to be true "on the angel's authority."[124] Augustine also notes that angels bear witness to events at which no other spectator could have been present, such as the creation of the world (Gen. 1) and the creation of humankind (Gen. 2–3), as discussed in chapter 1. They serve as an authoritative eyewitness to these events and are involved in handing it down to subsequent generations. Just as Augustine understands the angels to have perfect knowledge of the Word and of themselves, he correspondingly claims for them superior authority in revelatory matters. Augustine, therefore, offers a multifaceted reflection on the meaning of angelic heralding, which includes a contemplation of the doctrine of creation more broadly, as well as the aesthetic and authoritative quality of the angelic witness in particular.

Conclusion

In departing from the traditional view of Old Testament theophanies as appearances of Christ, and arguing instead that angels carry out visitations to the patriarchs, Augustine gives a prominent role to the angels in salvation history. The angels, like the prophets, remain always themselves

---

[121] My analysis of the use of wonder in Augustine is taken from John Cavadini, "The Anatomy of Wonder: An Augustinian Taxonomy," *Augustinian Studies* 42.2 (2011): 153–172.

[122] *lib. arb.* III.xii.32. He says that this is the case for all angels, whether they sin or not.

[123] *s. Morin* 17.6 (*testem uocem angeli uenturo Christo praenuntiantem intentis auribus audierunt*). The angels' witness at the ascension is likewise called "the plainest evidence of the angels" (*secundum euidentissimum angelicum testimonium*) in *s.* 214.9. See also *s.* 361.8.

[124] *s.* 51.16. The angel's commission for each of the parents to name the child is in turn a confirmation of their parental authority (*s.* 51.30).

and yet simultaneously facilitate a vision of God and speak on God's behalf. This type of heralding parallels his understanding of the beatific life, wherein we will be both completely conformed to God's will and show God to others, yet we will also remain ourselves and be embodied. Angels, moreover, do not fulfill the role of herald for lack of a better candidate, but their place in salvation history is intended from the beginning; their enlightenment in the *fiat lux* entails that they shed God's light and therefore bear witness to that light coming into the world. As the angels play their part in the history of Israel, therefore, they always participate in God's greater purpose and thus in the incarnational economy. The angels are Christ's angels, they herald him and are conformed to his humility. The angels understand God's design from the first, and enact it from the first. The angels serve as heralds for our sake as well as their own, because God created the angels good and created them for a purpose and for communion, just as he created humankind. But the angels also contribute in their own special way to God's plan, for example, because they are beautiful and because they are the cosmic witnesses of creation.

Augustine's suggestion that the beauty of angels gives their mediation a particular quality perhaps raises some further questions for theological aesthetics. Since he links the angelic vocation closely to the incarnation, we might well ask if the aesthetic quality of angelic mediation is tied to the incarnation or not. In other words, is Augustine's aesthetic of angels a revelatory aesthetics (and thus the kind of aesthetics taken up by modern theologians, e.g. Balthasar)? Since Augustine most often speaks about the beauty of the angels in relationship to the hierarchy of being, it would seem their aesthetic is more directly related to their sheer createdness. Rowan Williams rightly explains that, for Augustine, creation is beautiful as such because it is growing into its own good, which is defined by the beauty that is the will of God. Williams writes that, for Augustine, "creation, then, is the realm in which good or beauty or stability, the condition in which everything is most freely and harmoniously itself in balance with everything else, is *being* sought and *being* formed."[125] Perhaps in contemplating Augustine's view of the angels in particular, we can find some midway point between these two modes of aesthetic contemplation. The angels are more beautiful than us even though they have reached a place in which they are no longer "growing" or "becoming" properly speaking; they are held by and hold to God. But it is precisely because they fully embrace the sheer beauty of their createdness (i.e. they know

[125] Rowan Williams, *On Augustine* (London: Bloomsbury, 2016), 70.

they are not God and how they are related to God and to us) that they are also fully conformed to God's revelatory aesthetic. To borrow Williams' language (following Hanby), the angels are beautiful because they are their "doxological selves."[126] This image of self-as-praise captures both the beauty by which and for which the angels are created and also the beauty they communicate in their participation in God's self-revelation.

---

[126] Ibid., 76.

4

Augustine and Spiritual Warfare

Thus far, the contextual motivations for some of Augustine's views on angels have formed an important part of this study, but it is clear that the angels serve more than a polemical function in his thought. In other words, the angels are not simply objects to be positioned against Augustine's opponents. If one overemphasizes the polemical and political function of Augustine's angels, one could arrive at the conclusion that he shows little interest in our daily interaction with spiritual beings and our development in virtue in relationship to these beings.[1] Even in the overtly polemical *City of God*, however, his theology of angels far outstrips that of an anti-pagan rhetoric. More generally speaking, he frequently engages in discussions pertaining to spiritual warfare and our contact with angels and demons, particularly in his pastoral works. In this chapter, Augustine's myriad references to the struggle against the devil and his angels, primarily in his *Expositions of the Psalms*, will be used to demonstrate that his conception of the role of the devil and the spiritual world in everyday Christian experience is remarkably consistent with the angelology he lays out in other works. First, the common motifs of spiritual warfare present in these homilies will be presented, and the general features of Augustine's teaching on this subject will be sketched. He understands the daily temptations of Christians to originate from the

---

[1] Muehlberger reaches such a conclusion. Evagrius, in her view, "imagines angels as one part of a constantly changing constellation of rational beings, making progress on their return to God." Augustine, however, because his angels are already aligned with the will of God, is not as interested in what she terms "cultivation literature," which is concerned with growth in the spiritual life and spiritual warfare. See *Angels in Late Ancient Christianity*, 57.

devil, and in particular, from the allure of pride. His remedy is to rely on Christ and to be formed by liturgical activity (i.e. the remedy is humility). Secondly, the question of the role of the good angels in spiritual warfare will be discussed. Augustine rarely speaks of good angels fighting demons, but rather the good angels provide us a perspective on the state of the spiritual battlefield. The final part of the chapter will consist of a theological analysis of Augustine's preaching on spiritual warfare, which will demonstrate that his pastoral views reflect the same communal vision of sin and virtue (in which the good angels and demons have their place) that we have seen in *City of God* and elsewhere.

Augustine's Teaching on Spiritual Warfare in the *Expositions of the Psalms*

In his figurative interpretations of the Psalms, Augustine often has recourse to spiritual warfare as a paradigm through which to read a particular psalm. Virtually any psalm which speaks of combat, war, violence or victory is understood to pertain to the struggle of the church, of Christ or of the individual against the devil. In one instance the word "tent" is enough for Augustine to see the psalm as one framed by spiritual warfare.

The psalm begins "Lord who will sojourn in your tent?" (Ps. 14:1). Although the word tent is used sometimes to denote everlasting habitation, strictly speaking a tent (*tabernaculum*) is something associated with war. Hence soldiers are referred to as tent-companions (*contubernales*) because their tents are grouped together. The interpretation receives further backing from the words "who will sojourn?" For we do battle with the devil for a time, and we need a tent in which to regain our strength. This points in particular to faith under this temporal dispensation established for us within time by our Lord's incarnation.[2]

The psalm, according to Augustine, is addressed to Christian "tent-companions," that is, to those who participate in the temporal battle against the devil and who are refreshed in the tent of the incarnation. The word "enemy" and related terms such as "persecutor," however, serve as the most common cue for Augustine to interpret a psalm in this mode; a reference to an "enemy" in the singular is understood as the devil, whereas the plural "enemies" are the devil, his angels and occasionally, human beings under the power of the devil. For example, he interprets "I will say to your name, O most high, in turning my enemy back" as referring to

---

[2] *en. Ps.* 14.1.

Christ rebuking the devil,[3] he sees "the swords of the enemy" as the false words the devil uses to cut down the believer,[4] and he explains that when we are shut up "in the clutches of my enemy" we have fallen prey to the devil.[5] But Augustine casts the net even wider. He interprets names (such as Joab mentioned in the title of Ps. 59) to mean "enemy" and therefore the devil,[6] and he often understands figurative enemies, such as lions and snakes, to denote Satan and his followers as well.[7]

Even when Augustine allows that human opponents are denoted by the text, the notion of a human enemy is always subordinated to that of the one true enemy, and Augustine situates our conflict with other human beings in the greater scheme of a spiritual battle. For example, he explains that the shift in a plural reference (persecutors) to a singular (lion) in Ps. 7 is indicative of the psalmist's perfection, since he has come to know there is only one foe against whom he truly fights,

"Lord, in you I have hoped; make me safe from all my persecutors and pluck me out" (Ps. 7:2). The psalmist is speaking, it would seem, as someone already perfect, someone for whom the only remaining enemy is the devil, now that all warfare and resistance from its vices have been overcome. "Make me safe from all my persecutors, and pluck me out, lest he ever, like a lion, tear my soul" ... after saying in the plural, "save me from all my persecutors," the psalmist went on to use the singular ... he did not say "in case they tear" because he knows exactly which enemy, one violently opposed to the perfect soul, stands in his way ... for if God does not rescue or save, the devil snatches us away.[8]

For Augustine, in the everyday struggle against vice and the journey toward perfection, the true combatant knows the battle is "not against flesh and blood but the devil"[9] (cf. Eph. 6:12). The cry for help in the psalm is shifted entirely away from a petition for help against a human foe or even an abstract temptation. Rather, for Augustine, the perfected psalmist seeks aid against his only true adversary, the devil himself. The

---

[3] Ibid., 9.4.
[4] Ibid., 9.8.
[5] Ibid., 30.1.9. There are many other examples of Augustine interpreting the psalmist's enemies to be the devil and/or his angels; see *en. Ps.* 7.2–3, 12.3–12.5, 34.1.4, 40.4, 41.18, 54.4–6, 55.4, 60.5, 67.16, 93.20, 105.10, 139.7–8, 142.7, 142.16 and 148.4.
[6] *en. Ps.* 59.2. Augustine suggests a similar interpretation for the name Amahas (*en. Ps.* 55.4) and Assyria or Asshur (*en. Ps.* 82.8).
[7] See *en. Ps.* 7.2–3, 16.11, 39.1, 40.3–4, 49.29, 69.2, 73.22, 90.2.9 and 103.3.22. Sometimes Augustine introduces the image of the lion and/or snake unprompted by the text, or other animals serve as his starting-point (see, for example, *en. Ps.* 73.22).
[8] *en. Ps.* 7.2.
[9] Ibid., 55.4.

psalmist indicates his progress in spiritual warfare by making a clear, singular identification of Satan – the lion – which Augustine reminds us is a name used for the devil in 1 Peter 5:8.[10] Likewise, the petition "Lord, rise in your anger" (Ps. 7:5) found in the same psalm is only a righteous prayer because it is made against the devil and his angels, not against human beings.[11]

Augustine is careful to make a distinction between human and spiritual enemies, and how it is that we fight them. According to Augustine, when a psalm asks for help in battle or the defeat of the foe, it is calling for the overthrow of Satan, and not the punishment of an earthly adversary. In the example from Ps. 9:4 mentioned above, where the psalmist asks for the Lord to turn back his enemy, he interprets the prayer to be made against the devil.[12] He holds that this is the most fitting interpretation, but he does offer an alternative reading, namely, that "enemy" could refer to a pagan or a sinner more generally. If this kind of enemy is being denoted, however, then the meaning of "turn back" must be modified. To turn back a human enemy is "not a punishment but a kindness, and such a kindness as to be beyond comparison; for what is more blessed than to lay aside pride and not wanting to be in front of Christ?"[13] In other words, the human enemy who is "turned back" is converted, not obliterated. Likewise in Ps. 34, Augustine recognizes that human beings can be our persecutors in this life, and that they

are our enemies, to be sure; but we are taught to recognize other enemies too, against whom we are waging invisible warfare (*inuisibiliter dimicamus*). The apostle warns us about them: "it is not against flesh and blood that you have to struggle" – not against human adversaries, that is, whom you can see, – "but against the principalities and powers and rulers of this world of darkness" (Eph. 6:12). In saying "the rulers of this world" he obviously meant the devil and his angels.[14]

Augustine makes clear that by "flesh and blood" Paul is referring to other human beings, and therefore it is against the principalities, powers and rulers, that is, the devil and his angels, that the true contest takes place. Human persecutors who rob, injure or tempt us are indeed our adversaries, but only insofar as they are "the dark subjects ruled by the devil

[10] Ibid., 7.2.
[11] Ibid., 7.5.
[12] Ibid., 9.4.
[13] Ibid.
[14] Ibid., 31.1.4. For similar interpretations, see *en. Ps.* 76.7 and 143.4.

and his angels."[15] In the case of Ps. 9, therefore, we must understand
that the petition for the defeat of human foes is quite different than the
request that the devil be destroyed. In Ps. 34, the human adversary is
completely subordinated to the devil, and the increase of the righteous
would be – to borrow Augustine's words – the turning back both of evil
people (in conversion) and the devil (in his ultimate defeat and the loss
of his thralls).

In a number of other places Augustine simply asserts that we should
not mistake references to enemies as being references to human beings.
The enemies who were prevented from delighting in the death of Christ
in Ps. 29, for example, are not the Jews; "Hardly," he remarks, rather
these would-be gloaters are "the devil and his angels who fled in confusion when the Lord had risen."[16] Likewise, the prayer of Ps. 141 – "free
me from those who persecute me" – is not a request to be liberated
from human beings who do us harm: "from whom do you think he is
praying to be delivered? From human persecutors? Are human beings our
enemies, then? No, we have other foes, invisible enemies who persecute
us with other ends in view."[17] In Ps. 40, when we pray not to be delivered
into the hands of the enemy, we must understand that

this enemy is the devil. When we hear these words, none of us must refer them
to any human enemy we may have. Perhaps you were thinking of a neighbor, of
someone with whom you had a dispute in court, someone who tried to steal your
goods, or one who is attempting to coerce you into selling your house? No, do not
think along these lines; but refer the verse to the enemy of whom the Lord says
"an enemy has done this" (Matt. 13:28). This enemy is the one who suggests to
us that he should be worshiped to guarantee temporal prosperity.[18]

Augustine is insistent that his congregation understand that the pleas of
the psalmist pertain to a higher order of struggle, rather than to conflicts
with neighbors in the matter of earthly affairs. In fact, it is a typical ploy
of the true enemy to offer temporal prosperity in exchange for worship,
not of God.

In short, as Augustine says in his exposition of Ps. 139, when we suffer
at the hands of a human enemy, it is by the contrivance of the devil.[19]
We must never hate a fellow human being or think of him or her as an
enemy, he explains, but we should despair of correction in the case of the

[15] *en. Ps.* 31.1.4.
[16] Ibid., 29.2.11.
[17] Ibid., 141.14.
[18] Ibid., 40.4.
[19] Ibid., 139.7.

devil alone.[20] In fact, one of the principal ways to defeat the true enemy is never to abandon the love of our human enemies,[21] and, conversely, the one who tries to defeat human foes is in fact being overcome by the devil.[22] Augustine's consistent interpretation of "enemy" (and related terms) in the Psalms is just one example which demonstrates that spiritual warfare is a dominant theme in the *Expositions of the Psalms*, and that the evil angels are not treated as an abstract conception, but tangible spiritual beings whose presence affects our spiritual state on a regular basis. His sense of spiritual struggle and the threat of the devil are immediate and tangible. For example, when the psalmist pleads with God to rescue him from his enemies in Ps. 58, Augustine reminds us that these enemies are "the devil and his angels who constantly, daily, rise up against us and try to dupe us in our weakness and fragility. They are relentless in their attempts to ensnare us by their tricks, promptings, temptations and any traps they can devise, as long as we live on earth."[23]

Augustine understands the struggle against the devil to be real. It is constant and pressing. He therefore encourages his congregants to view their earthly trials through the lens of spiritual warfare rather than understanding them as merely human disputes. But in what ways is the struggle then carried out? We know who the true enemy is, but how does Augustine describe our battle against the devil and his angels?

First and foremost, for Augustine, our spiritual struggle often manifests itself in the daily and mundane resistance of vice, and in particular, pride. The antidote to this pride, and the key to winning a victory over the devil, is to rely on Christ and trust in God. Practically speaking, Augustine recommends prayer, love and certain liturgical practices as ways to strengthen oneself against the foe. He also sets up models for his congregation to follow in their spiritual struggle. Although martyrdom remains a predominant paradigm for understanding the spiritual life long after the time of persecution has ended, Augustine does not quite reimagine the struggle against vice as simply a kind of spiritual martyrdom. Rather, he understands both martyrdom and the resistance of temptation to be battles against the same adversaries, namely, the devil and his angels. The biblical figure of Job serves as his primary exemplar for contemporary Christians in their struggle against Satan. Let us turn to a consideration of these pastoral dimensions of Augustine's preaching on spiritual warfare.

[20] Ibid., 54.4.
[21] Ibid., 54.6. See also *en. Ps.* 93.28.
[22] Ibid., 7.3.
[23] Ibid., 58.1.4.

In general, Augustine often speaks of the devil working through temptation. By a constant and nagging prompting, Satan cultivates certain
desires designed to turn the believer from the right course; the "snake
never tires of whispering suggestions to lure you to iniquity"[24] and works
"through poisonous suggestions to make us lose hope."[25] Augustine often
uses the temptations of greed and temporal security as examples of the
persistent inducements of the devil.[26] Although the Lord teaches honesty,
we protest "how am I to eat then? Handicrafts need a little dishonesty to
succeed, and business cannot flourish without a little fraud."[27] We look at
the wealthy and complain, "that other fellow is rich, and I am poor. I fear
the Lord, but look how much wealth he has amassed by not fearing him,
while I through fearing him have been stripped of everything."[28] We must
resist saying such things to ourselves, Augustine cautions, because in so
doing "we are putting our head into the devil's noose; it tightens round
our throat and the devil holds us enslaved to wrongdoing."[29] If we follow
the devil's course, we will finally imitate the rich man and suffer his fate.
Augustine warns that if you let your love of money guide you, you will
certainly fall prey to the devil, for

when you let your desire lead you, you give the devil his chance. Imagine the
devil has dangled before you an opportunity to make money and invited you to
commit fraud. You can't have the money unless you consent to fraud too. Now
the money is a bait, and the fraud is a snare. Take a good look at the bait, so good
that you detect the snare as well.[30]

Christians must constantly be on guard both against loving the possessions
that they have and so fearing their loss, as well as coveting that which
they do not yet have, because such a desire will lead them into the devil's
trap.[31] This predicament, namely that "good fortune often corrupts the
soul," contributes to the sober realization that "human life on earth is
one long temptation" (cf. Job 7:1).[32] In an inversion of worldly avarice,
Augustine recommends instead that you should "clutch your innocence
like the greedy to a purse, guard it from the thief (i.e. the devil)."[33]

[24] Ibid., 93.20.
[25] Ibid., 3.10.
[26] In addition to the passages cited hereafter, see also *en. Ps.* 40.3–4, 103.4, 118.11.6, 139.1
and 143.5.
[27] *en. Ps.* 33.2.14.
[28] Ibid.
[29] Ibid.
[30] Ibid., 139.12.
[31] See, for example, his description of this dual temptation in *en. Ps.* 62.17 and 141.3–4.
[32] Ibid., 68.1.1.
[33] Ibid., 36.3.15.

There are other temptations which Augustine also attributes to the devil. The temptation to give up on the life of virtue because it is too hard is the very suggestion the devil made to Eve in the garden of Eden.[34] Likewise, iniquitous tongues that aim to convince us that we are too weak or too poor to pursue the path of Christ are instruments of the devil.[35] Various temptations of the eyes can be the devil transforming himself into an angel of light[36] and, as aforementioned, the hatred of human enemies is, at its root, a diabolical suggestion.[37] Physical attacks, such as illness and bodily suffering, as well as the despair that attends to such circumstances are also "often inflicted by Satan's messengers."[38] In other words, the spiritual struggle against the devil and his angels "whose power pervades our atmosphere and dominates the children of unbelief" undergirds all human struggle, the struggle against ourselves, our habits and our daily temptations.[39] These countless temptations, however, are not simply to be understood as the fruit of the devil's maliciousness, who is given free rein over the earth. Temptation, although intended for evil by the devil, is intended for good by God who uses this evil to increase our virtue or to keep from us that which would hinder us spiritually. If we pray to God for some temporal good, for example, and it is withheld from us, it is likely because it would not have been profitable for us to obtain that good. After all, when the devil wanted to tempt Job, the evil one had his request granted, but to his damnation. When Paul asked for the thorn to be removed from his side he was denied, but this was for his salvation.[40]

Whatever the temptation set before us, Augustine tends to subordinate it to that of pride. Our inclination toward greed, or any other sinful behavior, stems from a desire to possess that which belongs to God alone, and to replace God with ourselves. When Augustine encounters the psalmist's request to be "cleansed from the great transgression," he asks: "what else can this be but pride? For there is no greater transgression than apostasy from God and that is the point of departure for all the pride of humanity."[41] Pride is, then, the fundamental sin against which the Christian must strive in spiritual combat, because pride is the devil's

---

[34] Ibid., 47.9.
[35] Ibid., 119.5.
[36] Ibid., 134.20; cf. 2 Cor. 11:14.
[37] *en. Ps.*, 54.5.
[38] Ibid., 130.7.
[39] Ibid., 75.4.
[40] Ibid., 85.9.
[41] Ibid., 18.1.14.

particular sin, and he is the father of it. The psalmist's praise of God – "you broke the dragon's head" – for example, refers to Christ's defeat of the devil's pride,

Listen: "you broke the dragon's head in pieces" (Ps. 73:14). What dragon is meant here? By "dragons" in the plural we understand all the demons who fight under the command of the devil, so who but the devil himself can be meant by the singular dragon whose head was broken to pieces? What did Christ do to him? "You broke the dragon's head in pieces." Its head represents the beginning of sin; and on this head the curse was laid, that Eve's descendants would watch for the head of the serpent (cf. Gen. 3:15). The Church is warned to avoid the beginning of sin, and what else is the beginning of sin, but the serpent's head? We are told that "the starting-point of all sin is pride" (Sir. 10:15). The dragon's head was broken in pieces when the devil's pride was smashed.[42]

Pride is the root of all evil, and it is pride by which the devil fell.[43] Christ has defeated the devil, and our spiritual struggle consists primarily in resisting the diabolical pride which seeks to place the self above others and God. Peter is called Satan because he walked ahead of Christ; he is rebuked and told to get behind,[44] and even Paul, who is a model of virtue, needed the aforementioned thorn in his side to prevent him from becoming prideful.[45] In Ps. 139, the lament "the proud have laid a trap for me" (Ps. 139:5), therefore, perfectly articulates the state of the spiritual battleground, and "the psalm has summed the whole body of the devil in that brief phrase, 'the proud.'"[46] In his further exposition of this psalm, Augustine explains the ways in which the devil's body defines itself: by a dedication to self-righteousness, by its refusal to confess sin, by its envy and by its desire for riches, reputation and the like. In other words, pride is the root of all those mundane, daily temptations which we are required to resist if we wish to conquer the devil and to prevent ourselves from becoming a member of his company. The devil's seduction of Eve, by which he persuaded her to commit the sin of pride, is here the archetype of the attempt which is made against us even now, every day, by the devil and those under his power. Augustine often reminds his congregation of the human temptation to this most grave sin in regard to any spiritual or temporal good one might have; "I cannot emphasize enough

---

[42] Ibid., 73.16.
[43] See *en. Ps.* 120.5.
[44] Ibid., 69.4.
[45] See, for example, *en. Ps.* 130.7.
[46] Ibid., 139.8; *totum corpus diaboli explicauit breuiter, cum ait: superbi.*

to you, beloved, how perilous it is to be proud about any gift received from God."[47]

If Augustine is emphatic about the centrality of the sin of pride, so he is equally sure that the key to defeating the devil is to rely on God. Casting oneself upon God's mercy and imitating Christ, after all, requires humility, which is pride's cure. Those who are willing to "become poor and needy" (Ps. 71:12), that is, to forsake their pride and acknowledge their need for God's power are the ones who will benefit from Christ's victory over the devil,

> Powerful indeed he is who has been called the accuser. Yet it was not his own strength that brought men and women into subjection to this powerful tyrant and kept them there in captivity, but human sins. The powerful tyrant is also called in scripture "the strong man," but Christ, who humiliated the accuser, also broke into the strong man's domain to bind him and seize his possessions. Christ is the one who has "delivered the needy from the tyrant, that poor person who had no other champion," for no one else had the strength to accomplish that – no righteous person nor even an angel. There was no champion at all, therefore; but Christ came and saved them.[48]

Augustine's most important advice for combat against the devil, then, is not to depend on one's own ability to fight, but rather to trust in Christ's power. In several places, he fittingly images this reliance on grace for successful spiritual combat in military language. In Ps. 143, we are told to become the sword in Christ's hand as he slays the devil. Just as David took Goliath's own sword in order to cut off his head, so we who were once under the devil's power and used by him are now wielded by Christ.[49] In Ps. 70, Augustine speaks of our acquiescence to the devil's hints as defection: "we betrayed our commander and rallied to the standard of a deserter."[50] To fight on our own is to desert (pride); instead we should obey the orders issued to us by our commander (obedience). If, as Augustine understands it, our spiritual battle is one of resistance of temptation, and behind every temptation is the demonic inducement to join the proud, then the only way to conquer is in humility. We must face the (perhaps frightening) truth that the devil is stronger than we are,[51]

---

[47] Ibid., 130.7; *quam ergo timenda sit superbia de dono dei, etiam atque etiam commendandum est caritati uestrae.*

[48] Ibid., 71.14.

[49] Ibid., 143.4.

[50] Ibid., 70.2.2.

[51] Ibid., 34.1.15; "Our David will pluck the helpless person out of the strong-handed one, surely. Our David will pluck the helpless person out of the hand of the stronger foe.

and we will only overcome by being obedient to Christ who bound the strong man; "for those who do battle against their entrenched concupiscence, or against the devil and his angels, will not be victorious if they have trusted too much in their own valor."[52]

In more practical terms, Augustine recommends prayer and liturgical practice as fortifications against the devil.[53] Prayer demonstrates our reliance on God to resist temptation and to persist in love of our enemies,

> We are advised that in any trouble we may have, we should not cast about for a retort to make to our enemies, but look to how we may propitiate God by prayer, and especially pray that we not be overcome by temptation. And finally, we are taught to pray that even our persecutors may be brought back to spiritual health and righteousness. There is no greater thing we can do, no better way of dealing with temptation than to withdraw from the hubbub outside and enter the secret recesses of our minds and there call upon God, where no one else sees either the groaning suppliant or the one who comes to our help.[54]

This example of withdrawal and private prayer is set by Christ himself, who suffered the devil's temptations alone for forty days in the desert. Here, then, Augustine draws primarily on Matt. 6:5–13, which both commends private prayer behind a closed door and contains the text of the Lord's prayer. He mentions two features of the Lord's prayer – praying for one's enemies and for the resistance of temptation – and he elsewhere cites the Lord's prayer when speaking about how one ought to combat the devil. Although Christ has conquered the devil and released us from our captivity, still their "attacks on us are possible because they sense in us the residual trace of our weaknesses, those traces concerning which we pray 'forgive us our trespasses' and beg 'lead us not into temptation.'"[55]

Augustine's most frequently cited passage from Matthew's Gospel is, in fact, Matt. 6:12, "forgive us our trespasses as we forgive those who trespass against us," and this verse sums up his advice on spiritual warfare.[56] If we intend to overcome the devil, we must set aside pride and

When the devil captured you he proved the stronger, he overcame you because you consented."
[52] Ibid., 32.1.16.
[53] Gregory Wiebe likewise notes the centrality of the liturgy for engaging in spiritual combat, for Augustine: "incorporation into the church becomes the paradigm for humanity's opposition to demonic powers. In other words, the importance of the engagement with demons is, for Augustine, not its moral nature, *per se*, but rather the containment of that moral struggle within an ecclesial setting." Wiebe, "Demons in the Theology of Augustine," 4.
[54] *en. Ps.* 34.2.3.
[55] Ibid., 105.36.
[56] Matt. 6:12 is cited 295 times in Augustine's corpus, and 6:13 is cited 121 times. The only Gospel citation which exceeds this number is John 1:1 (which he cites 312 times).

recognize our need for God to redeem us from our sinful state, and we must pray for those who have sinned against us. Indeed, those who now oppose us can be won over by the grace proclaimed in this prayer,

> The time will come when there will be thousands of people beating their breasts and saying: "forgive us our trespasses as we forgive those who trespass against us" (Matt. 6:12). Even today, how few are left who are too ashamed to beat their breasts! Let these few find fault with us; we can bear with them. Let them find fault, hate us, accuse us and defame us: "wait a little, and my prayer will be very popular among them" (Ps. 140:5). The time will come when they will eagerly have recourse to my prayer. At first, they will arrogantly present themselves to be righteous by their own efforts, but they will be worsted in the struggle (*uincentur in lucta*) and then, because they reared up in their pride, they will be thrown down and dragged by their sins ... the keenest insight of their minds will be directed to their guilt, and they will seize with relief on the prayer "forgive us our trespasses as we forgive those who trespass against us."[57]

Augustine sees both communal and private acts of worship as acts of humility; the Lord's prayer is no exception. Since our chief sin is pride, and it is pride by which the devil fell, it naturally follows that prayer should heal us from this proclivity in particular. One of Augustine's favorite liturgical demonstrations of humility is the *sursum corda* invitation of the eucharistic liturgy.[58] In *City of God*, for example, he sees the response to these words as a communal renunciation of pride. Adam's fall was caused by his desire to live according to himself, he explains, and "therefore the holy scriptures designate the proud by another name, 'self-pleasers' (*sibi placentes*). For it is good to have the heart lifted up, yet not to one's self, for this is proud (*bonum est enim sursum habere cor; non tamen ad se ipsum, quod est superbiae*), but to the Lord, for this is obedient, and can be the act only of the humble."[59] In the *Expositions of the Psalms*, the message is similar; "it is not to earth but to the Lord that we are ordered to have our hearts raised (*sursum corda habere iubemur ad Dominum*)."[60]

---

[57] *en. Ps.* 140.18.

[58] This invitation is now commonly referred to as the *sursum corda*, and Augustine does sometimes use the plural, but in Augustine's liturgy the invitation appears to have been in the singular (*sursum cor*). For an overview of Augustine's eucharistic liturgy see Burns and Jensen, *Christianity in Roman Africa*, 261–287.

[59] *civ. Dei* XIV.13.

[60] *en. Ps.* 10.3. In this passage, as in Augustine's reflection on the Lord's prayer, having one's heart raised to the Lord reflects a kind of hiddenness; the prayer is directed toward God and not to other people. Prayer is here imaged by the dark side of the moon: prayer can be seen only by our conscience and by God, whereas good works are the light that radiate to everyone (in this analogy, the moon with both of its sides, represents the church).

The *sursum corda* appears explicitly in the context of spiritual warfare as well, in passages which have much the same character as others we have already seen. When we lift up our heart to the Lord, it means we renounce worldly attachment and therefore greed.[61] Lifting up your heart, then, means not loving the world, which in its present state is ruled by the dominions and powers of Satan.[62] Twice in the *Expositions of the Psalms*, Augustine uses the healing of the crippled woman (Luke 13:10–17) to explain how the *sursum corda* proclaims the devil's defeat.[63] This woman was bent over, he says, held captive by Satan and looking only toward earthly things for some eighteen years, but "no one who has heard and heeded the invitation 'lift up your hearts' can have a bent back. An erect stance characterizes one who looks to the hope laid up for us in heaven."[64] So when we proclaim our hearts are lifted up we proclaim that "we aren't bent double … always looking for earthly things," but rather that this weighty penalty which "comes from the domination of the devil" has been taken away, and so we can now look toward heaven.[65] The *sursum corda*, for Augustine, therefore, is like prayer in that it is an exhortation to humility, but it is also an affirmation of the fact that Christ has already healed us and enabled us to fix our eyes on heaven rather than earth.

In another passage from the *Expositions of the Psalms*, Augustine uses both the congregational response to the *sursum corda* and the rite of baptism to describe how we have escaped the devil's "flock,"

> Those who make themselves the devil's allies have death for their shepherd: but we whose thoughts are on future immortality and with good reason wear the sign of Christ on our foreheads (*in fronte signum crucis Christi portamus*) have no shepherd except life itself … What? Are we in heaven already? Yes, we are in heaven through our faith, if we are not what becomes of the invitation, 'lift up your heart' (*sursum cor*)?[66]

For Augustine, therefore, one's ongoing participation in the eucharistic liturgy, and the victory over Satan which it celebrates, is linked to baptismal identity. The sign of the cross to which he refers is the anointing of the forehead at baptism,[67] although there is no indication that this sermon

---

[61] See, *en. Ps.*39.28, 80.21, 90.2.13, 96.10 and 104.28.
[62] *en. Ps.* 141.15.
[63] See *en. Ps.* 37.10 and 68.2.8. The same analogy appears in *s. Dolbeau* 17.5–6, cited below.
[64] *en. Ps.* 68.2.8
[65] *s. Dolbeau* 17.6.
[66] *en. Ps.* 48.2.2.
[67] That Augustine is thinking of the baptismal rite is clear from the opening passage of the homily; see *en. Ps.* 48.2.1 and the ensuing footnote. For a summary of the baptismal

is being given to neophytes or is written for some baptismal occasion.[68] Rather, Augustine is alluding to the indelible seal, now invisible, left by the baptismal signing on the foreheads of his congregants.[69] Through baptism and the Eucharist (i.e. the rites of initiation), the Christian has been released from the clutches of Satan and now belongs to Christ, and the Eucharist continues to cultivate virtue in the baptized, allowing them to resist future temptation.

That baptism should come to Augustine's mind in this context is no surprise, since the renunciation of the devil was part of the North African baptismal liturgy from quite early,[70] and he refers to baptism as the means by which we are set free from the devil's bondage.[71] Following many exegetes before him, Augustine often uses the exodus as an allegory for our release from the devil's captivity through water.[72] He also interprets the postbaptismal anointing – the seal on the forehead – as a preparation for combat; the baptizand is being oiled like a wrestler for his or her struggle against the devil.[73] This understanding is not unique to Augustine, as associating the oil with spiritual combat is a common motif found elsewhere in writers of East and West, but it fits naturally with his

rite in Augustine's time, see Max Johnson, *The Rites of Christian Initiation* (Liturgical Press: Collegeville, 1999), 186–189.

[68] Augustine is prompted to reflect on baptism by the words of the psalm "their later doings are even worse than what they did earlier" (Ps. 48:14). He understands this to refer to people who are baptized but backslide into sin, sin which is now all the greater because their wickedness is hidden "under a veil of piety."

[69] He refers to this invisible sign elsewhere as being the mark which distinguishes the initiated from the pagan, but it does not guarantee good conduct or salvation. See, for example, *en. Ps.* 69.2. See also *en. Ps.* 59.9.

[70] By the fourth century, the renunciation of Satan was part of the prebaptismal rite in both East and West, but its earliest attestation comes from Cyprian and Tertullian in North Africa. For a helpful summary of pre-Nicene baptismal rites, see Johnson, *Rites of Christian Initiation*, 111. Augustine himself alludes to the repudiations before baptism in a few places in the *Expositions of the Psalms*; see *en. Ps.* 44.12, 44.25–26, 80.18–19 and 150.3.

[71] The prebaptismal rites also included exorcisms and exsufflation, further highlighting baptism's effect of driving out the devil. As Jane Merdinger has shown, Augustine (especially as a young priest) was incensed by the Donatists' practice of the re-exsufflation of Catholic converts. How could these people who have already received the Holy Spirit still need to have the devil driven out? See Merdinger, "In League with the Devil? Donatist and Catholic Perspective on Pre-baptismal Exsufflation" in *The Uniquely African Controversy*, ed. Anthony Dupont et al. (Leuven: Peeters, 2015), 153–179.

[72] In the *Expositions of the Psalms*, Augustine employs this analogy a number of times. For example, see *en. Ps.* 72.5, 113.1.4 and 135.9.

[73] See, for example, *Jo. ev. tr.* 33.3; "for the name of Christ comes from anointing (*chrisma*): it is called chrism (χρῖσμα) in Greek and unction (*unctio*) in Latin. Therefore he anointed us, because he makes us wrestlers against the devil (*luctatores contra diabolum*)."

understanding of the liturgy and prayer as the practical preparation for spiritual combat.[74]

In addition to highlighting prayer and liturgy as activities in which we ought to participate in order to engage successfully in spiritual warfare, Augustine also offers his congregation examples of those who have successfully waged war against the devil. The most obvious choice for such an exemplar is the martyrs, and Augustine does refer to martyrdom in the context of spiritual warfare a number of times in these psalm homilies. The way in which the martyrs serve as our model, however, is not so direct as we might imagine. Augustine does not often speak of resisting temptation in the terms of martyrdom, nor does he directly apply the imagery of martyrdom to the contemporary struggle against vice.[75] The martyrs surely fought the devil and won, and they did so by relying on God just as we must do.[76] The devil, however, has changed his tactics since these early days of persecution. Augustine explains this shift in the devil's strategy by describing the devil as both a lion and a snake. In the time of persecution the devil was a lion, raging against the church and attempting to devour it, but then he became the snake, using deception and seducing those within the church in order to undermine it.[77] In some ways, he says, the assault the devil makes in the later time is even more

---

[74] See Johnson, *Rites of Christian Initiation*, 188. As Johnson notes, most commentators associate the oil for combat with the prebaptismal anointing, not the postbaptismal anointing as Augustine does. This association suggests that Augustine conceptualizes baptism and anointing as preparation for our future struggle against temptation, rather than thinking of the prebaptismal anointing as a preparation for the spiritual combat which takes place in the font.

[75] Even when Augustine notes that he is preaching on a feast day, he does not always take advantage of the opportunity to use the martyrs as an exemplar. He often spends more time meditating on Christ, whose example the martyrs follow. See, for example, *en. Ps.* 40.9–10.

[76] Direct exhortations to imitation are sparing. Augustine, however, calls us to imitate the martyrs by imitating Christ; see a good example in *en. Ps.* 69.1–4. Given that reliance on God is central to his teaching on spiritual warfare, the martyrs do provide a good example of this principle in practice. The martyrs receive help to defeat the devil by imitating and depending on Christ; see *en. Ps.* 40.1, 63.1–2, 90.1.10, 108.33 and 141.4. That humility is required by the martyrs is discussed elsewhere, for example, in *civ. Dei* v. Here, Augustine comments that if the Romans were able to perform heroic and selfless acts for the glory of an earthly city, the martyrs should be all the more humble in their service; "let not the martyrs carry themselves proudly, as though they had done some meritorious thing for a share in that country where are eternal life and felicity, if even to the shedding of their blood, loving not only the brethren for whom is was shed, but, according as had been commanded them, even their enemies by whom it was being shed, they have vied with one another in faith of love and love of faith" (*civ. Dei* v.18). As in his Psalm homilies, the contest of the martyrs, the struggle in which they have overcome, is one of faith.

[77] See *en. Ps.* 39.1, 40.4 and 90.2.9.

dangerous, because it is more subtle and includes attacks from those with the appearance of piety.[78] Our solidarity with the martyrs, then, primarily comes from the fact that we are fighting the same enemy, and we have the common ally of Christ; "God did not hand the martyrs over to sinners, because they were not handed over by their own will. Pray then, with all your might, pray that God will not hand you over to a sinner by your own desire. When you let desire lead you, you give the devil his chance."[79] In both cases, we must resist the desire to hand ourselves over to the devil. In the case of the martyrs, this meant refusing to yield to the violence inflicted on them and to renounce Christ, and resisting the temptation to ascribe this accomplishment to themselves instead of to God. For us, it means refusing to yield to the temptations inflicted on us and follow false desires, and also recognizing, like the martyrs, that we are too weak to resist such temptation without God. For Augustine, then, private moral temptation should not be thought of as a less glorious contest than that of martyrdom, but a parallel struggle,

Many people are valiant when they endure persecution from human beings who are raging against them openly. They are aware that they are imitating Christ's sufferings when people persecute them outright; but if they are buffeted by hidden persecution from the devil, they think they are unworthy to be crowned by Christ. But you must not be afraid to be like Christ in this matter. When the devil tempted the Lord in the desert no one else was present. The devil tempted him in secret and was defeated, just as he was defeated when he raged openly.[80]

Martyrdom is the imitation of Christ's suffering on the cross, where the devil was defeated once for all. But in our struggle against temptation, we also imitate Christ who fought the same enemy in another way. As in the case of private prayer, Augustine holds up the solitary trial of Christ in the desert as an example for us when we consider how to carry out our own daily spiritual contest.

Christ in his humanity, therefore, is always the premier exemplar for both the martyr and for Augustine's congregation. In his assumed weakness Christ has provided "every soldier with a model how to fight."[81] In the

---

[78] See, for example, ibid., 69.2.
[79] Ibid., 139.12. Augustine makes a similar comparison in *en. Ps.* 36.3.12. The martyrs were saved because God did not allow them to be betrayed by their own desire, and we should hope for the same. This somewhat circuitous phrasing is consonant with Augustine's understanding of sin. We can only be captured by the devil through our own freely experienced consent. This is true in spite of the fact that we are not fully free from the first, due to original sin, so that we cannot choose God without his assistance.
[80] *en. Ps.* 90.1.1.
[81] Ibid., 29.2.7.

passage cited above, however, Augustine also goes on to single out a biblical figure after whom we might pattern our hidden struggle with temptation: Job.[82] Job is set up as a model of successful spiritual combat much more frequently than the martyrs, and Augustine uses the story of Job to reinforce or exemplify many aspects of his teaching on spiritual warfare.

First, Job faced a series of hardships which are typical of the devil's plot against all Christians: loss of worldly property and of health, as well as enduring the verbal abuse of other human beings.[83] Following his usual pattern, Augustine highlights the temptation of greed which Job endured, and he is fond of using Job as an example of someone who proved he did not love his own property. On a number of occasions, he cites Job 1:9 – the words of the devil, "Job hardly worships the Lord for nothing, does he (*numquid Iob gratis colit deum*)?" – as a representation of the challenge put to every Christian, namely, are we willing to worship God with worldly disinterest (or *gratis*, as Augustine likes to say, echoing the biblical text)?[84] Job was very wealthy and lost everything, yet he resisted the devil's temptation to covet his lost property and turn against God. Job also endures the trial of sickness, so that not only Job's property is threatened but even his own body, covered in sores. Job, moreover, is tempted to despair by others around him, particularly by his wife. Augustine likes to pair Job with Adam and Job's wife with Eve, since Job's wife urges him: "Curse God, and die" (Job 2:9). Job, however, refuses his wife's fatal suggestion, and responds that he must accept both good and bad from the Lord.[85]

Secondly, Job understands the true profit of temptation. Job does not ever see the devil and does not know the conditions under which God has allowed him to be tempted, but Job confesses that it is God who has permitted misfortune to befall him, and he does not curse God.[86] Augustine cites Job 1:21 – "the Lord gave, and the Lord has taken away; blessed be

---

[82] Ibid., 90.1.2.

[83] Augustine often speaks loosely of these three as the temptations of Job, but he divides them clearly into these three successive trials in *en. Ps.* 103.4.6–7.

[84] See *en. Ps.* 55.19–20, 71.7, 104.40, 118.11.16, 118.12.4 and 118.26.4.

[85] Augustine is fond of this parallel and likes to commend the Adam-on-the-dunghill (i.e. Job) who was able to resist where the Adam-in-paradise failed. See, for example, *en. Ps.* 47.9 and 103.4.6–7. His congregation must have been quite familiar with the analogy, since in one case he refers to Job's wife as Eve without explanation (*en. Ps.* 133.2).

[86] We may disagree with Augustine's interpretation of Job, and he acknowledges that some people interpret Job's discourse to contain harsh words against God. To these people, he responds that they have misinterpreted the biblical text and he offers some examples to counter their view (see *en. Ps.* 103.4.7–8).

the name of the Lord" – as proof of the fact that the devil has no power unless permitted by God, and that in all his suffering Job still "had a heart full of God (*deo plenum cor habebat*)."[87] Job recognizes that God is in control of all temptations and trials, whose purpose is to condemn the unjust and prove the righteous.[88] Job's attitude, therefore, also exemplifies the need for God's assistance to combat the devil, because both the ultimate source of the temptation and the power to overcome it rests with God. As in the exposition of Ps. 143 discussed above, the cooperation of Job with God's grace is described in terms of Job being fashioned into God's weapon: "The tempted man emerged victorious and the tempter was vanquished. God had allowed the devil to take Job's goods away, but he had not inwardly abandoned his servant, and out of his servant he should fashion for himself a sword to defeat the devil."[89] Job's submission to God's trial, and his remarkable ability to endure such extreme suffering, is nothing less than "a powerful grace from God (*magna gratia dei*)."[90] Job was totally reliant on this grace, since "God himself had given what was now being given back to him; he himself endowed Job with the means of offering him the kind of sacrifice he desires [i.e. the sacrifice of the heart]."[91] Also following the general pattern of Augustine's teaching on spiritual warfare, this grace of God which defeats the devil manifests in nothing other than Job's humility, humility which is expressed in Job's ceaseless act of worship. It is Job's ability to praise God always which proves he is not overcome by the devil, and Job demonstrates this by referring both his losses and his blessings to God. Job receives God's grace (*gratia*) in order to respond in worship "for nothing" (*gratis*). Augustine interprets a reference in Ps. 133 to praising God in the evening as an imperative to worship God even in times of trial.[92] The perfect example

---

[87] *en. Ps.* 120.8.
[88] This is the most common lesson which Augustine's draws from Job's ordeal; the devil has power only as far as he is permitted, and temptation has a divine purpose. See, for example, *en. Ps.* 21.2.5, 29.2.6–8, 34.1.7, 36.1.11, 55.19–20, 77.28, 90.1.1–2, 96.12, 97.6, 103.3.22, 103.4.6–8 and 103.4.11.
[89] *en. Ps.* 34.1.7. In another psalm, Augustine uses a similar analogy. He describes the trials of Job as a hammer pounding him into a ductile trumpet on which the note of grace is sounded, see *en. Ps.* 97.6.
[90] *en. Ps.* 133.2. See also *en. Ps.* 144.18–19.
[91] Ibid., 55.19.
[92] Although we have no distinctively liturgical language here, it is perhaps no coincidence that Ps. 133 was used in the West for evening prayer. When the congregation prays this prayer, then, they are emulating Job (and angels, as explained in chapter 1). The reference to Job's sacrifice of praise mentioned in *en. Ps.* 55.19 is also colored with liturgical

166

Augustine and Spiritual Warfare

of this behavior is, of course, Job, who praised God in the gloomiest of nights; "truly he must have praised always if he praised then," Augustine declares.[93] Like Job, we must believe God's mercy never leaves us, and make up our mind to praise God no matter the circumstance. Only then will we reap the profit of overcoming temptation and be victorious in our combat against the devil. In short, as Augustine says, "what God seeks from you is praise. Your confession is what God demands of you."[94]

Lastly, Augustine understands the figure of Job to have symbolic or allegorical value as a model. Just as the devil's constant attempt to coerce us to pride is a repetition of the suggestion made in the garden of Eden, so Job serves as a type of Adam who overcomes this temptation even in the most adverse circumstances. Job therefore prefigures Christ while remaining a real human being who withstood the temptation into which the first Adam fell. Job may also have been favored by Augustine in his sermons in particular because he considers Job to be an example of a righteous lay person. In his exposition on Ps. 132, Augustine explains that the psalm's reference to the three figures Noah, Daniel and Job is an allusion to the three classes of people in the church.[95] These three also correspond to the three types of people who are mentioned in Matt. 24:40–41: the workers in the field, the men in their beds and the women at the mill. All of these three are divided in judgment, with some being taken and the others left. The first class is the cleric. Clerics work in God's field and are symbolized by Noah, who led the people in the ark and established sacrifice. The second class, the men in bed, are ascetics who recline at peace from the world and are symbolized by Daniel. The last class is the laity. They are the women working at the mill, which is the business of the world. This last group is symbolized by Job, who was married and suffered temptation precisely by being deprived of his worldly wealth and family, and by the false words of his friends and his wife; that is, he suffered the kinds of temptations which were undoubtedly familiar to the churchgoers at Hippo.

Although the overcoming of persecution remains important for Augustine's conception of the church's struggle against the devil, and the courageous acts of the martyrs sometimes serve as inspiration in his sermons, he favors Job as an example for his congregation to follow in

language of sacrifice, which is similar to Augustine's description of the eucharistic sacrifice in book x of *City of God* discussed in chapter 2.
[93] *en. Ps.* 144.4.
[94] Ibid., 55.19 (*laudem a te quaerit deus, confessionem tuam quaerit deus*).
[95] See ibid.,132.4–5.

their present spiritual struggle. Job faces the mundane temptations which Augustine understands to come from the devil and which daily vex believers – the temptation to love money, health and family more than God. Job performs this heroic feat not by any outward physical act, but by constantly praising God through his affliction with divine aid. In these ways, Job's struggle with and defeat of the devil encapsulates Augustine's teaching on spiritual warfare.

The Role of Good Angels in Spiritual Warfare

When preaching about spiritual warfare Augustine emphasizes our reliance on God, as we have seen. Christ is always the soldier contending against the devil and he alone is the victor. Augustine, therefore, tends not to highlight the martyrs' personal virtue in overcoming their persecutors, but God's triumph in and through them. We should marvel at the gift given to strengthen these combatants and be assured that God can grant us the same strength as well, if we rely on him.[96] In this Christocentric view of spiritual warfare, the good angels are not understood to wage war against the devil on our behalf, since no one can defeat the devil except for Christ, no one but he can bind the strong man, "no righteous person nor even an angel."[97] As noted in chapter 2, moreover, although Augustine does not explicitly reject the doctrine of guardian angels, he virtually never mentions the possibility of personal angelic companionship, despite its popularity elsewhere in the Christian world. In the *Expositions of the Psalms*, he refers to the angelic protection of human beings only once. We are on our way to becoming angels of God,[98] Augustine explains, but until that time "there are angels who can deride the dragon and prevent him from hurting you (*sunt angeli qui illudant draconi, ne tibi noceat*)."[99] As the Latin shows, even this reference to angelic protection is vague. The angels mock the devil "lest he harm you" (*ne tibi noceat*). It is unclear how the derision of the devil provides us any protection, and Augustine certainly does not employ any military imagery of good angels waging war against the demons, nor does he describe further the conditions under which holy angels might be said to prevent harm from coming to

---

[96] See, for example, *en. Ps.* 108.33. The martyrs are proof of the assistance Christ will provide to his body.

[97] *en. Ps.* 71.4.

[98] On what it means for us to be angels of God, see chapter 2.

[99] *en. Ps.* 103.4.9.

us. In *On the Spirit and the Letter*, Augustine recognizes that the angels
are capable of fighting, but in the case of Christ's contest against the devil
they were not permitted, according to Matt. 26:53. He mentions this
fact only in passing, however, as he is using this verse from Matthew's
Gospel as an example of something which is possible even if it did not
actually occur; "you may read [i.e. in Matt. 26:53], too, that twelve thousand legions of angels could possibly have fought for Christ and rescued
him from suffering, but in fact did not."[100] In *en. Ps.* 117, he mentions
that good angels (and good people) can help us with genuine love, but
we must remember that "God who made them good in their measure is
helping us through their agency."[101]

The good angels are an example in the spiritual struggle in the same way
the martyrs are. The angels, like the martyrs, have power because they rely
entirely on Christ. The good angels cling to God, and in this orientation
they are the perfect models of worship and humility. Augustine describes the
saints, martyrs and angels all as adhering to Christ,[102] and, like the angels,
the martyrs obtain strength from looking to Christ,

Today is a festal celebration in honor of the passions of our holy martyrs. Let us
rejoice in commemorating them, and as we remember what they suffered, let us
understand where they fixed their gaze; for they could never have endured such
dreadful agony in their flesh if they had not been flooded with immense peace in
their minds.[103]

As is typical for him, even on a martyr's feast day, Augustine focuses on
a discussion of the Lord's passion as the inspiration for the martyr.[104]
By contemplating Christ, therefore, we do what the martyrs do, that
is, fix our gaze on Christ, rather than extol the particular heroic acts
of the martyrs themselves. Although Augustine does not conflate angel
with martyr, they are in some ways closely linked. Angels and martyrs
both obtain beatitude with God's help, and angels are therefore fittingly
imagined by Augustine as rewarding the martyrs or celebrating with
them. In both *City of God* and *On the Care of the Dead*, he suggests
that the angels help accomplish the miracles attributed to martyrs.[105]

---

[100] *spir. et. litt.* 1.
[101] *en. Ps.* 117.5.
[102] For an example of saints, martyrs and angels being described in this way, see *s. Dolbeau* 26.24 (here the verb *cohaerere* is used).
[103] *en. Ps.* 63.1.
[104] See Boulding's comment to this effect in her footnote to *en. Ps.* 63.1.
[105] *civ. Dei* XXII.9 and *cura mort.* 20.

As in the case of Perpetua and Felicity, the angels receive the martyrs in their glory after death,[106] and angels recognize the martyrs' crown in heaven.[107] And, as Augustine frequently likes to remind us, the angels and martyrs both prefer God to themselves, and refuse all worship that would be given to them.[108]

We are kept humble, therefore, by coming to understand that even the good angels rely on Christ to fight the devil, and humility is critical to our success in spiritual warfare, as we have seen; good angels have more power than demons do, but that is because they are aligned with Christ.[109] The martyrs, whose title, after all, means "witness," are able to answer prayer because they can ask favors from the one in whose name they were slain.[110] As icons of worship, as I have called the holy angels in chapter 2, the angels serve as the highest example of how we ought to conduct ourselves in spiritual warfare, since worship (in prayer and liturgy) and reliance on God is the foundation of any attempt to overcome the devil. As with the martyrs, however, Augustine does not frequently exhort us to direct imitation of the angels, nor does he mention their prowess at resisting the devil as a model for our own struggles.

There is one activity, however, in which the angels engage with respect to spiritual warfare. Taking his cue from Job 40:14 [LXX] ("this is the beginning of the creation of the Lord, which he made to be sport to his angels") and Job 41:24 [LXX] ("there is nothing like him on earth, made for my angels to deride"), Augustine understands the angels to have the special mandate in the present time of mocking the devil. We may have thought, he remarks, that God himself should wish to deride the devil, but Job tells us that he has handed over the mocking of the devil to others.[111] Augustine understands this mocking of the devil not as some kind of verbal abuse done by angels, but rather as a reference to the repeated failure of the devil's plans. When the devil's temptations and attacks result in our salvation rather than our destruction, the devil is derided; "the way he is made fun of is by his temptations being of benefit

---

[106] *s.* 280.4.
[107] *s. Denis* 16.1.
[108] See a lengthy discussion of this point in *s. Dolbeau* 26.46–48.
[109] Augustine discusses the strength of angels over demons and related topics in a number of places. For example, he says that angels can perform more miraculous things than demons (*civ. Dei* XXI.6) and that if you think the devil is powerful, you should think whence he fell (*en. Ps.* 103.4.9).
[110] *civ. Dei* XXII.9.
[111] *en. Ps.* 103.4.9. He also connects Ps. 103:26 with Job. 40:14 in *loc. in Hept.* 2.51 and *Gn. litt.* XI.27.

to the saints when he strives to debauch them by these means, so that malice, which he himself deliberately chose to be in the grip of, might prove useful against his will to the servants of the God who fashioned him with this in mind."[112] Declaring that the devil is the angels' sport "from the beginning," therefore, speaks to God's foreknowledge that the devil would fall, but also to the great good that would be brought about from his defection, namely the testing and refining of the saints.[113] Although the good angels presumably have not profited from the devil's sin, other than, perhaps, by being proved his better by it, still they mock the devil in our stead until that time when we too have proved true when tested.[114] In the meantime we should take care that we are not given over to our own desire, lest we instead become the laughingstock of the devil.[115]

The image of the good angels laughing at the devil is really another intimation of grace, perhaps we might say, on the far side. The angels, martyrs, saints and we who follow them conquer the devil not by our own strength, but by relying on God. Although the angels were not permitted to fight the devil, and Christ alone conquered him, it is still the angels who receive the charge of mocking the devil, and one day we will join them in this triumph. So we earn victory over the devil through God, but by God's leave we also fully experience that victory as our own because we are the ones who deride the devil in the very process of profiting from his evil. In a final act of self-emptying, we might say, Christ gives over to his angels – and then even to us – the privilege of mocking the devil which he alone merited by his death. This angelic derision is yet another image of both angelic worship and reciprocity, which has been highlighted throughout this study. Since the angels are aligned to the will of God and rely on his strength for their own, they are given back in their turn the privilege of mocking the devil which they did not earn, but which becomes their own.

The Theology of Spiritual Warfare

Having sketched Augustine's teaching on spiritual warfare in his psalm homilies, and the roles played by angels, demons, martyrs and saints in the everyday struggle against the devil, let us now turn to a consideration

[112] *Gn. litt.* XI.29.
[113] This interpretation of Job appears both in *civ. Dei* XI.15–17 and *Gn. litt.* XI.27–29.
[114] *en. Ps.* 103.4.9.
[115] See, for example, *c. Iul.* 5.11.

of his theology more broadly speaking, and discover how his teaching on spiritual warfare relates to the other aspects of his thought and to his other works. Although tuned to pastoral needs and audience, Augustine's teaching on spiritual warfare in these homilies is consistent with his ideas about the heavenly and earthly city present in *City of God* and elsewhere. In the *Expositions of the Psalms* as in other works, he identifies pride as the main sin of the devil, as well as of the demons and human beings under the power of the devil. In other words, pride is the sin which is the root of all cosmic and political disorder, but also disorder in one's everyday life. This emphasis on pride allows him to maintain his distinction between human and demonic enemies both in *City of God* and the *Expositions of the Psalms*. Since Augustine sees pride as the organizing (or, we might say, disorganizing) principle of the earthly city, he is able to develop a communal vision both of sin and repentance. Although we experience individual temptation, our trials often arise from the brokenness of society, and, conversely, it is through the communal life of the church that we may resist temptation. Ultimately, then, we return to the heart of Augustine's angelology, that is, to worship. The angelic life is characterized by perfect worship, and worship, being the chief act of the humble, is the only way for us to defeat the devil and his pride. In a more practical sense, this means, for Augustine, that one must avoid all magical and superstitious rites and instead participate in the rites of true worship.

As seen above, although Augustine identifies various enticements with the machinations of the devil, these temptations are all subordinated to that of pride. The desire to be self-reliant and self-worshiping leads us to distort proper relations with our neighbors, it leads us to covet property, to deceive others and to use our power over others for our own gain. This inducement to pride, however, is not merely individualistic, but it manifests as a communal act of self-destruction and disunity.[116] Augustine speaks this way both in the *Expositions of the Psalms* and *City of God*. In his exposition of Ps. 139, he explains that the devil and his whole city are denoted by the term "the proud,"

"The proud have hidden a trap for me" (Ps. 139:5). The Psalm has summed up the whole body of the devil in that brief phrase "the proud." It is pride that most

---

[116] The communal aspect of Augustine's teaching on spiritual warfare is characteristic of his spirituality more broadly. As Mary Clark writes of Augustinian spirituality: "It is interior and social, involving the individual and society. Like the Trinity, man's life with God is an interior one while being wholly relational." See Mary T. Clark, "Augustinian Spirituality," *Augustinian Studies* 15 (1986), 84.

often drives the devil's followers to proclaim themselves righteous when they are sinful. It is also because of this pride that they hate nothing more than confessing their sins. Bogus pretenders to justice as they are, they envy the truly just, for no one envies any quality in another unless he wants to possess it himself or at least to be thought to possess it ... the sham pretenders to righteousness want to appear righteous and holy, whereas they are not: and when they see someone who is truly righteous they necessarily envy him and deal with him in such a way as to make him lose the very endowment that is his glory, if they can.[117]

Pride is an attitude which not only leads to the coveting of material property, but also of righteousness. It not only induces us to appear better than our neighbor, but even to make our neighbor seem worse and to make sin appear like righteousness. Here, Augustine is counseling his congregation on how to conduct their everyday affairs and to avoid envy, since by begrudging beauty, wealth and success in another, you will not thereby gain it for yourself. But the view of pride here presented, as that which breaks down community at its most basic level by turning us against each other, is precisely how he describes pride in the less pastoral context of *City of God*. As discussed at length in chapter 2, the earthly city is united in its disunity. In imitation of the devil, every member of the earthly city builds up praise for him or herself. The appearance of goodness, which Augustine characterizes as the ultimate prize of the devil and his adherents in the homilies, is also a most powerful attraction for the proud in *City of God*. In the opening passage of *City of God*, he notes that, although proud, Rome loves nothing more than to appear humble. He demonstrates this hypocrisy by observing that Romans are proud of a passage in Virgil's *Aeneid*, which ironically proclaims their humility; "the inflated ambition of a proud spirit also affects, and dearly loves that this be numbered among its attributes, 'show pity to the humbled soul and crush the sons of pride.' "[118] The devil also ensnares the wise and powerful by an appeal to this same vanity. Theurgists, for example, are persuaded that they have special and superior knowledge through which they can curry favor with the divine. The devil induces them to their so-called craft by the illusion of wisdom, virtue and power.[119]

Whether encouraging his congregation to avoid the love of riches and to pursue the course of justice, or characterizing the Roman empire as one which has been dominated by proud demons, Augustine appeals to the same theological notion of pride. Pride is both an individual sin

---

[117] *en. Ps.* 139.8.
[118] *civ. Dei* I.1.
[119] See *civ. Dei* II. 26 and X.28. Theurgy is discussed at greater length in chapter 2.

perpetuated by our own consent to prideful deeds and attitudes, whether this be the attitude of the philosophers in coveting their own knowledge over Christ's humble way (as in *City of God*) or our tendency to defraud our neighbors for our own profit (as in the psalm homilies), but it is also the sin upon which our entire earthly society is built. In the case of *City of God*, Augustine is attempting to demonstrate that Rome, which is one manifestation of the city of the devil, is trapped in a false economy of worship, wherein not only every person, but also the Roman empire as a whole, attempts to attract glory and praise to itself rather than God (especially the glory of feigned virtue). In the case of the *Expositions of the Psalms*, he often mentions that our society is built on a system of pride which rewards the love of self. For example, fraud in business quite often results in success in business.[120] He describes the earthly cities in which the devil rules as places where "deceitful and fraudulent purposes have approached the status of government (*ciuitates autem in quibus diabolus regnat, ubi dolosa et fraudulenta consilia tamquam curiae locum obtinent*)."[121] Our temptation to commit fraud then is individual, but also the result of a fraudulent, demonic society. He laments that even many Christians have become persuaded that they can fully participate in this prideful economy and lust after worldly wealth, while still relying on God for eternal life in the hereafter. Augustine, however, reminds his congregation that this attitude is completely false and that such Christians in reality seek security from the devil, who tricks us into thinking that God does not care about earthly affairs.[122] That the sin of pride is both personal and communal is applicable to his view of daily spiritual warfare and to his conception of the sinfulness of the earthly city at large, and it allows him to maintain the nuanced view of the spiritual life we have seen him espousing. He insists that Satan is our enemy and not human beings, while at the same time confronting the real and personal nature of the devil's temptations.

By identifying pride as the basic attitude of the earthly city under the devil's dominion, Augustine is able to teach the lesson that our spiritual battle is waged against the devil alone, and he interprets the psalms that pray for the defeat of the foe (such as the psalms of imprecation) in that light. As we have seen, he is adamant that when we are perfected in the spiritual struggle, we can identify our true adversaries and will not be tempted to hate our human enemies, but rather to pray and hope for their

---

[120] See *en. Ps.* 33.2.14.
[121] Ibid., 9.8.
[122] See ibid., 26.2.19 and 40.3.

salvation. For Augustine's flock, this means that the temptations they face in their earthly lives are real and difficult, but ultimately fought invisibly. Gaining a victory over a human enemy is not to be conflated with winning a spiritual battle. In fact, such earthly victories can be both hollow and dangerous, and can signal that we are falling into the devil's prideful trap by finding satisfaction in gaining power over other human beings.[123] On a larger scale, this is the same paradigm we find in the *City of God* – the Romans in and of themselves are not the ultimate foes of the church, but rather the demons, who are the true rulers of their empire. This view of Rome prevents Augustine from espousing an overly triumphalistic view of the Christianization of the Roman empire which was popular with some theologians of his time. Just as defeating our earthly foes cannot be equated easily with a spiritual triumph, so the overcoming of Rome does not signal a spiritual victory of Christianity in the world. When the open raging of the devil against the church has ceased, Augustine warns, more insidious attacks begin, such as the attacks of heresy.[124] Once we recognize the destabilizing force of pride, however, we are able to identify its origin, who is the devil, and to resist his overtures even when they come through another human being. It allows Augustine to identify pride as a personal sin, one in which all the devil's followers are complicit, without thereby making those individuals our personal enemies. Our prayers therefore can pertain to our present situation or temptation without being directed against our earthly foe. Augustine's view of the terrain of the spiritual battleground is one where each individual who belongs to the earthly city is culpable – they are not puppets being mechanically operated by the devil without their consent. It is not that our human adversaries are always knowingly enslaving themselves to the devil, but they do actively accept and participate in the economy of pride which the devil has put in place. Such people cannot blame murder on Zeus, or adultery on Venus, nor the fates nor horoscopes nor the devil, for they consent to his persuasion.[125] Yet our final struggle is not against these people, but against the king whom they are imitating, lest we join their ranks. With human enemies, reconciliation is always possible, but we can never become reconciled to the devil.[126]

This balance between communal and personal sin also allows Augustine to have a view of demonic temptation which accepts the devil's

---

[123] Ibid., 7.3.
[124] See, for example, *en. Ps.* 39.1.
[125] *en. Ps.* 31.2.16. See also *en. Ps.* 80.18–19.
[126] Ibid., 76.7.

participation in our everyday trials as real, but does not conceive of a cartoonish devil who constantly appears. Temptation often comes, for Augustine, through other human beings. The devil's angels are not merely demons, but also human beings who are part of the body of the proud. Even a wife can play Eve to her husband, and a man can be the devil for his wife.[127] Augustine readily speaks about the devil's constant attacks on us; "the devil and his angels interfere with Christians every day, trying to pervert them with some kind of greed or sly suggestions."[128] He rarely describes those temptations, however, in terms of some kind of voice or apparition produced by the devil – either internal or external. The devil can make illusions, to be sure, and he can transform himself into an angel of light (cf. 2 Cor. 11:14),[129] but most often the devil's temptations come to us as if they are from ourselves, namely, in the guise of our entrenched habits which are formed by our life in the devil's city, or they are introduced to us by another human being who encourages us to sin or dissuades us from virtue. Augustine believes that temptations originate with the devil, but they are most often experienced as routine trials in the context of everyday human interaction. This view of temptation corresponds well with his understanding of sin which we have been discussing, namely, that sinful acts arise both out of the sinful society which the devil has put in place, but also from our own desires which are the result of original sin, and which we follow by our own free will. In *City of God*, the whole Roman empire is willingly subject to the devil and participates in his economy. Romans do this, for the most part, without being conscious of the fact they are worshiping demonic forces, but nevertheless are completely complicit in the prideful structures which the devil has erected. They are not personally innocent, since they are not being coerced by the devil without their own consent. Nevertheless, we can separate their actions from the source of the destabilizing evil in the earthly city, which is the devil. Likewise, when we are tempted, this temptation may not manifest in a way which is easily recognizable as demonic, and we will not experience our yielding to that temptation as anything other than our own free act. Nevertheless, the source of our inducement to pride truly is the devil, and when we recognize this fact we can throw ourselves upon the mercy of God so that we might not be delivered unto evil.

---

[127] Ibid., 93.20. These temptations which come from one's spouse are still considered to be the snake "whispering suggestions to lure to iniquity."
[128] Ibid., 62.17.
[129] See, for example. *Gn. litt.* XII.13.28–29, *ench.* 60 and *civ. Dei* II.26.

In the end, then, the heart of Augustine's teaching on spiritual warfare is the heart of his teaching on angelology more generally, which is worship. If we worship ourselves, which is pride, we are in league with the devil, we yield to his persuasion and we take part in his society. If we worship God, we are humble and rely on him, which is the only way to defeat the devil. The devil and his angels are heralds of pride, whereas the good angels, following Christ, are heralds of God. Practically speaking, for Augustine, this reorientation means participating in the liturgical life of the church. In the *Expositions of the Psalms*, we have seen that he recommends liturgical practice as fortification against the devil: baptism is preparation for spiritual combat, prayer and participation in the eucharistic liturgy are communal acts of humility. But he also urges his congregation to avoid all manner of false rites – forms of magic, theurgy, superstition and pagan worship. We briefly sketched the contours of Augustine's theory of magic in chapter 2, but it will now be considered at greater length. Joining in the worship of the church is central for the Christian soldier, but so also is eschewing magic.

A number of times in the *Expositions of the Psalms*, Augustine warns expressly against participation in or reliance on magical arts, as well as pagan rituals and festivals. Generally speaking, he denounces those who think they can look for a little extra worldly security by using such methods. To those who ask: "'what … aren't those gods necessary too, if we are to secure everyday things?'"[130] he answers emphatically in the negative. The practices in which these Christians engage to get ahead are demonstrably useless, and even dangerous:

> If any one of you thinks that this sort of worship is necessary to secure temporal well-being, the following example will help you to see the futility of it. Take all those who worship Neptune: are they immune to shipwreck? What about those who scoff at Neptune, does that mean they never reach harbor? And all those women who worship Juno, do they all give birth successfully? Or do all those who scoff at Juno miscarry? You must understand, beloved, that men and women bent on worshiping these gods are empty-headed, for if it were necessary to pay cult to them for earthly things, only people who worship them would have these earthly things in plentiful supply. Even if that were the case, we should nonetheless shun such gifts and seek from God only the one thing, and the more because the God who is slighted when such gods are worshiped gives us earthly things too.[131]

Augustine stresses that pagan rites have no assured benefits either in this life or the next – which is also his principal argument in the opening books of *City of God* – but even if they did, he warns, we should not dare risk offending the God who has power over all things. At the end of his exposition of Ps. 61, Augustine denounces astrology in particular. He singles out a penitent in their midst who was an astrologer, but who renounced his trade in order to rejoin the ranks of the church. This man, Augustine explains, "has come to abhor falsehood, and to realize that he, who enticed so many, had himself been enticed by the devil."[132] Augustine asks his audience to help this person be sincere in his repentance, and not to fall back into the devil's snare. But he also takes the opportunity to remind his congregation that he is not oblivious to Christian solicitation of such professionals; he asks "how much money do you think he took from Christians? How many Christians purchased falsehoods from him?"[133] In his exposition of Ps. 90, he comments that pious Christians are sometimes ridiculed for avoiding astrologers by their less scrupulous brothers and sisters, who consider this abstention to be a showy act of false righteousness.[134] Again in his exposition of Ps. 93, these same kinds of people taunt the devout, asking: "why do you live so unconventionally? Do you think you're the only Christian around? Why can't you behave like other people? Why don't you watch shows and fights along with the rest of us? Why don't you make use of spells and lucky charms? Why not consult astrologers and soothsayers like everyone else?"[135] One can surmise that visiting an astrologer, using charms and engaging in other so-called pagan activities was commonplace in Augustine's congregation, and that many considered the avoidance of these culturally accepted religious practices to be unnecessarily zealous. Frederick van der Meer concludes that, from the perspective of Augustine's congregants, "in cases of sickness and misfortune, and particularly in the matter of averting the evil eye and pacifying the ever-present demons, it was surely prudent to apply the principle of making doubly sure."[136]

How, then, does Augustine conceive of Christian liturgy as the opposite of, or even as a replacement for, magical rites? He recommends that in response to the scoffers mentioned above, for example, the true believer should "make the sign of the cross, and reply, 'I am a Christian.'"[137] Is

---

[132] Ibid., 61.23.
[133] Ibid.
[134] Ibid., 90.1.4.
[135] Ibid., 93.20.
[136] Frederick van der Meer, *Augustine the Bishop*, 57. He discusses the persistence of pagan practices among North Africans more generally and gives many more examples of Augustine denouncing them; see 56–75.
[137] *en. Ps.* 93.20. Augustine makes a similar comment in *en. Ps.* 91.7. Here again Christians protest that they need soothsayers, fortune-tellers and astrologers to protect their

the confession of the Christian name accompanied with this sign, then, a Christian form of a magic, a church-approved gesture and speech that will ward off demons just as certain rituals and incantations attract them? To begin to answer these questions, let us consider Augustine's theory of magic more broadly. R. A. Markus provides an excellent overview both of theories of magic in the ancient world generally, but also Augustine's views in particular.[138] The main text from which he draws is *On Christian Teaching*, but many similar ideas about magic can be found in the *Expositions of the Psalms* and *City of God* as well. Markus argues that, for Augustine, magicians are able to practice their art due to the pact they make with demons, that is, because of their association with demons (not due to a conscious contract of some sort). Magicians and demons trade in a shared set of signs and symbols, and in this they form a communion. Markus emphasizes Augustine's conception of "association" of magicians and demons, an association which is expressed in and constituted by an economy of signs which is learned. Magic functions, therefore, because of the communion between magicians and demons, but also because of theurgical skill, which is the mastery of the sign language of that community.[139] Ultimately magic is effective, therefore, because demons have so arranged that chosen signs and symbols should communicate with them, and have privately taught certain adherents this art in order that these magicians may deceive others also for their own gain. In turn, those who solicit magicians do so for their own worldly profit. Thus, the economy of magic does not work because of any inherent effectiveness of magical rites, but only because demons have invented them and established a tacit agreement between themselves, magicians and,

property, but Augustine notes that the sign of the cross marks the Christian as one who refuses pagan arts; "my good man, do you not sign yourself with the cross of Christ? The law forbids all those practices." He mentions the signification value of the sign of the cross elsewhere in the Psalm homilies. The sign of the cross is a "sign more precious than any jewel" (*en. Ps.* 32.3.13, 73.6), the mark that Christians belong to God and not the devil (*en. Ps.* 48.2.2; in reference to the baptismal signing), and a reason for the Christian to be bold when reproached for Christ's sake (*en. Ps.* 68.1.12; again, this seems to refer to the baptismal signing). Augustine sometimes refers to Christ's actual crucifixion as the original "sign of the cross" which defeated the devil as well (see, for example, *en. Ps.* 61.22 and 80.11).

[138] R. A. Markus "Augustine on Magic," 375–388.
[139] Markus himself does not want to pit the "association with demons" model for understanding magic against the "theurgical/natural skill" model. He notes that in the ancient world, these two ways of viewing the effectiveness of magic were complementary (see "Augustine on Magic," 377–378). In chapter 2, I emphasize magic as a form of theurgical skill.

by extension, the consumers of magic, that these signs should function in a certain way. In *City of God*, Augustine likewise notes that demons have invented magic,[140] but also that they are addicted to it.[141] Since the two cities are opposing systems of pride and humility, it makes sense that demons could become addicted to their own invention. Magic is a system intended to bring prestige and worship to the demons themselves, thus they are addicted to their own praise.

In a number of places, Augustine also discusses why demons should be able to work any signs or have any power in the first place. He explains that demons have more subtle senses and a keener awareness of the natural world because of their angelic nature, and even though they have lost many of their abilities due to their fall, still they retain some of the capabilities of the angelic race.[142] The effectiveness of demons becomes a topic of some interest on occasions when Augustine is discussing the wonders performed by Pharaoh's magi. In this case, the demons use their knowledge of corporeal things to achieve seeming wonders (like bringing forth snakes) in order to secure Egyptian allegiance. It is not that the snakes are produced *ex nihilo*, but rather the demons understand the basic elements of nature and so can transform one type of matter to another.[143] So the demons establish a relationship – or, we might say a pact – with the Egyptians on which the magicians rely to feign magical power. In reality, however, these signs are performed by the natural ability of demons and can be curtailed by God at any time, which is why Pharaoh's magicians failed to produce gnats. Being thwarted by the smallest of creatures, Augustine notes, is a blow to their pride. These demons, however are also cruel, and employ their ability to mock and ultimately punish the Egyptians in the form of the plagues. In both instances, whether demons are performing miracles or punishing, the demons are of course limited by God's will, but they are also always acting according to their own vicious intent, which God uses.[144] In *City of God* Augustine likewise alludes to the fact that all magic is created or coopted by demons and is not a true science.[145] Here he recounts the story of Numa, who uses hydromancy,

[140] *civ. Dei* XXI.6.
[141] Ibid., X.7–8.
[142] See *en. Ps.* 77.28 and *Gn. litt.* XI.37. That angels/demons have subtler bodies than our own was a common supposition in antiquity, and also explains how angels and demons perform miracles (they are not "supernatural" but are the result of the superior natural powers of an angel).
[143] See *qu.* 2.21 and *trin.* III.12–13.
[144] *en. Ps.* 77.28–29.
[145] *civ. Dei* VII.35.

but does not contact good angels or the dead as he intended. Rather, demons take delight in Numa's rites and come to be worshiped under the pretense of the summoned dead men. Thus the demons are attracted to magic because they can use it for their glory and establish a deceitful relationship with the likes of Numa, but his incantations are not actually operative in summoning them. Numa's "magical power" results from the pride of demons who use this opportunity to deceive him.

To conceive of liturgical practice or prayer as somehow a form of Christian magic, then, is to misunderstand Augustine's conception of magic in the first place. As it turns out, magic is not the basis for liturgical action, nor is magic a competitor with the liturgy properly speaking, in Augustine's view. Rather, as Markus also notes, magic is a parody. Because magic is based on the inverted economy of pride established by demons, whereby each person uses deceit to gain selfish power, it is a parody of the whole social order.[146] Due to the fact that magic is a performative act, it "belongs to phenomenologically the same realm of action as sacraments."[147] We can add, then, that magic is not just a parody of praise in general, but it is an even more perverse parody still, because it imitates Christian worship as it is actually practiced, that is, it parodies the sacramental economy. This exact parody is why the one form of outward worship (Christian sacraments and liturgical practices) helps us to prevail over the devil, while the other (magic) entails subjection to him. They are not types of the same, but opposed to one another. Christians, therefore, who consult an astrologer are not making doubly sure, but putting themselves in the precarious position of participating in the devil's sacraments, which oppose and mock the true worship of their Christian faith. Magic and the liturgy are the sign currencies, we might say, of their respective cities.

As an example of how these two communities of sign-making are opposed, let us return to a consideration of the sign of the cross. In his exposition of Ps. 73, Augustine speaks about different groups of signs; the sign of the cross on the one hand, and Roman imperial signs on the other. Here, he associates magic with signs used to communicate Roman glory. He interprets Ps. 73:5 ("they set up their signs, their emblematic signs, and knew not") to refer both to the various regalia flaunted by the Romans after the conquest of Jerusalem and destruction of the temple in 70 CE, and to the communication of demons. The victorious Romans

---

[146] Markus, "Augustine on Magic," 384.
[147] Ibid., 381.

had insignia, and they set them in the temple: their standards, their eagles, their dragons, their Roman emblems and perhaps too their statues, which they had placed in the temple on a previous occasion.[148] They had been given "signs" by the soothsayers who served their demons; and such oracles too may be meant when the psalm speaks of "their signs."[149]

The physical signs of human military domination and conquest, that is, Roman paraphernalia and religious icons, are ironically put in the same category as the signs by which the Romans are dominated. By making this connection, Augustine again demonstrates how prideful sign culture functions. The demons use their sign system – magic – to subjugate the Roman empire and so steal for themselves the worship due to God. In this case, the demons are even able to have their statues erected in the very temple that belongs to the one true God. The Romans, in turn, use their standards and emblems as a testimony to their own power, which highlights Roman glory and instills fear and admiration into the defeated foe. The capture of the temple, as Augustine points out, is especially horrific because of this inversion. It is an abomination that God's signs should be replaced by demonic ones; "'how great a devastation has the spiteful enemy wrought among your holy things' (Ps. 73:3) Among things sacred to you – in your temple, in your priesthood, among all the holy signs established at the time (*in illis omnibus sacramentis, quae illo tempore fuerunt*).'" As in the case of the Egyptian magi, however, God uses the Romans and their own evil will for his good, namely, for the punishment and correction of his people. The psalm also tells us, moreover, that these perverse signs have ultimately been defeated by one completely unlike it: "those who wield the scepter today submit to the wood of the cross ... on the foreheads of kings the sign of the cross is more highly prized than jewels set into their crowns (*in frontibus regum pretiosius est signum crucis, quam gemma diadematis*)."[150] As demonic oracles and Roman standards belong to the same community of signs, so does the wood of the cross and the baptismal seal on the foreheads of Christians.[151] The former group, of course, are the signs of the proud and

---

[148] See Boulding's footnote to *en. Ps.* 73.8 – Augustine could be thinking of Pilate's erection of standards in the temple, or of the infamous desecration of the temple by Antiochus IV Epiphanes in 167 BCE.
[149] *en. Ps.* 73.7.
[150] *en. Ps.* 73.6
[151] Boulding translates *signum crucis* here as "representations of the cross." Perhaps Augustine is speaking about the crosses on the heads of Christian rulers with a certain sort of irony; they should prize above all the sign of the cross on their foreheads which

the latter are the signs of the humble, because Christians have adopted a sign of humiliation and defeat as their standard.

The good angels, as we have shown above, are not often mentioned in terms of spiritual warfare, and likewise they do not frequently appear in Augustine's discussions of magic. Augustine, however, does speak about the angelic life in liturgical terms, as we have noted throughout this study. The good angels oppose demons not by fighting directly against them, but precisely by following Augustine's spiritual advice; they conquer through God. In this way, the good angels are not in direct competition with the demons, because although demons sometimes impersonate holy angels, they do not wish to steal worship or power from good angels, but from God himself. The good angels undermine this tactic by participating in the worship of the city of God alone. Unlike the lax in Augustine's congregation, the good angels never make the mistake of engaging in the false worship of demons. They are oriented toward God in whom they are secure, and they do not therefore seek praise or some other benefit from another source. Augustine makes a concerted effort to distance the good angels from magic and to make clear that good angels can never be called upon by means of magical arts, but rather holy angels worship the same God whom we are to worship. We have seen this idea elsewhere, and Augustine is relentless on this point. He avails himself of every opportunity to remind his readers or his congregants that good angels are not swayed or pleased with magical incantations, but only with praise of God.

Augustine rarely mentions the good angels by name, for example, but when he does it is not so that we might learn their names in order to call upon them, but in order to remind us that they are servants of God. For example, in *en. Ps.* 117 he connects a reference to the word "princes" to Michael (who is called prince in Dan. 10:21), but only in order to show that the psalm tells us not to invoke him; "'it is good to hope in the Lord,' therefore, 'better than to hope in princes.' Angels too are called princes; so we read in the Book of Daniel."[152] Likewise, even the mightiest of the holy angels, whom we know from the biblical text, would never induce a person to worship him,

It's not only though, if some human being, but also if any angel, seemingly, should wish to tempt you, either through some kind of apparition or through a dream and say "do this for me, celebrate this rite for me, because I am" – for example – "the

is the baptismal seal, but perhaps they have merely replaced the gems on the brow of their crown with a cross.
[152] *en. Ps.* 117.5.

angel Gabriel"; don't believe him. As for you, stick safely to worshiping the one God, who is Father and Son and Holy Spirit. If it's really an angel he will rejoice at your worshiping like that; but if he gets angry because you haven't given him something extra, then you must now understand him to be the one about whom the apostle says that he "transforms himself into an angel of light" (2 Cor. 11:14). He wants to block your way, he is intruding himself with evil intent; he is not the mediator who reconciles, but rather the one who separates ... that is not the kind of great household that our Lord runs. His servants love him, his children love them. If you want to corrupt any of them, as it were, on the side, in order to be admitted to their master, you will be expelled very far indeed from that great household.[153]

Augustine goes on to compare this so-called angelic household to the Christian community in the book of Acts. The angelic mode of life is one where everything is shared in common, there is no private property, and none of the good angels wants to keep something offered to them in private. Gifts must be accepted, but offered communally to God. Using this homely analogy, he reproduces his vision of angelic community found in *City of God*.[154] The good angels are not interested in the private possession of worship as the demons are, because the good angels reject the devil's prideful economy wherein each individual seeks power and praise for him or herself and becomes addicted to possessing what is due to God alone. The good angels, instead, oppose the devil by worshiping God and by encouraging others to join this community of praise. They exist now as the perfection of the community of Acts, that is, the church. As Augustine explains in the same sermon, the reason that the pagan gods have such varied rites and demand specific forms of veneration is precisely because they are false, and they arrogate to themselves diverse rites in order to win any scrap of praise they can find.[155] Contrast this with the Christian sacraments, he remarks, where neither martyrs nor holy angels are offered sacrifice, but only "the one through whom they defeated the devil."[156] He urges us not to listen to those who might say "invoke the angel Gabriel in this way, invoke Michael in that; offer the former this little ritual, the latter this other," due to the fact that the names of those angels can be found in scripture, but rather note that in the biblical text these angels never demand any "personal religious veneration for themselves (*priuatae religionis exegerint*)."[157] Spiritual warfare is centered

---

[153] *s. Dolbeau* 26.48.
[154] For a discussion of angelic community in *City of God*, see chapter 2.
[155] *s. Dolbeau* 26.47.
[156] Ibid.
[157] Ibid.

around properly ordered worship. Participation in magic is participation in a demonic system of worship which divides praise and builds pride. Participation in the Christian sacraments, on the other hand, praises God alone and cultivates humility. In terms of spiritual warfare, therefore, the angels occupy the same place as they do in Augustine's vision of worship and community more generally: good angels worship God perfectly. It is in this way that they oppose the demons, not by trusting in their own strength or valor, and not by winning individual praise through magic, cosmic battles or in any other fashion.

Conclusion

In the *Expositions of the Psalms* (and in his other homilies), Augustine shows a keen interest in the matter of spiritual warfare and often reminds his congregation of the true battle which is being waged in the course of their everyday lives. Spiritual warfare, in fact, serves as a hermen-eutical key for Augustine in his Psalm commentaries; if Christ – either as head or body – is the speaker of each one of the Psalms, then the devil must always be the enemy to whom the speaker is referring.[158] Augustine develops in these homilies a theory of spiritual warfare which demonstrates not only how the devil is the true enemy of the Christian, but how that enemy should be fought (by reliance on Christ to overcome temptation, by the practice of prayer and engagement in the liturgy, and by imitation of the martyrs and of Job, who demonstrate and exemplify a total reliance on God to conquer Satan). Although he does not speak about the good angels engaging in open combat with the demons, they are likewise exemplars of how one overcomes the devil through perfect

---

[158] For Augustine, therefore, in the Psalms there is the *totus Christus* but also the *totus Diabolus*. The whole Christ is speaking, but the whole devil (the devil as the head along with his body – his angels, human and celestial) wages war. The phrase the "body of the devil" appears, for example, in *en. Ps.* 139.8 discussed above. The idea of the body of the devil as a hermeneutical principle comes from the rules of Tyconius, which Augustine recounts in *On Christian Teaching* (see *doc. Chr.* III.55). Pamela Bright in "The Spiritual World, which is the Church: Hermeneutical Theory in the *Book of Rules of Tyconius*," *Studia Patristica* 22 (1989): 213–218 notes that Tyconius recommends a twofold spiritual reading of scripture. For example, the church is spiritually bipartite because there are currently both good and evil in the church (215). Augustine, she argues, shifts this paradigm largely to a carnal/spiritual model (for example, there is a carnal Israel and a spiritual one) rather than a church with two spiritual aspects (216). Perhaps here, however, we see Augustine following Tyconius more closely, as he employs a bipartite spiritual reading; the psalmist is a spiritual speaker with a spiritual enemy (not a carnal one).

worship and how, by God's leave, one comes to deride the devil. With the angels, we will one day mock the devil's attempts to overcome us when we rely on Christ's victory. Theologically speaking, this teaching on spiritual warfare is consonant with Augustine's other ideas pertaining to demonic and angelic community. We are not only personally culpable by yielding to the devil's temptation, but we help to create a demonic society which is based on pride rather than praise of God. The devil tempts us in real and personal ways, but also assails us through the perverse structure of our entire earthly city. An example of the devil's work in the realm of daily spiritual warfare comes in the form of magic, astrology and other pagan rites. Although these seem harmless and normative to Augustine's congregation, they are in fact part of the demonic society which seeks to redirect praise away from God and reduce worship to a skill; they are the sacraments of the devil's city. The liturgy of the church, by contrast, requires humility and reliance on God and as such is the complete inversion of magical practice. Augustine, therefore, rejects any notion that the good angels can be prevailed upon through magical means, since they are part of the city of God and, in fact, they perfectly embody the properly ordered worship which detests all forms of magic.

As a further implication, this analysis challenges us to remember that Augustine's pastoral concerns lie at the heart of his theological thinking, and are not secondary to it. The harmony of his pastoral understanding of spiritual warfare and his angelology stands as proof of that fact (not to mention the sheer volume of his homilies and letters in comparison to his other writings). Many scholars of Augustine are of course attentive to the everyday context of his theological efforts, but it can be easy to lose sight of it, and to think only of his polemical or intellectual motivations. Even in polemical situations, however, Augustine must be primarily concerned with persuading those near at hand. Likewise, the forms of the liturgy in which he is engaged daily are a constitutive part of his theological thinking.[159] There is a lack of scholarly interest in how the words and ritual actions of the liturgy form his imagination, and liturgical scholarship on Augustine often focuses simply on reconstructing the liturgy in North Africa in his time. These reconstructions are historically invaluable, but limited. In the discussion of Augustine's view of

---

[159] It may be worth bearing in mind that it is in Augustine's North Africa that we find the first solid evidence for daily eucharistic celebrations; this practice was not normal pre-Nicea. See Gregory Dix, *The Shape of the Liturgy* (London: Dacre Press, 1960), 592 and Burns and Jensen, "Christianity in Roman Africa," 269.

spiritual warfare, we have seen an absolute glut of liturgical references, particularly to the Lord's prayer and the *sursum corda*, although others remain to be investigated. Worship, moreover, is at the heart of his theology of angels (including his view of spiritual warfare) and a central theme of *City of God*, but also of other works such as *On the Trinity*. A consideration of the actual enactment and form of the liturgical worship which Augustine experienced should not be overlooked, and should be considered part of the raw material from which he forms his theological ideas. The liturgy should correspondingly be one of the places scholars instinctively look in order to understand Augustinian ideas.

Conclusion

Throughout the course of this study we have seen that Augustine speaks about the angels with surprising frequency in a variety of contexts. Despite the fact that he has no treatise on the angels, he has consistent ideas regarding the timeline for their creation and fall, the makeup of their heavenly community, as well as their role in salvation history and in spiritual warfare. Since his discussions of angels are dispersed throughout his corpus, however, we have cut a wide path through a mass of material, and in so doing pointed out many theological implications of the angels without always being able to discuss them in full. Nevertheless, we have seen that, for Augustine, the angels are not of peripheral interest, but are a significant concern for him when considering how to expound the creation story, how to understand the origin and end of the city of God, and how to conduct oneself everyday as a Christian. The sophistication with which he speaks about the angels should not lull us into thinking that for him they are merely abstractions, theological concepts which serve as window dressing or polemical fodder. For Augustine, as for his congregation and his pagan contemporaries, angels and demons are real. His many discussions about the nature of their heavenly life and their interaction with human beings – which, for example, dominate the central section of *City of God* – are part of a conversation. This conversation arises from a culture which perceives the mediation of spiritual creatures to be a basic element of religious life, and Augustine's theological consideration of their role is proof of that fact. He has taken the matter as seriously as any other theological issue of his day, and has dealt with it in a manner which is just as elevated as any other.

Any reader of Augustine will know that his thought is so complex and his theological ideas are woven together in such an intricate way that when one attempts to pull out a common thread of any given topic, one is in danger of undertaking the task of unraveling the whole. The topic of angels is no different, especially given that his references to angels are spread across a number of his major works. One of the most significant unifying themes that this study has presented, however, is that of his theology of the goodness of created communion. The angels, who are the primordial members of the city of God, are not just created good or created in communion with one another, but their goodness is constituted by their proper relationship to God, to each other and to us. This communion *is* the goodness of their created life. This single organizing thought can help to shed light on Augustine's understanding of the angels in a number of the contexts which have been discussed, but it also elucidates how a contemplation of the existence of the angels should have a significant impact on our understanding of Augustine's theology more generally speaking.

In *Literal Meaning of Genesis* Augustine expounds the idea of angels as created light. Their creation is indicated by the biblical phrase "let there be light" on day one. They are created from their first moment in a certain relationship with God, since they are illuminated first by knowledge of the Word. They know the Word in itself before they know themselves, Augustine explains, and then in the subsequent evening they come to see their creaturely status and understand themselves in themselves. They come to know themselves, in other words, but already in relationship with God and with each other. On the following morning, it is this community that finally becomes its own, when it refers its knowledge of itself, and of the beauty of creation, back to God. This motion, of seeing and knowing God, seeing and knowing oneself and creation and then turning back to God, is called worship. It is not just the stabilizing and cohering force of this community, it defines the community. For this reason, the demons who refuse to worship (who do not want to praise God for what they are) immediately and permanently fall out of communion with God and the good angels on that second morning, when light is separated from darkness. Since Augustine argues that angels are created light and that the unfolding of creation in seven days is the biblical way of describing the angels' witness of creation, the act of creation itself takes place already in the context of a community. The angels help in creation, bear witness to it, rejoice in it and see it from the perspective – as created light – of its final consummation, which will be achieved through the incarnation. Creation itself is realized from the first as communion, in communion and in preparation for a future perfected communion.

Although the good angels are stable, and Augustine believes that once they have made the choice to worship God they are unable to fall, this does not mean they are without free will but rather by a "free and love-inspired choice"[1] they are perfectly free and love perfectly by the grace of God. He envisions their community as one based on the love and active responsiveness of created rational beings. The angels receive their created goodness where the devil refuses it, they make it their own, and they praise God for it. Augustine images this reception and response in what we might call sacramental or liturgical language. The angels, for example, are said to read the Word of God forever.[2] They consult God when they act, as we do in prayer.[3] And their habit of praising God in the morning for his creation and recognizing their creaturely status in the evening also corresponds to our praying of the Psalms. Our own patterns of worship then are an echo of the heavenly, not only in mere imitation, but as a principle of creation, since the angels' original community is founded by and coheres because of their worship; so also with us, since we are one community with them. Time as we know it exists because time is the way in which angels witnessed creation and were taught about their own goodness. Worship (and, by extension, our outward forms of worship in the sacraments) is the life for which both we and the angels are created. It is not simply an activity, but the basis of our created freedom, because it is only when we love God and then ourselves that we can be said to be free and to be attuned to the logic of our own created life. This view of the angelic life and our participation in it is a strong critique of a mythological view of angels, and anti-Manichean concerns are ever present when Augustine comments on Genesis. In the angels, we do not see a cosmic struggle between what is good and what is evil, and we do not attempt to glimpse some primordial pre-biblical time when things were different. Rather, we see in the life of the angels proof of the goodness of creation proclaimed repeatedly by Gen. 1, and in the demons a failure to remain in the community which should have defined their very life.

Given the principle that the angels are created in community and that their life is worship, we should not be surprised to find that worship is

---

[1] *Gn. litt.* IV.42.
[2] *conf.* XIII.15.18. See also *s.* 57.7 and *en. Ps.* 119.6.
[3] *ep.* 140.69.

also a central issue (if not *the* central issue) of *City of God*. In book x of *City of God*, which is where his discussion of the good angels is primarily located, Augustine develops a theology of worship. This theology is his basis for describing the two cities and tracing their development throughout salvation history in the second half of the work. The city of the angels is, as it was in the Genesis commentaries, a community of worship which always attracts praise to God and clings to God in charity. This worship is defined primarily by humility, which is the foundation of created life. We must know that we are not God, and yet love God for who he is and who we are in God. The earthly city is defined by pride, which means to love yourself above all else and induce others to love you instead of God. The city of God, then, is founded by the angels and in them we are assured of its existence and of our destination. But this assurance is not primarily constituted by vague notions of happiness and stability in heaven which the angels already enjoy or even primarily of being located in a certain celestial place. Rather, the promise of the angelic life is made concrete because it is a community, and one to which we already belong, albeit as pilgrims. Although our blessedness in the future life will be one of incorruption and one free from pain or any perturbations, this blessedness is not primarily based on the bodies we will obtain. The demons have subtle bodies of air but suffer eternal damnation. Rather, our hope of the life to come is based on our full inclusion in angelic community and our complete incorporation into their worship. That "we will be equal to the angels" (Luke 20:36) – one of Augustine's favorite biblical citations for imagining the life to come – ultimately means we will be conformed to angelic society and fit for their company. This does not mean suited to their company primarily in a corporeal way, but again, conformed to their love and life of worship, cleansed from sin. Sin, the chief of which is pride, is what divides us from the angels, not our flesh.

Once again, this communal life of the angels which is shared with us is imaged by Augustine in sacramental language; this is what created community looks like. The angelic–human communion which is the church is constantly being sustained by God and constantly offering itself to God in return. On earth, the church learns to make this sacrifice of the heart in the Eucharist, and Augustine describes even the heavenly life of angels with the language of eating. What Christ has become in the incarnation is the milk which provides the sustenance on the altar, but is the very same food which sustains the angels in heaven. The necessity of eating in order to survive in the flesh will pass away, but even in heaven we must be fed by God. As Augustine says, the "daily bread" (i.e. the Eucharist) of this life will become the bread of one eternal day[4] – a fitting image for angelic eating, since they are themselves created light. The goodness of the community which exists first in the angels (the city of God) is the chief good of created life. And if we are created not just *for* God's communion but *as* a communion with God and each other, then the highest evil is the community we create for ourselves. This is the devil's city, which is based not on worship of God, but worship of self, not of service to one another, but self-service. This is the exact perversion of the life for which all rational beings were created. Augustine's angelology is therefore political, but in the broadest sense, since it defines the perfection of our proper relations, and demonstrates that both human beings and angels are in essence political creatures.

In *City of God*, then, as in the Genesis commentaries, the angelic life demonstrates that we (that is, all of us rational creatures) are created as a communion and destined for perfect communion with God and each other. This idea is reflected also in the role which Augustine gives to angels in salvation history. The created community of angels and human beings is not just an abstract conception nor something we look forward to in the future, but the benefits of this communion are already in place, so to speak. The angels are perfectly aligned to God's will, but this does not mean that they are trapped in ecstatic contemplation, or that they prefer to play the harp all day long, but rather that they empty themselves in loving service as God does. As created light, they were enlightened at the moment of their creation, and their enlightenment includes a realization of their fundamentally communal nature, but also of Christ's pivotal role in the drama of human salvation, that is, the healing of the communion. The angelic community is by definition a working community; they were enlightened but in turn shed light. They are cooperators in God's plan, like farmers who sow but cannot cause growth, or as window-makers who cannot cause light but still show it forth.[5] Christ who is great in the day of the angels becomes little in the day of man,[6] but this light in which the angels are begotten is the same light which comes into the world – the angels are made in the knowledge of the incarnation and have their vocation from that same light.

---

[4] *s.* 57.7.

[5] Agricultural imagery for the cooperation of the angels is a common one throughout Augustine's corpus and is discussed in chapter 1. On angels as window-makers, see *en. Ps.* 118.18.4.

[6] *s.* 187.1.

The angels, therefore, are always understood by Augustine to be Christ's angels. The very name by which they are known to us – angel – indicates this, since the word "angel" is an office and not a nature. The angelic vocation, that of announcing, is a vocation which the angels actually receive from Christ, who is the angel of great counsel and who is the perfect herald of God's will. The angels announce by heralding Christ (as the prophets do in the Old Testament) and continue to prepare for and rejoice at his coming in the incarnation. The angels do not perform this function because God needs them, and they do not merely stand in for God as robot-like creatures any more than the apostles or prophets do (the groups with which the angels are most often paired). Rather, in keeping with his theology of the goodness of created communion, Augustine maintains that the angels participate in salvation history because they want to do so and because it is good for them to do so. Their angelic heralding does not inform God, but conforms them to God.[7] This is true also of human messengers (apostles, prophets and all Christians) whom God uses. God does not need to work through human agency, but it is good for us that he do so, and it demonstrates respect for creation. The angelic work in salvation history then is not different in kind from human work, but only in degree. Because angels are in perfect communion with God, they can speak on his behalf with absolute authority, while also remaining completely who they are. Perhaps we can understand this angelic transparency by reflecting on Augustine's vision of heaven in *City of God*: when we see an angelic messenger what we see is God himself, not because the angel disappears, but because in the beatific life we will be able to see God in each other and in all creation.[8]

Augustine's conception of the goodness of created communion is also essential to his teaching on spiritual warfare. As a survey of the *Expositions of the Psalms* reveals, he does not doubt the real and persistent temptations of the devil, which plague Christians every day and induce them to sin. We are tempted in every possible way, by being enticed by wealth and reputation, frightened by loss, oppressed by illness, or distracted by laziness. All of these temptations, however, are symptoms of pride, which is, as we saw, is the desire to make ourselves God; self-sustaining and self-defining. These temptations, moreover, are not strictly the personal encouragements of a devil who sits

---

[7] As Augustine says, in prayer God is not instructed (*instruatur*) but the creature is built up (*construatur*). See *ep.* 140.69.
[8] *civ. Dei* XXII.29.

on our shoulder. Rather, the inducement to pride is fundamentally communal. We are living already in a community of pride, a society whose structure is based on attracting wealth and accolades to ourselves. Our yielding to temptation, then, is not only a personal sin but also a complicity in the sinful structures which organize the whole of society. To resist these powerful and systematic evils then, one must give up pride and rely completely on Christ. As pride is our chief sin, humility is its cure. This humility means reliance on God, which is realized in our incorporation into the community of humility, that is, the church. Augustine advises us, in practical terms, to participate in the Christian liturgy and the sacraments in order to fight the devil. We must pray, which is an act of the humble, remember the grace of our baptism, and we must lift up our hearts in order to receive the Eucharist. The devil parodies this liturgical life not only by inverting the economy of grace and replacing it with one of pride, but also by creating a false sacramental system, namely, magic. Participation in magical or theurgical rites binds us to a community obsessed with skill and the attainment of worldly benefit, and conversely through Christian liturgical practice we become united to a community which does not seek achievement, but rather God himself. The examples set up for us – the martyrs and Job – are models not because they possess inhuman or heroic virtue, but because they worship God and rely on his strength. In short, our ability to fight the devil (or our failure to do so) comes from our association with a community.

The good angels have little part in directly combating the devil, because they too rely on Christ and point us toward him as our help, and not to themselves. Augustine rarely speaks of personal angelic protection or aid. Yet, as created light the angels embody the final perspective which we will attain with respect to the devil and his angels, that is, we will join in their mocking of the devil. Our final spiritual triumph will be to see in the light the angels do, or more properly, in the light that angels are, and from that point of view the devil is ridiculous. His pride and his constant thrashing against the will of God will no longer be a temptation for us but an object of mirth, since we will finally see his false city and false promises from the perspective of the love and sacrifice of Christ, that is, we will see him as the angels do because we will be in their company. The light of the angels is the radiance of a perfected community, it is the light in which we see God, ourselves and creation as they really are, but it is also what we become, being conformed to God and shedding light on each other.

For Augustine, in the angels we see both the foundation and perfection of our created communion. The angels' life is worship, but in this worship they do not forfeit themselves, rather they gain themselves and are themselves. This is the vision Augustine has also of our own beatific life, and it structures the way he thinks about our life now – about what constitutes our sin (pride), what gives our created life its meaning (God), and how we express our love for God and neighbor (in communal life, in the sacraments, in service). Like the angels, we are made to give our-selves over to God, to adhere to God and thereby to receive ourselves back again, "for we are all his temple, each of us severally and all of us together."[9]

[9] Ibid., x.3.

Bibliography

Primary

The works of Augustine are referred to by their English titles and with the standard Latin abbreviations (as listed below).

Where many references to Augustine's works appear together, they are listed in chronological order, followed by letters and sermons (which are difficult to date). When the biblical text is cited, it is cited from Augustine's own text when possible. Otherwise, it is cited from the New Revised Standard Version.

Augustine. *Against the Letters of Petilianus (c. litt. Pet.)*. In the *Nicene and Post-Nicene Fathers*, Series 1, Vol. 4. Translated by Philip Schaff. Buffalo, NY: Christian Literature Publishing Co., 1887.

Commentary on Galatians: Introduction, Text, Translation and Notes (exp. Gal.). Oxford Early Christian Studies. Edited by Eric Plumer. Oxford: Oxford University Press, 2003.

Answer to Faustus, A Manichean (c. Faust.). Translated by Roland Teske. New York: New City Press, 2007.

The Confessions (conf.). Translated by John K. Ryan. New York: Doubleday, 1960.

On the Care of the Dead (cura mort.). In the *Nicene and Post-Nicene Fathers*, Series 1, Vol. 3. Translated by H. Browne. Buffalo, NY: Christian Literature Publishing Co., 1887.

The City of God (civ. Dei). Translated by Marcus Dods. New York: Modern Library, 2000.

Expositions of the Psalms (en. Ps.), vol. 1–6. Translated by Maria Boulding. New York: New City Press, 2000.

Enchiridion on Faith, Hope and Charity (ench.). In *On Christian Belief*. Translated by Edmund Hill. New York: New City Press, 2005.

On Free Will (lib. arb.). In *Augustine: Earlier Works*. Translated by J. S. Burleigh. Philadelphia: Westminster Press, 1953.

195

Genesis Commentary Against the Manichees (Gn. adv. Man.). In *On Genesis*. Translated by Edmund Hill. New York: New City Press, 2002.

The Grace of Christ and Original Sin (gr. et pecc. or.) in *Answer to the Pelagians I*. Translated by Roland Teske. New York: New City Press, 1997.

Homilies on the First Epistle of John (ep. Jo.). Translated by Boniface Ramsey. New York: New City Press, 2008.

Homilies on the Gospel of John (Jo. ev. tr.). Translated by Edmund Hill. New York: New City Press, 2009.

Letters (ep.), vol. 1–4. Translated by Edmund Hill. New York, New City Press, 1990–1997.

Literal Meaning of Genesis (Gn. litt.). In *On Genesis*. Translated by Edmund Hill. New York: New City Press, 2002.

Notes on Job (adn. Job). Latin only, from the Latin text below.

Sermons (s.), vol. 1–11. Translated by Roland Teske. New York, New City Press, 2001–2005.

On the Spirit and the Letter (spir. et litt.) in *Answer to the Pelagians I*. Translated by Roland Teske. New York: New City Press, 1997.

Teaching Christianity (doc. Chr.). Translated by Edmund Hill. New York: New City Press, 1996.

On the Trinity (trin.). Translated by Edmund Hill. New York: New City Press, 1991.

Unfinished Literal Commentary on Genesis (Gn. litt. imp.). In *On Genesis*. Translated by Edmund Hill. New York: New City Press, 2002.

On the Usefulness of Belief (util. cred.). In *Augustine: Earlier Works*. Translated by J. S. Burleigh. Philadelphia: Westminster Press, 1953.

Latin texts:

Corpus augustinianum gissense. Edited by Cornelius Mayer. Basel: Schwabe, 1995.

In addition, I sometimes use the Latin with French translation and commentary found in

Bibliothèque Augustinienne. Paris: Institut D'Etudes Augustiniennes, 1939–present.

Secondary

Ayres, Lewis. *Augustine and the Trinity*. Cambridge: Cambridge University Press, 2010.

Babcock, William S. "The Human and the Angelic Fall: Will and Moral Agency in Augustine's City of God." In *Augustine: From Rhetor to Theologian*, 133–151. Toronto: Wilfred Laurier Press, 1992.

Barnes, Michel. "Exegesis and Polemic in Augustine's *De Trinitate*." *Augustinian Studies* 30.1 (1999): 43–59.

"The Visible Christ and the Invisible Trinity: Mt. 5:8 in Augustine's Trinitarian Theology of 400." *Modern Theology* 19.3 (July 2003): 329–355.

Bauckham, Richard. *Jesus and the Eyewitnesses*. Grand Rapids: Eerdmans, 2017.

The Testimony of the Beloved Disciple. Grand Rapids: Baker Academic, 2007.

Bonner, Gerald. "The Church and the Eucharist in the Theology of St. Augustine." *Sobornost* ser. 7, no. 6 (1978): 448–461.

Boulnois, Marie-Odile. "L'éxègese de la théophanie de Mambré dans le *De Trinitate* d'Augustin: enjeux et ruptures." In *Le De Trinitate de Saint Augustine: Exégèse, logique et noétique*, edited by Emmanuel Bermon and Gerard O'Daly, 35–67. Paris: Institut d'Études Augustiniennes, 2012.

Bright, Pamela. "The Spiritual World, Which Is the Church: Hermeneutical Theory in the *Book of Rules of Tyconius.*" *Studia Patristica* 22 (1989): 213–218.

Brox, N. "Magie und Aberglaube an den Anfängen des Christentums." *Trierer theologische Zeitschrift* 83 (1974): 157–180.

Bucur, Bogdon G. "Theophanies and Vision of God in Augustine's *De Trinitate*: An Eastern Orthodox Perspective." *St. Vladimir's Theological Quarterly* 52.1 (2008): 67–93.

Burns, Patout. *The Development of Augustine's Doctrine of Operative Grace.* Paris: Études Augustiniennes, 1980.

Burns, Patout and Jensen, Robin. *Christianity in Roman Africa.* Grand Rapids: Eerdmans, 2014.

Bradshaw, Paul. *Two Ways of Praying.* Nashville: Abingdon Press, 1995.

Bradshaw, Paul and Johnson, Maxwell. *Eucharistic Liturgies.* Collegeville: Liturgical Press, 2012.

Cary, Phillip. *Outward Signs: The Powerlessness of External Things in Augustine's Thought.* Oxford: Oxford University Press, 2008.

Cavadini, John. "The Anatomy of Wonder: An Augustinian Taxonomy." *Augustinian Studies* 42.2 (2011): 153–172.

"God's Eternal Knowledge according to Augustine." In *The Cambridge Companion to Augustine* (second edition), edited by David Meconi and Eleanore Stump, 37–49. Cambridge: Cambridge University Press, 2014.

"The Structure and Intention of Augustine's *De trinitate.*" *Augustinian Studies* 23 (1992): 103–123.

"Trinity and Apologetics in the Theology of St. Augustine," *Modern Theology* 29.1 (Jan. 2013): 48–82.

Chase, Steven. *Angelic Spirituality: Medieval Perspectives.* Mahwah: Paulist Press, 2002.

Clark, Mary T. "Augustinian Spirituality." *Augustinian Studies* 15 (1986): 83–92.

Cline, Rangar. *Ancient Angels: Conceptualizing Angeloi in the Roman Empire.* Leiden: Brill, 2011.

Couenhoven, Jesse. "Augustine's Rejection of the Free-Will Defence: An Overview of the Late Augustine's Theodicy." *Religious Studies* 43.3 (2007): 279–298.

Coyle, J. Kevin. "Saint Augustine's Manichean Legacy." *Augustinian Studies* 34 (2003): 1–22.

Daley, Brian. *The Hope of the Early Church: A Handbook of Patristic Eschatology.* Cambridge: Cambridge University Press, 1991.

Daniélou, Jean. *The Angels and Their Mission According to the Fathers of the Church.* Translated by David Heimann. New York: Newman Press, 1957. Originally published as *Les anges et leur missions d'après les Pères de l'église.* Chevetogne: éditions de Chevetogne, 1953.

Dix, Gregory. *The Shape of the Liturgy.* London: Dacre Press, 1960.

Dunkle, Brian "Humility, Prophecy and Augustine's Harmony of the Gospels." *Augustinian Studies* 44.2 (2013): 207–225.

Evans, Christopher. "Augustine's Theology of Divine Inspiration in the Production and Reading of Ecclesiastical Writings." Ph.D. Diss., St. Louis University, 2005.

Farkasfalvy, Denis. *Inspiration & Interpretation: A Theological Introduction to Sacred Scripture*. Washington, D.C.: The Catholic University of America Press, 2010.

Frederickson, Paula. *Augustine and the Jews*. New Haven: Yale University Press, 2010.

Freedman, David Noel et al., ed. "Kingdom." In *The Anchor Bible Dictionary* vol. 4, 57–58. New York: Doubleday, 1992.

Gavrilov, A. K. "Techniques of Reading in Classical Antiquity." *The Classical Quarterly* 47.1 (1997): 56–73.

Harrison, Carol. *The Art of Listening in the Early Church*. Oxford: Oxford University Press, 2013.

Hoffman, Tobias, ed. *A Companion to Angels in Medieval Philosophy*. Leiden: Brill, 2012.

Jackson, Pamela. "Eucharist." In *Augustine through the Ages*, edited by Allan Fitzgerald et. al., 330–334. Grand Rapids: Eerdmans, 2009 (1999).

Johnson, Maxwell. *The Rites of Christian Initiation*. Collegeville: Liturgical Press, 1999.

Keck, David. *Angels and Angelology in the Middle Ages*. Oxford: Oxford University Press, 1998.

Kloos, Kari. *Christ, Creation, and the Vision of God: Augustine's Transformation of Early Christian Theophany Interpretation*. Leiden: Brill, 2011.

Kuntz, Paul G. "'From the angel to the worm': Augustine's hierarchical vision." In *Jacob's Ladder and the Tree of Life: Concepts of Hierarchy and the Great Chain of Being*, edited by Marion L. Kuntz and Paul G. Kuntz, 41–53. New York: Peter Lang, 1987.

Lamirande, Émilien. *L'église celeste selon st. Augustin*. Paris: Études Augustiniennes, 1963.

Lancel, Serge. "Augustin et le miracle." In *Les miracles de St. Etienne*, 69–77. Turnhout: Brepols, 2006.

Lotz, J. B. "Augustinus über die Freundschaft." In *Die Drei-Enheit der Liebe: Eros – Philia – Agape*, 264–282. Frankfurt: 1979.

Madec, Goulven. "Angelus." In *Augustinus Lexicon* vol. 1, edited by Cornelius Mayer, 304–315. Basel: Shwabe & Co., 1986.

Markus, R. A. "Augustine on Magic: A Neglected Semiotic Theory." *Revue des Études Augustiniennes* 40 (1994): 375–388.

Saeculum: History and Society in the Theology of St. Augustine. Cambridge: Cambridge University Press, 1970.

McEvoy, James. "Anima et Cor Unum: Friendship and Spiritual Unity in Augustine." *Recherches de théologie ancienne et médiévale* 53 (1986): 40–92.

Merdinger, Jane "In League with the Devil? Donatist and Catholic Perspective on Pre-baptismal Exsufflation." In *The Uniquely African Controversy* edited by Anthony Dupont et al., 153–179. Leuven: Peeters, 2015.

Muehlberger, Ellen. *Angels in Late Ancient Christianity*. Oxford: Oxford University Press, 2013.

Murphy, Austin. "The Bible as Inspired, Authoritative and True according to Saint Augustine." Ph.D. Diss., University of Notre Dame, 2016.

O'Daly, Gerard. *Augustine's City of God: A Reader's Guide*. Oxford: Oxford University Press, 1999.

O'Donnell, James J. *Augustine: Confessions, a Text and Commentary*. Oxford: Oxford University Press, 1992.

Pépin, Jean. "Les Influences Païennes sur L'angelologie et Demonologie de Saint Augustin." In *Ex Platonicorum Persona: Études sur les Lectures Philosophique de Saint Augustin*, 27–36. Amsterdam: Adolf M. Hakkert, 1977.

Rist, John. *Augustine: Ancient Thought Baptized*. Cambridge: Cambridge University Press, 1994.

"On the Nature and Worth of Christian Philosophy: Evidence from the *City of God*." In *Augustine's City of God: A Critical Guide*, edited by James Wetzel, 205–225. Cambridge: Cambridge University Press, 2012.

Ruokanen, Miikka. *Theology of Social Life in Augustine's De Civitate Dei*. Göttingen: Vandenhoeck & Ruprecht, 1993.

Russell, Jeffery Burton. *Lucifer: The Devil in the Middle Ages*. Ithaca: Cornell University Press, 1984.

Saussine, Emile Perreau. "Heaven as a political theme in *the City of God*." In *Paradise in Antiquity*, edited by M. Bockmuehl and G. Strousma, 179–192. Cambridge: Cambridge University Press, 2010.

Simonetti, Manlio. "Gli angeli e Origene nel *De civitate Dei*." In *Il De Civitate Dei* edited by Elena Cavacanti, 167–181. Rome: Herder, 1996.

Smith, Gregory A. "How Thin is a Demon?" *Journal of Early Christian Studies* 16 (2008): 479–512.

Solignac, Aimé. "Exégèse et Métaphysique, Genèse 1,1–3 chez saint Augustin." In *In Principio: Interpretations des premiers versets de la Genèse*, 154–171. Paris: Études augustiniennes, 1973.

Studer, Basil. *Zur Theophanie-Exegese Augustins: Untersuchungen zu einem Ambrosius-Zitat in der Schrift* De videndo Deo *(ep. 147)*. Studia Anselmiana 58. Rome: Herder, 1971.

TeSelle, Eugene. "The Civic Vision in Augustine's *City of God*." *Thought* 62 (1987): 268–280.

Timotin, Andrei. *La démonologie platonicienne. Histoire de la notion de Daimon de Platon aux derniers néoplatoniciens*. Leiden: Brill, 2012.

Torchia, Joseph N. *'Creatio Ex Nihilo' and the Theology of St. Augustine*. New York: Peter Lang, 1999.

Van der Meer, F. *Augustine the Bishop*. London: Sheed and Ward, 1961.

Van Fleteren, Frederick. "Angels." In *Augustine through the Ages*, edited by Allan Fitzgerald et al., 20–22. Grand Rapids: Eerdmans, 2009 (1999).

Van Riel, Gerd. "Augustine's Exegesis of 'Heaven and Earth' in Conf. XII." *Quaestio: Annuario di storia della metafisica* 7 (2007): 191–228.

Weaver, Rebecca. "Prayer." In *Augustine through the Ages*, edited by Allan Fitzgerald et al., 671–674. Grand Rapids: Eerdmans, 2009 (1999).

Wetzel, James. "Augustine on the Origin of Evil: Myth and Metaphysics." In *Augustine's City of God: A Critical Guide*, edited by James Wetzel, 167–186. Cambridge: Cambridge University Press, 2012.

Wiebe, Gregory. "Demons in the Theology of Augustine." Ph.D. Diss., McMaster University, 2015.

Williams, Rowan. *On Augustine*. London: Bloomsbury, 2016.

"*Sapientia* and the Trinity, Reflections on the *De Trinitate*." In *Collectanea Augustiniana: Mélanges T. J. van Bavel*, edited by B. Bruning, M. Lamberigts and J. van Houten, 317–332. Leuven: Peeters, 1990.

Willis, G. G. *St. Augustine's Lectionary*. London: SPCK, 1962.

Young, Frances. *Exegesis and the Formation of Christian Culture*. Cambridge: Cambridge University Press, 1997.

General Index

Adam, 22, 35, 47, 48, 50, 51, 52, 53, 71,
   72, 130–131, 133, 134, 159, 164, 166
   body of, 88
   fall of, 14, 22
adherence of the good angels to God, 21,
   49, 56, 168
aesthetics, 84, 139, 144, 145, 146–147
angel of great counsel, 126, 127, 192
angels
   authority of, 55, 76, 111, 119, 145
   bodies of. *See* body, of angels
   free will of, 35–40, 119, 121, 189
   friendship with, 4, 74–75, 76–77, 79, 80,
      81, 83, 94, 95, 128
   guardian, 80, 138, 167
   knowledge of the, 24, 26–45, 53, 54, 188
   meaning of the word, 53, 124–125, 126,
      128, 129, 192
   our equality with, 85–95, 97, 107, 108, 190
   stability of, 20, 35, 36, 85, 87, 113, 189
   and time, 17, 19, 20, 23, 28, 31, 42–44,
      46, 48, 49, 189
annunciation, 115
Apuleius, 90
ascension, 133–135, 136, 139, 145
astrology, 132, 174, 177, 180, 185

Balthasar, Hans Urs von, 146
baptism, 42, 160–162, 176, 193
   by angels, 76, 77–78
   of the unnamed friend, 77
baptismal anointing, 160, 161, 181
Barnabas, 62

Bauckham, Richard, 55
beatific vision, 4, 6, 25, 37, 40, 41, 43, 63,
   84, 85–97, 103, 104, 105, 107, 108,
   120, 131, 133, 160, 190, 192, 194
body
   of Adam and Eve, 50, 52, 88
   of angels, 88–89, 103, 113–114, 135
   of Christ, 66, 93, 97, 99, 106, 124, 134,
      135, 136, 184
   of demons, 89, 90–91, 134, 179
   of the devil, 156, 171, 175
   meaning of, 4, 52, 53, 64–65, 66,
      88–92, 120
   resurrection, 87, 88–90, 103
bread of angels, 101–102
burning bush, 111, 112, 113, 114, 115, 119
Burns, Patout, 38

Cary, Phillip, 40–42, 64
Christmas. *See* nativity
citizens, angels as, 4, 7, 20, 30, 73, 75, 79,
   80, 83, 96, 109
Cornelius, 76, 77, 79
creation. *See* chapter 1
Crispina, 74, 83, 95

Daniélou, Jean, 1, 3, 74
demon, 3, 5, 8, 9, 57–58, 59–72, 74, 75, 80,
   82, 85, 89, 90–91, 95, 104–105, 107,
   108, 109, 127, 128–129, 134, 148, 149,
   156, 167, 169, 172, 173, 174, 175,
   177–182, 183, 184, 187, 188, 189, 190
   prophecies of, 71

Biblical Index